MANAGERIAL CAPITALISM IN RETROSPECT

Managerial Capitalism in Retrospect

Robin Marris
Professor Emeritus of Economics
Birkbeck College
University of London

First published in Great Britain 1998 by
MACMILLAN PRESS LTD
Houndmills, Basingstoke, Hampshire RG21 6XS and London
Companies and representatives throughout the world

A catalogue record for this book is available from the British Library.

ISBN 0–333–58888–6

First published in the United States of America 1998 by
ST. MARTIN'S PRESS, INC.,
Scholarly and Reference Division,
175 Fifth Avenue, New York, N.Y. 10010

ISBN 0–312–21578–9

Library of Congress Cataloging-in-Publication Data
Marris, Robin Lapthorn, 1924–
Managerial capitalism in retrospect / Robin Marris.
p.   cm.
Rev. ed. of: The economic theory of managerial capitalism.
Includes bibliographical references and index.
ISBN 0–312–21578–9 (cloth)
1. Managerial economics.   2. Capitalism.   3. Industrial
management.   I. Marris, Robin Lapthorn, 1924–   Economic theory of
managerial capitalism.   II. Title.
HD30.22.M378   1998
658'.001'5118—dc21   98–16540
                                                                              CIP

This book is printed on paper suitable for recycling and made from fully managed and
sustained forest sources.

10   9   8   7   6   5   4   3   2   1
07   06   05   04   03   02   01   00   99   98

Printed and bound in Great Britain by
Antony Rowe Ltd, Chippenham, Wiltshire

Re-dedication
To Jane

Contents

New Introduction

This book is an abridged and edited version of a book (*The Economic Theory of Managerial Capitalism*) on which I started work in the late 1950s, was eventually published in 1964 and has now been out of print for many years. The essential purpose of the book was to attempt to analyze the theoretical consequences of what is often called the separation of ownership from control, but which I prefer to call separation of ownership from management. The book is reissued now because a number of people have suggested it should be, and because interest in it, as evidenced by citations and so on, seems to have increased since the beginning of the 1980s. One reason for the revival of interest, almost certainly, is that the original book contained the first-known attempt at an economic theory of 'involuntary' take-over (that is, the event where one firm acquires another by making a direct offer to the target shareholders over the heads and against the wishes of the incumbent management, who may expect to lose their jobs if the offer succeeds). That element, however, was only one among a number of conceptual and theoretical innovations that I believed I had introduced. It is also the case that what I said on that topic has been rather widely misunderstood. What I said was that, although what is now called 'the market for corporate control' represented a basic constraint on managerial freedom *vis-à-vis* shareholders, it was highly imperfect – that is, it left management with a considerable degree of what is now called 'discretion'.[1] By contrast, many of my interpreters have implied that I conceived of this market as if it were, in the economists' sense of the term, virtually perfect.[2] The difference is that, on my assumption, if management allows the stock-market value of the firm to decline, only the *probability* of take-over is increased; on the other assumption, take-over becomes virtually certain if management permits stock-market value to fall only slightly below the possible maximum. I think it is fair to say that subsequent research by others than myself has tended to confirm my view.

Another reason for the reissue is that the theoretical model at the heart of the book, as the late and highly lamented Edith Penrose delicately said privately to the author, 'lacked focus'. In that model, building on Edith Penrose's own great work[3] the firm was seen as a continuing organization with constant or increasing returns to scale. Its absolute size was unlimited, the essential variable was the rate of growth. In order to maintain sustainable growth with a constant rate of profit, the firm must on the one hand undertake the effort and cost of continuous creation of new markets for its own services and products, and on the other provide itself with the necessary supplies of finance, which latter, in turn, must come either from external sources or retained profits. In other words, the growth of 'demand' (the saleable volume of all products and services consistent with a given profit rate or average margin) must balance the growth of 'supply' (finance and administrative resources and capacity). But the sustainable growth rate was not unique; rather, there was a family of them. More precisely there was a trade-off between the level of the sustainable growth rate and the level of the firm's stock-market value. How would management choose? The answer I gave was that, for various motivational reasons discussed in the original Chapter 2, they would choose the maximum sustainable rate consistent with a stock-market value that gave a reasonable level of security from involuntary take-over. Alternatively, they would maximize a utility function containing two arguments: growth rate and stock-market value. Thus management had the power to choose an optimum growth rate from its own point of view.

WEAKNESSES OF THE ORIGINAL EXPOSITION

There were three problems with the way the foregoing model was originally presented. The first was that the mathematical treatment was unnecessarily complex, if not obscure. The second was that I did not make sufficiently clear that the model was, in fact, profit-driven. Anything that increased the firm's profits from existing operations helped provide the finance to permit faster sustainable growth rates with given stock-market value levels: increased underlying profitability improved the trade-off between growth and valuation, and hence between growth and security, all along the line. The third weakness stemmed from the second. I failed to make clear that if the model is valid, management has no disincentive to be efficient. The more efficient the management, the greater the underlying profitability of the firm, and the greater the level of management utility when the managerially-optimum growth rate is chosen. This conclusion brings the theory into head-on collision with 'bureaucratic' theories of managerial discretion, which argue that all managerial organizations (that is, all organizations with a high degree of separation of management from ownership) are necessarily inefficient. In my model the only sense in which management is inefficient is that, having earned as much profit as possible from existing operations, they may devote a greater share of cash-flow and effort to long-run expansion of the scale and scope of the firm than would be optimal from the point of view of the shareholders. In turn,

that conclusion raises questions over the implications for societal economic welfare. Today, in the late 1990s, virtually every professional economist in the world bar myself appears to believe, almost axiomatically, that
the exercise of managerial discretion is bad for society. Apart from being
generally inefficient, managerially-influenced firms are trying to grow 'too
fast'. But in my view it is quite impossible to prove that an economy consisting mainly of managerially motivated firms would deliver less overall
social welfare through time than one where firms were mainly neo-classical. The reason is that the efforts of firms to grow mean efforts of research
and development that spill over into the general economy. I believe this
argument is well supported by the macroeconomic international history of
the 'First World' in the period 1950 to 1990.

A number of good economists have published papers clarifying, cor-
recting and extending the original theory.[4] I have also published work on
these lines myself.[5] Consequently, in the present work I have entirely
deleted the original theoretical chapters (original Chapter 5, 'Supply', and
original Chapter 6, 'Completed Micro Models') and replaced them first
with a reprint of an article that was first published in the recent
International Encyclopedia of Business and Management[6] and concerned
with both the theory and empirical testing of managerial theories of the
firm in general (new Chapter 5); and a newly-written theoretical synthesis
(new Chapter 6).

Since the early 1970s two outstandingly important developments – one
academic and the other technological – have had a profound influence on
the perception of modern capitalism. The first is the body of ideas that go
under the general umbrella of the economic theory of property rights, prin-
cipal-and-agent relations and transactions costs. The second is the information technology (IT) revolution.

THE SIGNIFICANCE OF AGENCY AND TRANSACTIONS-COST THEORY[7]

When I wrote my original book, like most other economists at that time, I
had not encountered Ronald Coase's now-celebrated article, published in
1937, posing the question, 'Why do firms exist?' If the market system is
so efficient, why is not all economic activity carried on by one-person
businesses? I just assumed that the answer was 'teams' (that is, that firms
did exist) and carried on from there. But a formidable body of scholars,[8]
led and inspired by Oliver Williamson, who rediscovered Coase, have
shown that in so doing one leaves out a line of inquiry that has proved to

be extraordinarily fruitful in economics. The answer Coase gave was 'transactions costs'. These are various costs of using the market to organize an economic activity as opposed to organizing it within the firm. By contrast, the costs of in-house organization may be placed under the label of 'agency costs': as a firm expands it must employ an increasing number of people who have little or no ownership stake in the enterprise and who therefore lack incentive to be efficient. Coase's original words were as follows:

> When we are considering how large a firm will be the principle of marginalism works smoothly ... At the margin, the costs of organising within the firm will be equal either to the costs of organising within another firm or to the costs involved in leaving the transaction to be 'organised' by the price mechanism.[9]

It is evident that Coase was implicitly describing a diagram in which the absolute size of the firm was represented on the horizontal axis and either marginal agency costs or marginal transactions costs on the vertical. There would be a curve of the former that was rising, and of the latter that was falling. And lo and behold, where they intersected we had the optimum size of the firm! If this was the representative firm in the economy, and all firms reached the optimum, then the total industrial structure was optimized: society achieves a macro-optimal balance between agency costs and transactions costs. The market was a self-organizing system which optimized its own structure.

The problem with this beautiful idea is that no one has produced any strong general theory to make the marginal agency–cost curve inevitably upward-sloping. As one takes on increasing numbers of people lacking ownership rights, why should the average non-incentive effect necessarily increase more than proportionately to their output? Why not a simple law of constant unit effect?[10] Frankly, I do not think this question has been answered. Consequently, I assert that a general hypothesis of constant or increasing returns to the scale of organizations, which is essential to my theory of the growth of the firm, continues to stand up.

VERTICAL VERSUS HORIZONTAL EXPANSION

A more powerful, and in my opinion much more successful, application of transactions-cost theory is found in Oliver Williamson's brilliant explanation of vertical integration. This was not a topic to which I paid any attention, but the more one thinks about it the more one can see that, in a sense, vertical integration is the essence of the concept of the firm. More precisely, it is the essence of the beginning of the firm. It is Adam Smith's pin factory. If an already-integrated firm is considering an act of vertical disintegration, it must take account of the fact that the profitability of its sunk investment in its central equipment is now partly dependent on an outside supplier of an intermediate product. Also, the outside supplier is dependent on the final producer. In theory, it should be possible for the two parties to write a long-term contract dealing with all possible eventualities in their future relations. In practice, such a document would be too complex to be feasible. Such contracts, in Oliver Williamson's terminology, are in practice inevitably 'incomplete'. The problem of the incompletability of contracts lies at the heart of transactions costs.

In determining the optimum degree of vertical disintegration these transactions costs are set against the presumed marginally increasing agency costs (but see above) of vertical expansion. A major merit of this theory is that previous explanations of vertical integration were theoretically woolly and were unable to account for the observation of fluctuating trends of integration and disintegration that have occurred historically in industries and economies.

But, but, but – what about the outstanding feature of the massive growth in the twentieth-century sizes of individual firms, namely *horizontal*, or lateral, expansion?[11] It is my contention that, at the end of the day, for all its achievements, the transactions-cost theory does not succeed in providing a comprehensive analysis or explanation of the process of expansion by diversification which lay, and still lies, at the heart of my own theory. My explanation, of course, is managerial motivation combined with constant returns to scale.[12] The implication is that, provided there are not barriers to firms' achieving the minimum size required for economies of scale and 'scope',[13] the efficiency of the economy is more-or-less independent of the size distribution of firms. As many have argued,[14] the notoriously skewed (apparently log-normal) macro size distribution of firms in general in a modern market economy is surely the result of an essentially probabilistic process, which I have elsewhere argued[15] can well be derived from my own micro theory.[16]

The great Harvard historian of business and economics, Alfred Chandler, who flatteringly adopted my term 'managerial capitalism', produced a series of classic works[17] providing strong evidence that managerial organizations, rather than displaying constant returns to scope and scale, in practice, over a wide range, had increasing returns. I have no difficulty with this (among economists) notoriously unpopular conclusion.

My assumption of constant returns represents a kind of minimalism. What I and like-minded others are agreed on is the absence of a strong general law of decreasing returns. It must be pointed out, however, that the general theoretical consequences of widespread increasing returns are much more awkward. In this connection the papers[18] of a recent conference held in the presence and in honour of Kenneth Arrow at Monash University in Australia, are rather significant.

So, in the face of all the powerful, fruitful, useful and elegant theory that has emerged since the 1960s, I feel bloody but unbowed. Twentieth-century managerial capitalism, for all its supposed undesirability, has proved to be the most successful economic system ever known so far.

THE IT REVOLUTION

No one can seriously doubt that the revolution in IT lies at the core of the transition from twentieth-century managerial capitalism to whatever it is we are going to have in the twenty-first century. In my opinion, the process began around 1985, which may also have been the end of the classic managerial era that had begun in the early nineteen 1900s.[19] Mainframe computers began to have a major influence on science, technology and some branches of commerce as early as 1960, but two important developments that brought the computer into the realm of the general population did not really begin until the 1970s. The first of these was the extremely rapid miniaturization of the hardware – that is, micro-chip technology – and the second was the development of effective software to ease communication between the machine, which works serially in numbers, and the human brain, essentially a pattern-recognizing entity, which works with a high degree of parallelism in words. The second development was, in truth, driven by the first. Although, software has become the industrial product of our time, everything that has happened in recent years has been made possible by the less-publicized hardware developments that have produced the amazingly rapid declines in the size and cost of given amounts of memory, and computing speed and power.

There are two aspects of the implications: the nature of the IT industry itself, and the effects on industry at large. As regards the first, it is quite obvious that the developments, especially on the software side, have not fitted at all well into my picture of managerial capitalism. That picture, as I painted it, had a strong physical capital-intensive industrial bias. 'People-based' firms such as Microsoft[20] have grown at explosive rates in terms of profits and value added, but do not employ huge amounts of labour and even less of material capital. They have often rewarded all their employees (not just top managers) with shares. In effect, they have spread both risks and rewards through the business at large. Is this a form of collective owner-management? Not exactly; employee shares still represent only a minority voting block.

The financial process is also different. A major capital requirement for building software products must be salaries (and other rewards) for professional staff during the development period. If projects succeed, the *ex-post* ratio of capital required per unit of saleable output may be quite moderate. The key financial problem, therefore, is the possibility of cash shortage for a relatively short time during development. One answer is to pay professionals a rather modest cash wage, plus shares.[21] When things have settled down, and some employees have sold their shares while others have stayed in the firm, what will the institutional and financial structure of the mature firm look like?

What of the general influence of IT? On the one hand, it may increase the effectiveness of the control of large organizations, thus reducing agency costs and increasing tendencies to economies of scale. Alternatively, in increasing the comparative efficiency of small administrative units, and possibly in other ways, it may reduce transactions costs. The quarter of a century since the early 1970s has certainly seen strong tendencies such as 'downsizing' and 'outsourcing'. The former means a radical reduction in the number of managers required to organize a given output, and the latter means vertical disintegration. On 'downsizing', one scholar has written that it is 'the most pervasive yet unsuccessful phenomenon in the modern business world'.[22] These are strong words, but one suspects that, in a general way, what is being observed is a tendency for computerized information monitoring to appear to reduce the need for middle management. The implication is not so much that firms are getting smaller in terms of output, but that they may be in terms of management numbers. The other side of the coin is the potentiality of IT to permit effective control of gigantic global organizations, some of which, in terms of value added, have become enormous. Yet another (apparently countervailing) aspect of the current situation in the Anglo-Saxon economies has been the wave of management buy-outs.[23]

The question then remains, has IT produced a general tendency to vertical disintegration? Most people believe it has, but the conclusion is not, in fact, so obvious. Some of the most dynamic large firms in currently fast-growing regions of South Asia, such as the Indian state of Gujarat, are already highly vertically integrated and fast becoming more so. As already indicated, the reasons why IT should reduce external transactions costs are somewhat elusive. But if IT does not explain the late-twentieth-century trend to 'outsourcing' in the mature Western economies, what does? Only fashion?

Finally, I must say what the reader will now expect me to say, namely that the effect of IT on diversification and *horizontal* expansion is also not obvious. And as to owner-management, while most of the United States' current crop of new billionaires come from the IT industry, and, in the case of Bill Gates, can attribute a major part of their success to breaking away from IBM, the latter entity, managerialist *par excellence*, after an awkward corner, is very much still with us.

MACRO IMPLICATIONS AND ENDOGENOUS GROWTH

The final chapter, Chapter 8, of the original book was entitled 'Possible Macro Implications'. It was essentially concerned with the theoretical vista that emerges if the strength of the growth efforts made by firms are (a) endogenous to the micro theory of the growth of the firm, and hence (b) endogenous to macro features of the environment (such as institutional barriers to take-overs), (c) spill over to affect the rate of growth of the productivity of the whole economy – that is, what was then called (in conjunction with population growth) the macroeconomic 'natural' rate of growth. Thus the natural rate, an essential constant in early post-Keynesian growth theory, became a variable – that is, became endogenous. In consequence, I believe it is the case that I was the first economist to write a line of prose in which the words 'growth' and 'endogenous' appeared together.[24] But my train of thought was different from that mainly pursued by subsequent writers in the field.[25] In that extremely exciting and interesting research programme, the objective is to explain macro growth rates by variables such as material or human capital that may have the property of feeding back on themselves (material capital via technology, and human capital via general spill-over) so that enhanced growth of total output creates enhanced growth of output per head. In my conception there was a similar outcome with a different causal chain: the micro efforts of firms to enhance their own growth rates involved various activities, such as research development, that spill over to enhance the natural growth rate of the economy. The main person to follow this up was Hiro Odagiri, whose work is discussed in a comment at the end of the present book.[26]

With the benefit of hindsight I can see the basis of a more specific macro model that I could have erected on my original micro foundations. Firms exist and many are large; some very large. They compete at two levels. At the 'lower' level they compete on price and advertising in the markets for existing products. These markets are inherently imperfect so this is a general game of monopolistic competition (or 'imperfect polipoly') or of oligopoly, including strategies involving entry, exit and threats of entry. The structure of these markets (which is, in fact, the long-term result of competition at the 'higher' level) determines the various parameters (conjectural demand-elasticities and entry costs or 'contestability' factors) that in turn determine the average profit margins resulting from rational play of these market games. The profit margins in turn determine the optimal choice of capital/labour ratios rather than, as in the neo-classical model, the other way about. The games thus determine rates of profit of individual firms before deducting the various costs[27] that firms must incur in order to enhance their own growth.

At the 'higher' level, the competition is the economy-wide competition to grow. Subject to the whole micro-model involved in the original book, and now synthesized in the new Chapter 6 in this volume, firms choose their desired growth rates. Other things being equal, the higher the pre-growth-cost rate of profit, the faster that desired rate will be. Therefore, high profits encourage firms' growth efforts, which, in turn, may spill over to enhance the growth rate of the economy. Therefore, the less 'competitive' the market structure in the technical sense of the word (for example, lower conjectural demand elasticities and thus higher average profit margins), the faster, other things being equal, will be the growth of the economy.[28] In short, although I failed to emphasize this at the time, any macro model based on the micro model must be heavily profit-driven.

Odagiri also pointed out another dramatic and counter-conventional conclusion. For a given profit margin and other factors, managerially motivated firms will choose faster growth rates if there high institutional and transactions costs or barriers to take-over. The implication is that, other things being equal, countries whose capital markets are strongly 'imperfect' in this sense will tend to grow faster. This is emphatically supported by the cases of France, Germany and Japan who, after the Second World War, went through long periods of rapid macroeconomic growth at a time when, in all three countries, barriers to involuntary take-over were virtually infinite.

More generally, unlike many or most economists, I believe managerial capitalism was a Good Thing. It was responsible for, or at least closely associated with, the historically unique period of economic growth that occurred in North America, Australasia, Western Europe and Japan over the twentieth century as a whole. I dare anyone to claim seriously that if there had been all kinds of laws and other constraints compelling firms to be always small or, if large, always exceptionally owner-orientated, the level of social welfare, in the economists' sense of the word, would have been better.

ECONOMIC CONCENTRATION

If the model of internal growth is combined with the theory of merger, the general theory of business concentration can be both strengthened and broadened. I did not pursue this until the late 1970s, when I published an attempt in this direction.[29] Let operating profit rates in any given short period, such as a year, be distributed symmetrically among the general population of quoted corporations. Then according to the micro theory, the desired or planned growth rates of the firms will be similarly distributed. Let the distribution actual growth rates be generated by the distribution of planned growth rates, and thus be symmetrical. Assume no serial correlation but assume it is possible that the expected reported profit of a firm is correlated, positively or negatively, with the current size of the firm. Then, in the absence of mergers, if this correlation is zero, the distribution of the logs of the sizes of firms will converge to symmetry, but the variance of these logarithms will increase persistently and linearly over time. If the correlation is positive, the process will explode. If it is negative, the logarithmic variance will converge to an asymptote. This variance is a measure of concentration. It also has a one-to-one relationship with other measures of concentration, such as the share in size of the hundred largest corporations and so on. So, under managerial capitalism, without mergers, a reasonable stochastic process in the factors affecting reported profit rates may lead to inexorable, ever-increasing concentration. The only damping factor is the new entry of medium-sized firms into the general population of large firms. This appears to be the explanation of the slow-down or cessation of the increase in concentration that has occurred in the USA and a few other countries since the 1970s.

If, to the above model, a plausible stochastic model of mergers is added (based on a matrix of probabilities of firms of size x taking over firms of size y in any given period), the above described process is likely to be augmented. Thus the merger process that partly disciplines managerial capitalism may also increase its concentrating tendencies. This does not necessarily mean a loss of competitiveness. Competition among giants, especially 'high-level' competition for growth, may be at least as fierce, if not fiercer, than competition among non-giants.

EDITING AND FORMAT

Most chapters have been shortened considerably, and some, as already mentioned, have been deleted entirely. In addition, a certain amount of small-scale editing has also been done. Only where[31] major cuts have occurred is there a corresponding indication for the current reader.

Within passages that have been retained there are additional italicized comments inserted by myself at the present time.

Notes to each chapter are gathered at the end of the book, in 'Notes and References'. New footnotes of current comment have also been added; these are indicated by text markers and note numbers in bold type. Old references retained and new references added have been dealt with in the notes. Where a reference is repeated it is usually repeated in a shortened form, and to assist in the use of references, there is an index of names.

Finally, it is necessary to apologize for the extraordinarily dated male chauvinism of much of the original style. At first I attempted to purge it all, but the grammatical ramifications were too extensive. I have, however, cut out some of the most blatant examples.

1997

Original Introduction and Preface

This essay was inspired by a growing sense of frustration at the divorce between the motivational axioms employed in the established microeconomic theories and the type of behaviour most believe to be real. We drill our students in analytical exercises based on these theories. We warn them not to believe the assumptions, but offer only incompletely developed alternatives. By the same token, applied research is weakened.

Yet ever since the publication of 'Berle and Means', most of the profession has recognized the existence of some kind of 'managerial' capitalism based on separation of ownership from control. Some have argued that, in practice, this system behaves little differently from 'traditional' capitalism. Others have asserted the opposite. And recently, one or two writers have suggested plausible models based on more appropriate assumptions. So far, however, such models have not been worked out in great detail or integrated into comprehensive theories of the firm.

We therefore feel justified in attempting to carry the development a stage further. We start from the proposition that corporate directors may subject corporate policy decisions to utility functions of their own. We ask after the probable nature of the resulting preference system, given the character of the institutional environment and the nature of the managerial task. We also consider the extent to which the environment will permit such preferences to count. These foundations are then employed in an attempt to reconstruct the 'internal' theory of the firm.

A summary of one of the resulting models appeared in the *Quarterly Journal of Economics* in May 1963, but the reader is warned that the author's ideas have developed considerably since that paper was written. In this book,[1] the first two chapters discuss the interrelationship between institutional framework and utility system, always against the background of the existence of an organized market for corporate securities. The third chapter relates the results of the first two to the conventional economic environment, defines concepts, and explains the analytical methods to be employed later. The next three chapters work out two specific micromodels, which at the end of the sixth are more or less integrated into a single final model. Chapter 7 attempts to apply the models to real behaviour, taking account of known statistical evidence. Finally, Chapter 8 ventures to speculate about possible macro-implications.

On the empirical side, we have drawn heavily from existing material, both qualitative and econometric. We also deploy the results of some limited experiments of our own. But the main weight of testing must await the results of a substantial programme of research based on the analysis of ten years' data derived from the accounts of all British quoted companies, which is currently in progress at the Cambridge University Department of Applied Economics. We make no apology whatsoever for publishing the theory in advance.[2]

So many people on both sides of the Atlantic have contributed criticism and advice that it is difficult to guarantee that acknowledgments will be adequately comprehensive. A significant debt is owed at least to all of the following economists and associated institutions: Kenneth Arrow, A. K. Bagchi, Lee Bawden, William Baumol, Alan Brown, Robert Dorfman, James Duesenberry, Christopher Farrow, Sargent Florence, Gordon Fisher, Aaron Gordon, Frank Hahn, P. E. Hart, Benjamin Higgins, Herschel Kanter, Carl Kaysen, Richard Kahn, Nicholas Kaldor, Harvey Leibenstein, John Lintner, Siro Lombardini, Fritz Machlup, Julius Margolis, John Meyer, Luigi Pasinetti, Michael Posner, Jack Revell, Joan Robinson, Janet Rothenberg, Richard Ruggles, Eugene Rostow, David Snell and Peter Wiles; members of the staff seminar of the Economics Department, University of Texas, Fall 1960; members of the author's graduate classes at Berkeley in 1961; seminarists at Harvard, Princeton, Texas A & M, UCLA and Yale in 1960 and 1961; a group of economists in Cambridge, England; and The Institute of Business and Economic Research at Berkeley. Mrs Robinson, however, must be singled out for special thanks. She has given constant support, encouragement and constructive criticism, and her recent thinking has almost certainly had a considerable influence on the author's.

Another name for special mention is that of Ajit Singh. Acting as the author's assistant, first at Berkeley and later at Cambridge, he not only carried out the econometric work described in Chapter 2, but also read the whole final manuscript, corrected many errors and revised certain passages. The author is greatly in his debt for most efficient and perceptive advice.

Among persons associated with disciplines other than economics, we should mention Noel Annan, John Goldthorpe and Bill Wedderburn. Dr Goldthorpe's sociological contribution, which resulted from a collaboration between himself and the author in a course of lectures given in Cambridge, was particularly important, as will be apparent to any reader who gets as far as Chapter 2.

Appreciation should also be expressed to the Fulbright Commission and to the Departments of Economics at the Universities of Texas and

California (at Berkeley) for facilitating the author's visit to the USA in 1960 and thus materially assisting in the research. To the then Chairman of the former Department, Ben Higgins, thanks are due for advice, encouragement and the provision of captive audiences; to the then Chairman of the latter, Aaron Gordon, thanks are due not only for giving the benefit of his very considerable experience in this field, but also for lending his substantial stock of research material connected with the Preface to the 1961 edition of *Business Leadership*.

Finally, if the book is readable, this is entirely the responsibility of the author's wife, who being, unlike himself, literate, has struggled womanfully over a long period to improve the prose. What more could a person ask?

1964

1 The Institutional Framework

Two forms of property appear, one above the other, related but not the same. At the bottom is the physical property itself, still immobile, still there, still demanding the service of human beings, managers and operators. Related to this is a set of tokens, passing from hand to hand, liquid to a degree, requiring little or no human attention, which attain an actual value in exchange or market price only in part dependent on the underlying property ... A first-rate manager would not increase the values of the properties were they to be sold; but he will increase the value of tokens representing that property. A poor management will have the opposite result. (Berle and Means, 1932)[1]

THE DISAPPEARANCE OF THE ENTREPRENEUR

'Managerial' capitalism is a name for the economic system of North America and Western Europe in the mid-twentieth century, a system in which production is concentrated in the hands of large joint-stock companies. In many sectors of economic activity the classical entrepreneur has virtually disappeared. His role was essentially active and unitary; once dismembered, no device of collective abstraction could put him together again. As a result (so a substantial body of writers have suggested),[2] entrepreneurship in the modern corporation has been taken over by transcendent management, whose functions differ in kind from those of the traditional subordinate or 'mere manager'. These people, it is argued, can wield considerable power without necessarily holding equity, sharing profits or carrying risks.

Of course, there never was a managerial revolution. Like the Industrial Revolution, the development from traditional capitalism to the contemporary form represented the slow replacement of one type of economic organization by another, a process that has not yet ended. The nature of the result is by no means obvious, and indeed puzzles even Marxists. Human societies, however, rarely arrange their institutions of production with the rules of behaviour, as seen from the economist's viewpoint, fully specified. In traditional capitalism, the decision-taker has private-property

1

rights over his instruments. He has the rights of exclusive use and enjoyment subject only to certain limited restraints on his freedom to damage others. (He may burn down the factory, but must ensure that the workers have left, and must not negligently allow the fire to spread to his neighbour's property.) There is also the implicit 'rule' that a capitalist who makes continuing losses will eventually cease to be a capitalist: both financially and morally he is encouraged to aim for profit. But how much profit is not stated.

A similar ambiguity applies to the directors of the modern corporation: in law, they owe a duty to the shareholders, but its extent is not defined. Directors who refuse to *maximize* profits because, for example, they pay attention to competing social interests such as those of employees, cannot legally be penalized: indeed, they are likely to be popular. And the position is not very different in the socialist forms of managerial society. The manager of an industrial plant under Communism is given specific instructions, usually consisting of quantitative production targets which it may literally cost him his life to ignore, but the rules as a whole, when examined, commonly prove quite inadequate to define the implied system of national resource allocation. The significant difference between managerial capitalism and managerial socialism lies less in the character of the rules of the game than in who sets them. In socialism, the rules are set by political government. In capitalism, they emerge indirectly from a body of law and custom, founded on the concepts of private property and slowly developed.

Because they are so rudimentary, they tell us little about the game. Implicitly, they define a field (the economy), some players (producers and consumers) and some balls (goods and money). Violence to other players (theft) is illegal; certain coalitions (companies) are permitted if approved by the referee, others (combinations in restraint of trade) are not. But as to goals we know strangely little. We may perhaps infer that a player who has no ball under his control for more than a certain period is eliminated (starves), and there are reasons for believing that, other things being equal, players will prefer more time with the ball than less, but we know little of their views about ball-holding by others. If coalitions are formed, we do not know how these will behave – what goals, if any, they will set themselves, or how they will determine the interior distribution of any utility they may acquire. To date, most theories of capitalism have proceeded on particular simplifying assumptions about these questions, many of which now seem doubtful when applied to the special type of coalition represented in the modern corporation. In order to see why this is so, it is necessary to begin by re-examining the traditional system.

The essence of the traditional method of economic organization is the unification of the functions of risk-carrying, reward-receiving and operational decision-taking in one individual. By combining ownership with management, the person who carries much of the risk also makes most of the decisions determining its extent. As owner, he receives the rewards of success, and is therefore motivated to optimize the balance between boldness and prudence. Economic theory has often overlooked this interdependence between risk and organization. Risk is seen as arising mainly from exogenous uncertainty, for example, from uncertainty concerning the future demand for the product of a particular asset. The shape of the resulting probability distribution of returns is therefore outside the control of anyone within the firm. Risk-taking, in this concept, consists only in choosing between lists of projects, with given, unalterable probability distributions. Real commercial life is much more flexible. If the demand for one product turns out badly, a nimble decision-taker may restore his position by changing the line of production, or at least he may minimize losses by timely retrenchment. A slow decision-taker, on the other hand, may fall into a vicious spiral of financial decline; by acting too late, he incurs losses; thereby inducing actions causing further losses, and so on. Thus the probability distribution of financial results is not only differently shaped from the exogenous parent distribution (because in the latter, disturbances are independent, in the former, not so), but also depends intimately on decision-taking skill and will-power. It is difficult for an outsider to assess the ability and integrity of a particular professional manager or team. The assessment itself involves considerable uncertainty and represents perhaps the greater part of an investment. As such, it must be paid for. By contrast, an individual entrepreneur carrying his own risks considerably reduces this uncertainty, at least subjectively. He believes he knows his own ability, and appreciates a continuous discipline to do his best. Therefore, by combining risk-taking with decision-taking, traditional capitalism reduces the cost of the former while increasing the efficiency of the latter. That is why there is still quite an amount of it about.

The offsetting disadvantage, of course, is that owner-management imposes severe restraints on scale, restraints deriving not only from difficulties of delegation but also from the inevitable emphasis on internal financing and consequent restriction on the firm's rate of growth. Important economies may therefore remain unexploited. It was to overcome these disadvantages that the social architects of the nineteenth century invented the public, joint-stock, limited-liability company, and thus invented modern capitalism. In that complex and somewhat peculiar institution, the managerial restraint on scale was overcome by resort to collective ownership and delegated control, while the financial restraint was handled by the issue of marketable shares carrying limited liability.

In England, where the invention occurred,[3] it was greeted by considerable public criticism, so effective for a time that the necessary legislation was delayed for several decades. The critics realized that a major change was involved. They saw the advantages of owner-management being lost; they could not see the advantages to be gained because they did not believe in large scale organization. Nevertheless, as everyone knows, the public joint-stock company arrived, prospered and multiplied, until, by the mid-twentieth century, not only was an overwhelming proportion of the national income in Britain and North America produced by companies, but the greater part came from firms of the type in which shareholders were numerous and their holding dispersed.

In effect, then, we now have an economic system in which the traditional and the corporate methods are legally and economically permitted to coexist, and in which each may predominate where its relative advantages are greatest. But it is by no means necessary that, in order to survive, both types of firm must adopt the same internal rules of behaviour; either or both, for example, may well dispense with profit maximization. This is not only because the relative advantages of the one or the other are in some areas so overwhelming that differences in behaviour are easily offset, but also because the competitive environment has been made highly imperfect. Once large-scale organizations appear, they have the capacity to mould the environment in directions convenient to themselves, and whether they are profit maximizers, other maximizers or 'satisficers'[4] they soon find that, rather than competing perfectly in a given environment, it is better to strive to create conditions of monopoly, monopolistic competition or oligopoly. In practice, in the sectors where corporations prevail, the predominant condition is oligopoly.

Economic theory struggled manfully with the 'external' conditions of oligopoly, but persistently refused to attempt to penetrate deeper. Until very recently, almost all 'micro' analysis implicitly regarded the corporation as a form of collective entrepreneurship, to be treated in much the same way as the one-man business, and nearly twenty years elapsed between the discovery of the managerial revolution and the appearance of related theories of the firm.[5]

A particularly serious consequence of the refusal of economic analysis to 'go behind' these assumptions has been a failure to consider whether the assumed behaviour of *organizations*, such as companies, could logically be expected to arise from rational behaviour by their members, even when rational behaviour is confined to more-or-less orthodox utility maximization. A person's utility system is the result of his social situation, of the society around him, and of the way it has moulded his psyche. But his social situation depends in turn on economic organization. (The conventional separation of economic and social theory was false from birth.) For example, it is by no means obvious that action intended to maximize the utility of a company's stockholders is consistent with maximizing the utility of the action-takers: that is, of the management.

THE TRADITIONAL PRE-HISTORY OF A CORPORATION

Most large companies have grown out of smaller businesses of a more-or-less traditional type. For the moment, however, let us postulate a situation in which, when new economic activities are to be organized, there is a straight choice between the one or the other form only. Given that a person has noticed an opportunity for profit, how should he decide between a traditional business and floating a company? If he proceeds traditionally, he must have access to initial capital, and he must be prepared to carry a high proportion of the risk. He will receive the whole income from both management and risk-taking, will have the absolute right to dispose of that income, and will have absolute and unquestioned control. But the income, the wealth and the empire of power will be constrained by the scale limitations of traditional organization. If, on the other hand, a company is floated, some of the constraints are lifted, while the founder is yet able to secure for himself an important position as manager, chairman or president. This may provide him with prospects of both financial and 'psychological' rewards. But unless he has put up more than half of the capital (in which case the organization can be regarded as being effectively more-or-less traditional) none of these positions is absolutely guaranteed. Each depends on the consent of others as well as, in principle, on the service he has to sell – as, for example, a special knowledge of the trade. His income will be a salary determined by complex factors by no means entirely under his control. But to the extent that the larger-scale organization is more efficient, the income prospects may be better than the profit prospects of the traditional organization; in some ways more risky, in some ways more secure. We might say that, in general, as compared with the pure entrepreneur, the pure manager is safer on capital account, while, on balance, a little less secure on income account. But his total satisfaction will depend also on non-financial considerations, such as his personal evaluation of the relative merits of the two types of role. A manager is a different type of person from an entrepreneur, with different ideals and different personal values. A man might prefer flotation then, if he liked a salaried status, if he had little capital to invest, and if the advantages of large-scale organization were considerable. In other words, taking all things into account, in some circumstances, pure flotation might mean greater utility.

But in practice, whatever might be preferred, wherever exploitation of the economic opportunity requires the development of a significant amount of organization, as is usual, for example, in manufacturing industry, pure flotation is rarely practicable. Investors are not readily induced to subscribe to the shares of non-existent organization. The overwhelming proportion of operations involving the formation of new public companies represents reorganization of traditional enterprises sufficiently successfully to command confidence, and attempting to break through their constraints. Let us consider the process of growth that occurred before this point was reached.

Suppose, for the sake of argument, that previous growth has not been limited by demand: either demand exceeds capacity, or the entrepreneur knows how to develop new markets when old ones are saturated. His constraints are thus mainly managerial and financial. The management problem has been widely discussed in orthodox literature, and arises essentially from the difficulties of delegation and co-ordination in an organization originally designed for one-man control. This has usually been regarded as a limit on absolute size rather than on the rate of growth. The financial constraint, on the other hand (which has been less discussed) apparently limits only the rate of growth. For finance to limit ultimate size, special assumptions are required.

If a traditional capitalist firm does not borrow, it can grow no faster than the rate of net profit (after tax, depreciation and subsistence for the entrepreneur) earned on capital employed, and the growth of the owner's wealth and of the firm's assets are synonymous. If, however, borrowing is allowed and is practiced, the rate of growth of the size of the firm, measured by capital employed, is no longer necessarily the same as the growth rate of the entrepreneurial property. But, provided the profit rate exceeds the interest rate, both can grow faster than the maximum possible when borrowing is not allowed, because the annual difference between profit and interest may be used as a source of capital for further reinvestment. Therefore, whether he derives utility from his own wealth, from the size of the firm, or from both, it appears at first sight however, that rational behaviour requires the traditional capitalist to borrow as much as he can. At second sight, however, the answer is not so simple.

For if at each round of growth more is borrowed than is reinvested from the previous period's profits, the ratio of borrowed to reinvested money in the capital structure will rise steadily; in effect, the firm will become increasingly 'levered', or, in British terminology, 'geared'. Leverage or gearing increases the risks of both lenders and borrower. Lenders know that, as the leverage ratio rises, the margin of assets covering their loan must be reduced proportionately, so there is increasing danger that, in the event of an unexpected decline in earning power, the value of assets would become less than liabilities. The borrower (the entrepreneur), on the other hand, is more likely to see the problem in terms of the burden of interest charges against his profits: if profits fall, he is liable to default on payments, and may be forced into liquidation in circumstances where, were it not for the leverage, he would have been able to continue in business. Put more generally, the effect of leverage (for both borrower and lender) is to increase the risk of insolvency for any given probability distribution of earnings.

If, therefore, it is desired nevertheless to increase the rate of growth, 'non-contractual' borrowing will be necessary. But lenders with no contractual rights to interest nor security for their capital inevitably require a share in ownership and control. They otherwise have no protection from wilful withholding of dividends, refusal to earn profits, or negligent inefficiency. It follows that a traditional enterprise cannot grow rapidly by means of indefinitely increasing leverage and still remain traditional.

If, for convenience, we define a maximum-leverage point (that is, maximum consistent with retaining the traditional organization) by reference to some ratio of outstanding debt-to-book-value of total assets, the financial constraint on the growth rate of a traditional firm can be made precise. Once the maximum-leverage ratio has been reached, growth is constrained by the need to ensure that at each subsequent round of expansion, the proportionate increase in debt does not exceed the proportionate increase in total capital: if debt is permitted to expand more quickly, the leverage ratio will again begin to rise.[6]

The limits on size can be penetrated by changing the structure of the firm. By corporate reorganization the autocratic figure of the founder is replaced by a management team, and the financing problem is eased by acquiring shareholders (although, as we shall see, the financial growth rate of a company is by no means without limit). Thus, by 'going public' (a British expression for the conversion of a closed corporation into an open one) traditional enterprises can continue to grow in a new form, and this has been the origin of an overwhelming proportion of established public corporations. The advantages to the firm are obvious; less obvious are the advantages to the owner-founder. Before the change, the growth of the enterprise was closely associated with the growth of his personal wealth;

after the change, the connection is considerably weakened. Why, then, does he agree? He may be approaching retirement and seeking a convenient method of realising his gains, a motive that is particularly powerful where taxation discriminates against income. Or he may have concluded that the economies of scale he had been losing were so considerable that co-operation with other people and other capital would, on balance, increase the growth of the value of his own equity, despite the fact that he would no longer be sole owner. Finally, he may in truth be more interested in promoting the continued growth of the organization he has founded, for its own sake, even though his personal financial position will not be significantly improved. The organization may have become an expression of his ego, and its growth as such may provide direct utility. There is nothing in the rules of traditional capitalism to require an owner-manager to exclude all forms of satisfaction other than money. Where the founder can make arrangements that will guarantee him an important continuing role until such time as he chooses to retire, this motive of continuity is particularly likely to be effective, but even where he cannot make such arrangements, the founder may nevertheless obtain pleasure from watching the further development of his 'baby' long after he has ceased to direct it.

R. H. Tawney showed how Protestantism released commerce from ethical restraints on money-making; Protestantism was thus associated with capitalism in a two-way relationship of cause and effect.[7] Max Weber suggested how the Protestant ethic directly provided a drive for accumulation.[8] This originated in a special aspect of the doctrine of predestination. Society was divided into the elect and the 'rest', with the latter being irrevocably damned. The profits earned by a man in his business were to be regarded as manifestations not of a stochastic process but of the hand of God. Business success could be interpreted as a sign of grace (that is, of membership of the elect) and if, therefore, God showed one of His elect a good investment opportunity, the beneficiary was duty bound to take it. Combined with the Puritan moral injunction against consumption, the resulting morality implied a continual attempt to maximize profits and to reinvest most of the proceeds. The 'Puritan' was thus a man with an almost unlimited appetite for future wealth who could have been interpreted by economic theory as endowed with a negative rate of time discount. His utility function contained only one variable, and this Divine index was the logarithm of net assets. Of course, if one was not of the elect, nothing was of any use anyway, but, fortunately for society, one did not discover the truth until one died.

It might be possible to reinterpret the motives of traditional business in terms of modern analytic psychology, although, as far as the present author is aware, not much has been done on these lines. Evidently, the business drive is sublimated libido, and perhaps the business itself represents a castrated son. The position is more complicated, however, when actual (uncastrated) sons are employed in the enterprise, and intended to inherit it. The psychological conflicts set up in these situations are familiar, and it is often unclear what the father really wants. The usual conclusion of observers is that he would rather his son succeeded in an organizational environment of his own – the father's – making, than that he genuinely made his way in the world, thus demonstrating manliness. *En-tout-cas*, whether as a sign of grace or to satisfy his ego, the father attaches utility to the continuity of the organization he has founded, as such, irrespective of the direct financial advantage.

As a matter of fact, most organizations have inherent tendencies to attempt to perpetuate themselves. Even though a traditional capitalist would wish his firm to express no more than himself, the firm itself contains individuals who may feel differently. Thus the baby cannot always be prevented from growing and showing signs of independence, whatever the parent may desire. If the baby succeeds, it is almost certain, sooner or later, to be transformed into a modern corporation, an institution of considerable ambiguity, to which we now turn.

THE CORPORATE COLLECTIVE

Unlike many human institutions, the legal 'constitution' of a joint-stock company is carefully specified. The law, however, is mainly concerned to protect creditors and investors from obvious fraud, and has done little to push these great productive institutions in any particular economic or social direction. Thus company law represents no more than a special aspect of the general protection of property in the ordinary legal framework of capitalism. But, however 'non-economic' are the purposes of the corporate constitution, it is the framework within which the game is played and must therefore be taken seriously. A joint-stock company is a legal person intended to engage in trade or business, although it is not compelled to trade and may, in practice, undertake almost any known human activity. This person, which is really a specially defined collective, may sue and be sued, prosecute and be prosecuted, employ labour, own assets, incur debts, and be subjected to taxation. Its management is vested in a board of directors who sign documents, bind the company and generally behave as its agents. None of the directors, however, need necessarily hold a significant equity in the company, nor must the directors necessarily be employees of the company in any other capacity. But directors *may* be substantial equity holders and may be full-time managerial employees.

The company, then, is a legal institution owning productive assets as if it were an individual. Who, then, owns the company? The law provides for a body of shareholders, or more precisely for a body of shares. These are the property of individual holders and, like other property, are transferable to other real persons, either as gifts or for a consideration. They can also be owned by other legal persons. They entitle the owner to a bundle of rights in the company, and generally, but not always, are originally issued in return for some specific consideration such as the subscription of capital. Usually, the resulting rights attaching to the share are *equitable* relative to the consideration – for example, if the consideration is capital, then capital dividend and voting rights are awarded in proportion to the amount of capital supplied. Thus the *company* issues the shares, but the rights inherent in the shares give real persons some aspects of part-ownership of the company. Strictly, however, all that a shareholder owns is a bundle of rights. His shares are his property; the company is not. The shareholders are not the legal owners of the assets of the company, nor even, in many countries, of the current profits before distribution.

The directors, on the other hand, are servants of the company, and not, apparently, of the shareholders. But do the rights inherent in the shares not provide the holders with virtual *de facto* ownership and control? Many people believe this to be the case (and, indeed, many believe, erroneously, that shareholders are proprietors *de jure*), and it is certainly true that if a company is not owned by its members, it is owned by no one. Almost universally, the company meeting appoints the directors; therefore the right to vote at the meeting apparently provides definite indirect collective control. Similarly, the rights to dividend and capital imply a position which, if a long way from that of sole owner, is by no means that of a true *rentier*. This, however, is far from the end of the matter. For it is the directors who determine the dividend, and they have gradually acquired discretion to withhold considerable proportions of current profits, which then, either as fixed or liquid assets, become the property of the company. This capital accumulated from retained profits 'belongs' to the shareholders only to the extent provided by their specific rights. The increased capital behind each share should lead to increased earnings, from which shareholders will benefit provided these are distributed. Shareholders also benefit if the directors decide on a capital distribution, or if the business is sold. But the shareholders cannot, in general, directly initiate a capital distribution except by enforcing total liquidation: that is, by causing the assets to be sold at break-up value.

In social accounting terms, company law creates concepts of corporate income and corporate capital, distinct from and by no means identical with the more familiar concepts of personal income and personal capital: the value of company assets is not necessarily equal to the market value of corresponding stocks. Through gradual development of the practice of substantial dividend retentions, corporate assets – created from corporate income – have become a partly autonomous factor in the economic system, and the industrial capital of Western democracies is no longer divided into two classes, 'public' and 'private', but rather into three: 'public', 'private' and 'corporate'. The corporate sector likes to be described as 'private', but this may represent no more than a desire to conceal, and thus protect, the underlying independence.

Corresponding to the third concept of capital, we may identify a third body of persons, rivalling the shareholders for its control. These are 'the managers' – a term of art which, since Burnham,[9] has been generally applied to people who control and operate, but do not substantially 'own' productive institutions. To Veblen[10] and Burnham they were technicians, and Veblen thought they were not powerful. Berle and Means saw them as neither technicians nor capitalists, but rather as disembodied entrepreneurs enjoying many of the fruits of capitalism without themselves providing much capital or taking proportionate risks. More recent writers have emphasized their role as organizers and administrators. This is surely correct. It was by providing virtually a new factor of production – the capacity for large-scale organization – that the new system broke the restraints on traditional capitalist production. Large-scale production depends uniquely on large-scale organization. The profits and dividends of large companies are derived from the professional abilities of people who know how to flatten the U-shaped cost curve. This ability gives them considerable influence and bargaining power.

It is sometimes supposed that, in the corporate sector, boards of directors may be regarded as trustees for shareholders, that they are, in fact, akin to watchdog committees set up to keep management in its place. This view, however, is not supported by legal authorities, and in any case the managers have themselves considerably assimilated the directorial system. Legally, the function of the board is to operate the company. For the purpose, it employs executives who may themselves, as we have seen, be directors. But board members who are also full-time employees command the power of organization and hence must, in general, dominate. Thus, by combining the functions of employee and employer, the management body is considerably freed from direct external restraints, a condition that is emphasized by the fact that the vast majority of board nominations are proposed by existing directors. In practice, in many firms, the board itself recedes into the background and operations are taken over by committees of senior executives, not all of whom are necessarily directors.

For these reasons, the distinction between 'management' and stockholders is a valid one, and the two groups may properly be regarded as separate elements in the corporate structure. More precisely, we define 'the management' as the particular in-group, consisting of directors and others, that effectively carries out the functions legally vested in the board. This does not mean that shareholders and management are necessarily opposed, or that policy will necessarily differ from that which might be pursued in a system where managers were immanent. All we are saying is that the two groups are sufficiently distinct, and the managers sufficiently autonomous, for the existence of a harmony of interests not to be regarded as axiomatic. Therefore, in order to understand the economic system of the corporations, it is essential to assess the factors determining the relative influence of, or balance of power between, these two forces operating within them.

The pull of the management in an individual company greatly exceeds the sum of the values of the individuals' qualifications on the open market. The management is a team that has been built up over a period of time and has acquired the unique ability to operate a particular business. The profits earned by the assets depend on the management; they by no means reside entirely in the character of the assets themselves. Indeed, to a considerable extent, the physical assets are notably subordinate to the human assets in the general economic picture of the firm: an investor can far more realistically be said to be buying a share in (that is, interest in) the organization than a share in a particular set of physical assets. In truth, he is buying a compound of the assets and the organization. The organization has special knowledge and ability in managing the assets and the assets have been built up to match the special talents of the organization. This is what is meant by a 'going concern'. Hence the value of the team is very much greater than the sum of the salaries the members could earn if disbanded.

Of course, management can always be replaced. But the new team will not be familiar with the firm's particular operation, even if it has considerable experience of the particular trade. A complete change of management is likely to increase the rate of return on the company's capital only if the existing management is very inefficient. This point is of crucial importance because, as we have seen, in cases where a concentration of shareholders is in a position to impose sanctions on the board, their legal weapon essentially resolves into the threat of dismissal. Shareholders cannot legally interfere with any other aspect of management. In order to remove a senior manager not on the board, against the wishes of the existing board, they must at least threaten to replace a majority of the existing directors with their own nominees. Both sides therefore possess a 'deterrent' of sorts, and the outcome is uncertain. Even in a fairly closely-held company, the management has considerable autonomy through economic influence, because its members represent an organization capable of operating the assets, while the shareholders, in general, do not. It follows as a corollary that the relative strength of a management's position depends *inter alia* on its relative commercial efficiency.

The factor of commercial efficiency, however, is specific to individual firms. More general factors in the balance of power are the procedural facility with which the directors can be dismissed, the distribution of holdings and the various economic consequences of shares being saleable. The right to elect is of little influence if the procedure for dismissal is cumbersome, and the votes themselves are of little influence if they are statistically dispersed and their holders unorganized. But dispersed votes regain their potency if the firm can be threatened with take-over, or if selling activity 'punishes' management in any other way – for example, by affecting future supplies of finance or by damaging managerial prestige.

In England, since the Second World War, all the directors in any public company can be removed by simple majority at a properly constituted meeting. In the USA, where the law varies from state to state, the position is sometimes more circumscribed. In England, shareholders are also restrained by the effect of the law relating to contracts between directors and their companies. And, in general, both in the UK and the USA, dismissal of directors is in practice rare, except where an individual or small organized group has acquired a majority holding and is engaged in a take-over raid.

As to the statistical distribution of holdings, the familiar facts are that the proportion of British and North American manufacturing output produced by companies of the type where a single person or family holds impregnable control has been small for some time past; that by the late 1930s, in two-thirds of large and medium-sized English companies, and in four-fifths of large US companies, in each case not even the top twenty shareholders had between them sufficient stock to command an absolute majority; and that since then dispersion has continued to increase, and in England, at least, the trend appears to have been accelerating. It follows that only by organizing could shareholders, in the majority of cases, make effective use of their votes. But typical shareholders are unorganized almost by definition. They spread their holdings in order to avoid, among other risks, the hazards of finding themselves locked into a firm with whose policies they are dissatisfied, and if, in fact, they are dissatisfied, generally prefer to sell rather than to go to the trouble and expense of organizing opposition. The directors, on the other hand, usually have a small collective holding sufficient to dominate meetings in the absence of concentrated or resolute opposition. Typically, boards hold 1 to 2 per cent of the total equity, a fact that has often been adduced to demonstrate separation of control from ownership. The reinforcing effect on control has received less emphasis. It is particularly significant that while managements do not usually hold large blocks of shares, their holdings are rarely negligible. They are not owner-managers. Perhaps they could be described as 'controller-managers'.

We are forced inevitably to the conclusion that, if shareholders in general possess countervailing power, it must be found mainly in the factors we have yet to discuss – that is, in the transferability of shares and in the existence of an organized stock market. The subject is so important that we begin a separate section.

THE INFLUENCE OF THE STOCK MARKET

Because shares are bought and sold in an organized market, management policies must affect their prices. But these, in turn, react on management in several ways. First, it is by no means unlikely that the market valuation of a company directly enters the managerial utility function. They may feel prestige associated with healthy prices – a sign of approbation from the investing class; they may feel loyalty to their shareholders; or they may have a sense of conscience towards the shares as such: under modern conditions, the share *holders*, as a body of persons, are changing every day, but the shares, though abstract, are constant, and their market price well known. The shares may be thought to represent a collective super-ego, enforcing 'good' (that is, traditional) managerial behaviour. This possibility and its implications are discussed in the next chapter. Note, however, that what we are concerned with is the influence of the stock market as a whole, including potential buyers and actual sellers – that is, we are not merely concerned with the particular individuals who happen to be holding the company's shares at a particular moment. The price of a company's shares may change substantially without any significant change in membership (turnover of stock), and the membership may change substantially without any significant change in price. We are concerned only with the price, with the way it is affected by management policy, and with the way policy may be affected by it. This is the impersonal logic of the corporate system.

Second, share prices may also affect supplies of finance, not only new-issue finance but also, by permeation, borrowing-power in the bond market. There is a double implication. Managers may desire expansion, in which case their utility is affected directly, or, alternatively, if firms pursuing certain policies are unable to expand, in the long run others will predominate: in other words, financial policies inimical to growth do not have survival value.

Third, share prices may favour a radical change in the voting distribution; that is, a take-over raid. Some policies may depress prices so far that the aggregate market value of the equity becomes significantly less than the value, to a single outsider, of the assets behind the equity. The 'outsider' would be a person or organized group who could value the assets on the assumption that sufficient stock was obtained to guarantee easy dismissal of the present directors and a suitable change of policy. Take-over raids are difficult and risky, but if the prospective gain is large enough, the attempt will seem worthwhile. Potential raids are, therefore, and always have been, a real factor to any management wishing to stay in office. Investors value voting rights[11] not so much because they expect to use them, but because they can be sold to someone who might. The balance of power between investor and manager involves two institutions: on the one hand, the stock market, essentially an exchange for *rentier* paper; and on the other, the voting share, something of a pre-managerial phenomenon. Take-overs, as against voluntary mergers, are feared because, typically, after a successful raid, the whole top management is dismissed, losing jobs, prestige and perquisites of office. Thus policies likely to induce raids also lack survival value.

A take-over raider is a person or company aiming for virtual ownership. He or they intend to acquire sufficient stock to be able to dismiss and appoint directors at will, to distribute capital, to amalgamate with other firms controlled, perhaps, by themselves, to appoint executives at salaries of their own choosing – to appoint, perhaps, themselves, their relatives or their friends. They may plan to reorganize the firm, sell the assets, distribute capital and realise quick capital gains. Alternatively, they may intend to continue the business on existing lines, but managed with greater efficiency or with a different pay-out policy. *En-tous-cas*, they require at least 51 per cent of the voting stock and probably more; the precise requirement will depend on the existing distribution of holdings, on the terms of the charter, and on the laws of the country.

Two methods are typically available. Either the raider may attempt to buy the necessary shares on the open market, or he may announce publicly that he will buy all the existing stock at a stated price provided sufficient acceptances are received to ensure the desired degree of control – the so-called conditional offer in a procedure known as a take-over 'bid'.[12] The open-market method suffers from the disadvantage that, unless the market is perfect and the operations perfectly secret, the price is almost certain to rise as the purchases develop. The 'bid' method, on the other hand, suffers because, the announcement being public, the offer price will almost certainly have to be higher than the pre-existing market price, and part of the benefits of the raid will necessarily be shared with the old stockholders. Often, the announcement will also bring other bidders into the field, as the raider's commercial competitors strive to prevent him from increasing his domination of their industry. In practice, the cheapest method is usually some combination of the two, but the average price paid for stock will still almost always exceed the price ruling in the market before the operation began or was rumoured.

For the moment, however, let us assume most of these tiresome details away. The raider can acquire all the stock he needs by secret open-market purchases without affecting the price at all: the average price he pays for stock is the price quoted by dealers the day before he began buying. There are no substantial blocks of votes held by persons or groups who value them above the ruling market price, and the raid is not discovered by the existing management until it is too late; so they cannot defend themselves by announcing policy changes. The purchase price therefore reflects the market valuation based on the expected results of existing managerial policies.

We then ask how the existing management's policies must be constrained if they desire to avoid creating market conditions in which a raid (on our assumptions, necessarily successful) would be likely to occur. Policies lying within the constraints will be called 'safe'. In real life, because markets are imperfect and raiders unable to maintain secrecy, managements will be fairly secure if they pursue policies considerably more dangerous than the most dangerous of those that are safe on this definition; but we can assume validly that the economic characteristics of 'reasonably' safe policies are determined by, and vary with, the characteristics of those defined theoretically as being safe; therefore, by analysing the latter we may also roughly delineate the former (for obvious reasons, the 'limiting case' method is more convenient).

When one takes over a large company, one acquires a particular set of assets associated with a partly specific labour force and a rather more specific body of middle and junior managers; one also acquires various other ingredients known as 'goodwill'. But whatever or whoever one is, if the assets are to continue to earn, one will have to be able to provide a more or less complete new high management. This is evidently a considerable restriction, because circumstances where the assets can be realised in a quick capital gain involving no continuing management are rare, though lucrative. In this book we are concerned with the large companies that produce the bulk of industrial output, and he who wishes to raid these must be able to provide at least the rudiments of the high management needed for large-scale organization. Alternatively, he must accept a lower level of efficiency. If 'he' is some kind of traditional capitalist he should not, in principle, be so well-equipped for the purpose as the typical professional managerial team, and must therefore set his organizational disadvantage against the possible benefits of changes of policy; for this reason, in manufacturing industry, successful raids by traditional capitalists are almost unknown.

However, the 'pure' traditional capitalist is by no means the only species of wolf in the forest. Some raiders combine traditional characteristics with modern; incorporated, but closely held; and concerned mainly with getting rich, but nevertheless capable of considerable organization. Some with apparently traditional motivation are, in fact, akin to management specialists. Finally, of course, powerful raids are made frequently by other purely managerial organizations. The successful among those represent involuntary mergers imposed by one professional team on another, for motives which, at least in principle, may differ considerably from the traditional.

One requirement, however, is common to all raiders: they must have the means of payment. They must either possess or be able to borrow large sums in cash, or, if incorporated, they must either have large reserves or mortgageable assets, or be able to offer to issue new shares in their own company in payment for the shares of the raided company at a rate of exchange that is both acceptable to the recipients and does not dilute the raider's own old stock to a greater extent than is considered desirable or safe. This last method is not compatible with our assumption of secrecy, but the fact that it is widely used in conditional offers only serves to emphasize that, unlike us, real raiders assume real stock markets to be highly imperfect. On our assumptions, raiders must have cash.

In the course of the managerial evolution, the quantity of organizational talent in society has been vastly increased, but in the process it has become professionalized, bureaucratized and largely separated from finance. The majority of professional top managers spend a large part of their working lives in a single firm, and at any one time only a few are seeking to move.[13] When they do move, their method of transfer is professional rather than capitalistic; that is, they do not take capital with them. In the small-business sector, conditions are reversed, and lying between the small and large-scale sectors there is a significant penumbra where traditional and modern methods are mixed. Some of these businesses have large turnovers and yield large profits, but it is noticeable that they are rarely found in industries typically requiring genuine large-scale organization. It follows that, in the modern world, take-over raiders, wherever they occur, are scarce, and being scarce, in order to function, must be appropriately rewarded.

But although they are scarce, they exist, and if sufficiently tempted, will pounce. In measuring the temptation represented by a particular firm, a 'traditional' raider can value the assets on the basis of any pay-out ratio he chooses (because, if successful, the choice will be his), on his own, rather than the market's, rate of discount, and on the rate of return he expects to obtain with the management he intends to install and the investment policy he intends to pursue. Because he is scarce, his discount rate (reflecting the next most profitable use for his capital) will be high, and because he is traditional we may assume that, although of no great managerial efficiency, he will attempt to pursue the investment policy expected to yield the maximum rate of return, given the nature of the business, the character of the assets and his actual organizational capacity.

Because we are not yet ready to discuss theories of managerial motivation, the case of the 'managerial' raider is more vague. We shall, however, be reasonably consistent with our own later arguments if we assume that he or they apply a rate of discount equivalent to the rate of return obtainable with unchanged policies within 'their' own firm and a rate of return no lower than the rate expected from the highest-yielding policy, in the merged organization, consistent with a rate of expansion at least as fast as the rate associated with the existing policy in the raider's present organization. If the managerial raider pays cash, he will also assume a zero retention ratio. (If, violating our assumptions, he uses the exchange-of-share method, he must take account of the fact that any newly-created stock will rank equally for dividend with his own old stock, and the result is therefore affected by the terms of the offer and his own expected retention ratio.) We may then say that a successful managerial raid requires that the return in the merged organization exceeds not only the average of the two old rates, but also the rate expected by the market were the unified firm itself to be taken over by the defending management (if not, the defenders could successfully form a company to retake captor and prize). In other words, the market must believe not only that the merger would be profitable, but also that the new combine would be better managed by the aggressor management than by the defendant. Here again, however, we are wandering into a world that violates the analytical assumptions, because, on these, the market never has an opportunity of assessing the raider.

We thus see how the institutional framework, as specifically represented in an organized market for voting shares, restrains managerial independence in general and, more particularly, the freedom to grow. Unlike the restraints discussed in the earlier part of the chapter, this one is definite and effective, and will be with us for the rest of the book.

TAKE-OVERS FROM THE POINT OF VIEW OF THE ACQUIRING FIRM

The theory of take-over, as described above in the original book, considered the problem mainly from the point of view of the potential target or 'acquired' firm. Not much was said, it will be seen, about acquiring firms as such. In reality, the process of acquisition is a major method whereby firms grow. In effect, by this means firms can to some extent break the contraints on internal growth that were the main concern of the book. Thus the theory and practice of take-over from the point of view of the acquiring firm should be a a major feature of any theory of managerial capitalism. The original text returned to the subject in the context of a discussion of the organizational constraints on growth in Chapter 3 (reproduced largely uncut below).

When the book was written, the disciplines of economics, finance and business management had, to my knowledge, made almost no studies of take-overs. Shortly after the book was published, however, a wave of mergers and take-overs occurred in the Anglo-Saxon countries, followed by a partial relapse in the early 1970s, followed by an explosion in the late 1970s which has continued unchecked ever since. As a result, a very substantial amount of research has been stimulated. A comprehensive bibliography, containing more than a hundred items can be found in Dennis Mueller's (1995) classic paper, 'Mergers: Theory and Evidence'.[14]

All the results confirm the proposition that firms with low market value are liable to be taken-over. This was hardly surprising. More significant, however, are the data concerning the effects of take-overs on the general wealth of the stockholding class. Shareholders in acquired firms make capital gains. What happens to shareholders in acquiring firms? The general evidence is that, on balance, they lose. After making take-overs, the shares of acquiring firms, on balance, decline. Dennis Mueller calculates that the net effect, for shareholders as a class, is probably negative. It is very difficult to reconcile this with the proposition that managerial raiders are motivated solely by the desire to benefit their own shareholders. But once a managerial bias towards growth is hypothesized, the results fall into place.[15]

I conclude with a final reported quotation from the newly-appointed chief executive of Abbey National savings bank, one of Britain's most popular shares (which had recently failed in an attempt to merge with the leading retail bank, Natwest): 'He also raised the prospect of returning up to £500 million of excess capital to shareholders. In the absence of an acquisition or rapid internal growth, he would not be opposed to a share buyback'. (The Times, *Business News, 24 October, 1997, p. 26). Different people can interpret the nuances in different ways. Why not ask the shareholders whether they would prefer a distribution or an acquisition?*

POSTSCRIPT: A REPLY FROM DENNIS MUELLER

I sent the foregoing passage to Dennis Mueller for comment, and believe I can best serve the reader by quoting his reply in full, as follows:

When you first described the takeover mechanism in the early 1960s, they were fairly rare in North America, and large firms were essentially immune from the threat due to the transaction costs of financing them. In the mid-80s, however, raiders like Boone Pickens appeared and began borrowing money from banks based on the value of the assets of the firms that they were trying to takeover, M. Milliken invented the junk bond to finance takeovers, etc. The constraints placed on managers by 'the market for corporate control' tightened. The reactions of managers were interesting. On the one hand, they tried to protect their skins by introducing poison pills, golden parachutes, and getting the legislatures of the states in which they were incorporated to pass legislation that made takeovers more expensive. On the other hand, they did try and improve the performance of their firms. This took the form of spin-offs, downsizing, and a return to 'core competencies'. Firms also began to repurchase their shares to add value. Thus, the 1980s and their aftermath is exactly what your theory predicts would happen by a structural change that reduces the costs of takeovers.

In this regard, I think these events cast doubt on both Oliver Williamson's claims about the efficiency gains from vertical integra-

tion, and your claims that firms can expand indefinitely via diversification without running into diminishing returns. If vertically integrated firms were more efficient, then managers would not react to a tightening of the takeover constraint by spinning off parts of their vertical chains and shifting to 'outsourcing'. Ditto diversification. The finance literature is now full of articles that show that diversified firms are less efficient and explain this via 'agency problems'. But it is essentially your theory. You might also want to comment on the rediscovery of your theory as the theory as the 'free-cash-flow' theory.[16]

When I wrote in my merger survey, 'Those who espouse this hypothesis...' I meant by 'this hypothesis' the claim that all mergers and takeovers can be explained as attempts by well-managed firms to replace the bad managers of the acquired companies, i.e. not your 'managerial' hypothesis.

2 Motives and Morals

We believe the arguments of Chapter 1 are sufficient to establish that, in the modern system, management has considerable freedom of action. Shareholders may impose minimum constraints on, for example, investment policy, but there is no evidence that general equilibrium of the system requires these minima to become maxima. Most of the relevant markets are imperfect, and in one case, that of the capital market, this is a critical factor in the intracorporate balance of power itself. In some cases, notably those of the markets for manual labour and for products, the resulting problems have been studied intensively by both economists and sociologists, but this work has not been matched by equivalent work in relation to management. Economists have investigated management attitudes to particular problems, such as price determination and, more recently, investment policy, but there exists not one comprehensive or rigorous study of the basic motivational forces determining business decisions in general.

Whether or not this state of affairs is a cause for surprise, it is certainly a considerable hindrance to understanding the working of a modern economic system. The present chapter therefore represents an attempt, albeit tentative, to explore the neglected area in a fuller and more systematic manner. We offer no apology for the fact that in our subsequent analysis manual workers are rarely mentioned: we do not fail to recognize that they, as producers and consumers, are the primary citizens of the system, but we feel they have already been adequately studied elsewhere, whereas, by contrast, insufficient attention has been paid to the men who make, rather than merely experience, the contemporary capitalist environment. We are not in a position to offer a major contribution to the study of managerial motivation as such. In the present state of knowledge we can do no more than produce reasoned arguments for hypotheses we believe to be plausible in order to form the basis for a theoretical economic analysis. Ultimately, only the reader can decide whether he feels the hypotheses suggested are in fact sufficiently plausible to justify the uses to which they will be put.

We start from the premise, previously discussed, that there are no rigid rules of the game which bind managers to a particular set of policies or to a particular goal in their capacity as organizers and administrators of modern corporations. They have the freedom to chose from a wide range of policies, a number of which affect the rules of the game. Our central problem in this chapter is to discover the policies that managers seem most likely to pursue in their conduct of the corporations; what objectives they are supposed to follow, or which they set for themselves, to follow and why they do so. In answering this question and in exploring managerial motivation, we shall try to take the problem out of the narrow, utilitarian mould of conventional economic analysis and to consider it from a wider perspective. We shall bring to bear on the subject available information from other social sciences and from the behavioural school, and we shall eventually suggest a utility system possessing a number of psychological, sociological and economic elements such as desire for power, status, wealth and personal security. Similarly, we shall find that internal sociology of working in a team, the managerial code of professional competence, the system of rewards for the managers in the form of salary, bonus or stock-option schemes, and the objective nature of the organization of the modern corporation can be made to yield definite behavioural implications. The main concluding theorem is that the various pressures mentioned above lead managers to maximize the rate of growth of the firm they are employed in subject to a constraint imposed by the security motive.

THEORIES OF MOTIVATION

There are three main approaches to any problem in human motivation, loosely, the psychological, the sociological and the economic, the last being further divisible into two, which we may call the 'broad' and the 'narrow'. The psychological approach concentrates on the individual's inner wants and drives. The sociological approach modifies psychological drives by systematic reference to the effects of his social situation, and of his involvement – that is, with other individuals at work and at play. The two economic approaches are not alternatives; both represent a calculus of rationality founded in utilitarianism; both endow humans with psychological, sociological and material needs, expressed in utility functions which, once specified, serve as vehicles for the analysis of consistent behaviour – the latter representing the main problem of interest. The distinction lies in the feature that the 'broad' considers all variates, while the other concentrates on so-called 'narrow' economic factors such as income, wealth, tangible consumption and saving.

The psychological method may also be subdivided: into that of the 'behaviourist' school on the one hand, and that which, for want of a better word, might be called the 'purposive' on the other. It is convenient to defer discussion of the behaviourists until later in the chapter: briefly, rather than asking what it is the individual want or needs, this school asks how, given his neuronic equipment and informational situation, he appears likely to be induced to behave.[1]

PSYCHOLOGICAL MOTIVES

'Purposive' psychological studies of the type required for suggesting ways in which psychology may influence business decisions are as rare as any. Some studies have been made of the character-types of successful executives, but in no case is it clear whether the elements discovered may not also be typical of any successful professional man, or at least of any successful administrator. The work of two writers, however, deserves attention. As long ago as 1948, W. E. Henry published the results of interviews with a sample of a hundred successful top managers, concisely describing his findings as those of a 'study in the psycho-dynamics of a social role'.[2] He noted that these men tended to be psychologically well-integrated people who nevertheless possessed strong drives towards achievement. As might be expected from the fact that only the successful were selected for interview, these drives were found to be pressing and continuous; as fast as objectives were achieved, new aspirations arose. Also unsurprisingly, the subjects were not merely ambitious but also active; not dreamers, but doers. They were impelled, it seems, to move continually onward and upward, at least until nearing retirement. The implications for the theory of the firm would be that whatever it is the executive wishes to do with his organization, he is always attempting to repeat and enlarge the performance; and while the drive is personal, the dynamic effect must surely wash over into the behaviour of the firm as such. An individual may partly satisfy dynamic aspirations by rising within one firm or by successive inter-firm transfers, but as he approaches the top, unless transfers are easy, he can progress further only by inducing the firm itself to grow. In other words, the motive for collective expansion may be founded directly in personal ambition.

The second psychological contribution to be mentioned is that of George Katona.[3] In a book concerned with the psychological aspects of economic behaviour as a whole, this author argues forcefully that the executive is likely to identify his own ego with 'his' own firm. Rather than seeing the firm as a mere apparatus for satisfying personal wants, he sees the prosperity and success of the firm as an actual proxy for his wants. In the extreme, this hypothesis would predict that a man would not mind suffering personal privation provided only that the firm was doing well. Unfortunately, because the relevant criteria of a firm's success are not defined, the policy implications are ambiguous. Katona suggests that business success is defined by profits, but, except to the extent that profits are required to expand other possible indices, such as turnover, this is no more than an induction. William Baumol, for example[4] – one of only two economists to have previously attempted an overtly managerial theory of the firm – states that in his experience as a business consultant he found a dominant desire for maximum turnover, and suggested that this end was generally pursued, subject to a minimum profit constraint. Baumol's experience is supported by the common observation of anyone with contacts in the business world, or who has studied business periodicals. In the periodical literature, for example, 'profits' and 'turnover' seem to be used indiscriminately as synonyms for 'good'. The real distinction, however, as we shall soon see, lies between indices such as aggregate turnover, aggregate profits or aggregate assets, which necessarily vary with the scale of the firm, and others, such as rate of return or profit margin, which do not. If Katona's motive of self-identification is applied to indices which vary with scale, it reinforces our deductions from the findings of Henry, because, if executives tend to identify with the organizations in which they already happen to be employed, they are less likely to seek an outlet for ambition by transfer, and more likely to choose the method of internal expansion. With this conclusion we move on to sociology.

SOCIOLOGICAL MOTIVES[5]

To apply the sociological method to business motivation it is necessary to characterize the businessman's social role and his place in the social structure; in particular, we need valid descriptions of the class to which he generally belongs, and of the norms, if any, to which he is predominantly subject. Is he merely another species of professional man, like a doctor, a teacher or a technician – the ideal type envisaged by the originators of the idea of the managerial revolution? Is he the possessor of a distinct professional ethic based on a clear perception of duty to society, leading by implication to the concept of a corporate conscience? Is he, as Kenn Rodgers has suggested, governed mainly by unconscious prejudice? Is he the helpless prisoner of William Whyte's conformist organizational ethic?

Or is he fundamentally no more than a loyal member of the class identified by C. Wright Mills as the 'corporate rich' – intermarried, interdependent and intermotivated with the small group of families who still own the great proportion of most (non-socialist) nations' private wealth. The answers, of course, are all affirmative. More than any other type, the business executive is many-sided and multi-motivated. He has professional ethics, he feels a sense of public service, and is not insensitive to public opinion. He is both a member of the corporate rich and an Organization Man. But it seems that the nearer he gets to the top, the more he is of the former and the less of the latter (Whyte's account, it will be remembered, related particularly to middle managers, and he noted that chief executives and such appeared to be rather different). Or, to switch to David Riesman's language, it would seem that top men are still characteristically 'inner-directed'. Neo-Marxists of the Wright Mills school might argue that these men were, of course, the ones most closely connected with the propertied class, and that the other-directedness of middle management arose from its relative impotence in face of the power realities in the strata above them. In the present book, however, we are not primarily concerned with the politics or general sociology of contemporary capitalism. We need only the minimum 'non-economic' hypotheses required for the bases of valid models of the system's microeconomics. We are not interested in the way top executives vote, lobby or otherwise pressurize society. We are interested only in the way their norms affect their internal or 'operational' decisions. Thus a good part of the material in debate between those who regard managers as deinstitutionalised professional men, and those who regard them a institutionalised tycoons, can be ignored. The implications of what remain prove tenuous, while not, however, unsuggestive.

The Wright Mills thesis implies that managers should have a marked sense of loyalty towards the propertied class as a whole, including both those who are managers and those who are not. Being himself relatively rich, the typical manager holds considerably more equity stock than the average citizen, and while the bulk of his portfolio does not typically consist of shares in the corporation that employs him, he may nevertheless feel precisely that sense of 'conscience towards the shares' at which we first hinted in Chapter 1. He may be inhibited from pursuing policies which, in his secondary role as a man of property, he would not like to see pursued by another firm of which he was himself a shareholder. If valid, this would seem a very powerful consideration indeed; as powerful, perhaps, as that represented in the fear of take-over raids.

Ambiguities, however, remain. In the Neo-Marxist conception, the 'corporate rich' are by no means typical investors: they are people of power with important minority holdings in relative small numbers of strategically placed companies. Towards more typical shareholders, managers may feel no more and no less a sense of duty than they do towards, say, manual employees or customers. (In nasty old Britain we would say it all depends on whether managers think of themselves as middle-class or upper-class, the answer being that some are middle-class, and some upper.) But if we are prepared to ignore this difficulty, we can with reasonable confidence adopt the hypothesis that some kind of stockholder-orientated conscience does usually exist in the managerial breast and that this is best expressed by saying that the current market quotation of the shares may enter the managers' utility function as an independent variate.

A conscience, however, is as much a source of potential conflict as of harmony. Managers, in considering how they would expect other managers to behave, and hence how they themselves should behave, must surely recognize the legitimacy of self-interest, particularly if, as has been suggested earlier, their world is unusually materialistic. If, for example, policies required to maximize the market value of the stock would conflict with policies required to further some other recognized managerial end, moral behaviour need not insist that the former should always take precedence over the latter, because managers will expect other managers to sympathize with the position. Consequently, the most likely result is compromise.[6] If the resulting policies are criticized for failing to *maximize* market value, the corporate leader may argue that he, and he alone, knows what is best for the corporation and its shares in the long run. Such an attitude may be seen as the other face of managerial paternalism.

All ethics conflict with self-interest, and few societies rely on the effectiveness of conscience alone. Sanctions are universal. But if moral behaviour depends exclusively on enforcement (as is still the case in unfortunate countries where the people lack a well-developed sense of public morality), the outcome is notoriously inefficient and not infrequently results in social and economic stagnation. By contrast, in better-balanced societies, internalized discipline effectively reinforces external sanction, and the social mechanism is permitted to function with the minimum of policing. The analogy must surely be valid for business. In adhering to a reasonable minimum stock market value, the firm not only satisfies conscience but also avoids the sanction of take-over. We do not argue that managers' attitudes to the stock market were governed solely by fear of raiders; we believe their attitudes in this area to be almost precisely analogous to that of middle-class children in relation to stealing and the police.

The idea of a conscience reinforced by a discipline can be applied to other aspects of corporate policy, in particular to the double restraint on excessive leverage which should be imposed by fear of the personal consequences of financial failure (that is, of loss of employment) on the one hand, and by a conscience towards the equity-holders on the other.

A NORM OF PROFESSIONAL COMPETENCE

To whatever class he belongs in the context of his home, his club or his general culture, the manager at work is in continuous contact with colleagues from whom he experiences both pressures and stimuli. What form will these take? In attempting an answer, we are faced with an almost complete *lacuna* in established knowledge and are virtually forced to improvise.

Groups of people collaborating in teams tend to develop what might be described as 'a norm of professional competence' in relation to the efficiency of individual performance. When one member is inefficient, the others inevitably suffer, if only because they are often compelled to take on part of his work. Consequently, the delinquent may experience contempt and even hatred.[7]

The norm, however, has positive as well as negative aspects. Not only are incompetents despised, but competent individuals, even when personally unattractive, are admired. And the desire for professional approbation being one of the most powerful features middle-class masculine psychology, the most competent and aspiring members of any team will tend to favour 'testing' policies – that is, policies which provide opportunities for demonstrating prowess and by the same token increase the group's relative need for people of ability. In other words, such men will favour the setting of difficult rather than easy goals, and in business they will press for the adoption of policies that emphasize the least routine aspects of the collective function. Of course, their views will not always prevail. Internal social equilibrium (and hence efficiency) will require that attention also be paid to the needs of the weaker vessels. How the balance is struck will vary considerably between organizations, those in which the tearaways dominate usually being described as 'go-ahead' or 'dynamic'. In all cases, however, because ability to persuade others is in business life fairly well correlated with ability in general (persuasive ability being so much a requirement of the general function), there should be a tendency for the more aggressive policies to push to the front and to be restrained (in a sociological sense) only by the specific 'drag' of the weaker members; apparent exceptions usually turn out to involve firms containing strong residual traditional-capitalist elements.

Unfortunately, to say that executives will be influenced by a norm of professional competence does not provide immediate policy implications, because, in the absence of clearly defined goals (unlike the case of football) we have no established criteria by which competence is to be judged, or methods by which ability is to be demonstrated. A man may be judged competent by the quality of his decisions, but if we do not know the organization's goals, how do we tell whether a decision is 'good'? The answer, perhaps, is a criterion based less on the nature of the decisions than on the manner of their taking and execution; alternatively, perhaps, on the ability to persuade others of their desirability. In other words, the criterion of competence may be derived mainly from the character of the function.

We have previously argued that the functional essence of management lay in the provision of organization. Organization involves not only taking decisions, but also co-ordinating decisions and generally seeing that they are made swiftly, consistently, and apparently in accordance with policy. In principle, the 'pure' organizer is not supposed to make policy but only to carry it out. But the power of management, we have seen, lies in the fact that wherever an organizational task is of a high order – as is necessarily the case in business – people entrusted with executing policy in practice inevitably acquire considerable influence over its determination.

As we have already emphasized, the testing tasks of business are those that are the least routine: the development and marketing of new products and of new methods of production, the planning and execution of expansion, and the creation of organization where none previously existed. Business administration differs from other administration in that the unit of organization, the firm, is autonomous and expandable. A business organization has the peculiar capacity to promote its own growth, because it can seek its own supplies of factors of production (including those of managerial personnel) and is free to attempt to develop demand for its own products. Unlike a government department, a business has no 'establishment' laid down by Treasury, Parliament or Congress which can be varied only by negotiation. If sales can be made to expand, the resulting revenue is sufficient justification and means for hiring new personnel, and the necessary capital can be obtained directly or indirectly from the profits of previous successes. But all expansion requires organization and planning, and if not carefully organized and planned may be halted by various failures expressed economically in reduced profitability. Well-planned and well-executed expansion, on the other hand, is both stimulating and self-sustaining, and thus represents to the executive a challenge similar to the challenge of difficult climbs in mountaineering. But in both mountaineering and business there is little sympathy for those who overreach themselves. Here, then, we perhaps have the beginning of a theory. It is difficult to award the accolade of professional ability to a chief executive who competently maintains a constant output, with constant profits, constant product mix, and constant methods of production in a constant market! In order to demonstrate ability he must develop new markets, increase his share of old ones, develop new methods of production, organize a merger, or at the very least do *something*.

There are reasons for supposing that the professional environment will not only favour organizational expansion, but it will also influence both the quality and direction of expansion and the means employed to achieve it. No one really believes that real-life traditional capitalists are necessarily interested only in money, albeit with a peculiar rate of time discount. Given imperfect markets, and hence an element of transcendence, traditional capitalists are able to choose products because they like them, or at least like producing for them. In general, the social sense of the traditional capitalist, where it exists (and, of course, there are some who lack any), consists in producing goods he feels he might want to consume himself; alternatively, he may enjoy their vicarious consumption, convinced that at least one major class of consumers will not only buy but also need them. Traditional capitalists also derive considerable satisfaction from providing employment; the sense of true paternalism, of having provided new opportunities for earning income, being very noticeable in this type of manufacturer.

The 'bureaucratic' environment of the large corporation, on the other hand, is likely to divert emphasis from the character of the goods and services produced to the skill with which these activities are organized. To the extent that professional competence is tested by expansion, any new product that sells will serve, and turnover, profits and organizational facility may become the exclusive criteria of assessment. Reputations will be built not only on the ability to notice products likely to succeed, but also on the ability to plan development, push sales and control the relationship between input and output. Finally, there may develop a rather cynical attitude to both customers and workers. The concept of consumer-need disappears, and the on question of interest in connection with a proposed new product, whether a sufficient number of consumers, irrespective of 'need', can be persuaded to buy it. The professional manager may feel less paternalism towards, and greater social distance from, the manual workers. 'Workers' become analogous to irritating pieces of machinery, always going wrong and interfering with the essential activity of the organization, whatever that may be: the correct solution to labour troubles is a skilful personnel officer, himself another brand of technician.

In other words, the existence of a 'managerial' norm of competence is a possible explanation for some of the alleged irrational purposelessness and soullessness of which modern capitalism is accused by many liberal critics. The point should not be overdrawn; purposelessness may be inherent in all conditions of capitalist affluence, whether or not the institutional form is traditional managerial. Furthermore, it is by no means certain that organizations of the modern type may not also develop biases for and again particular types of product. Such biases might be mainly unconscious, but are none the less effective for that.

The theoretical implications would be as follows. Managerial organizations would favour growth, and this, we shall see, usually involves diversification. In principle, given the powers of large-scale organization, no firm is restricted to any one product group: in principle it is free to roam the economy, ever seeking new outlets. In practice, the extent of the search will be limited not only by dynamic restraints, but also, perhaps, by this unconscious bias. Some products will not be considered at all, others will be rejected for economically inadequate reasons, and yet others taken up only to fail because feet were dragged in promoting them. Similarly, favoured products will be adopted and made to succeed, from allied causes. Given the very considerable uncertainty involved in assessing the economic prospects of any new product, such suggestions are not implausible. They are reinforced, as we shall see later, by similar factors operating from the side of technology. In the meantime, we suggest the best short description of the motivation induced by social existence in a managerial group is that of a drive towards efficient, well-organized expansion, associated with a persistent search for new opportunities from a set that is perceived as being finite, at least at any one moment of time. With these hypotheses, we are ready to enter the supposedly better charted areas of both 'broad' and 'narrow' economic motivation proper.

ECONOMIC MOTIVES (BROAD)

Until fairly recently, economists tended to argue that the distinction between broad and narrow economic approaches, as we have defined them, represented mainly a question of convenience: because the effects of the narrower variates in the utility function, such as income and wealth, were more easily analyzed, the profession felt justified in concentrating on them alone, and in assuming that the introduction of others would be unlikely seriously to modify the qualitative, if not the quantitative, character of conclusions. In the field of consumer behaviour, the dangers of this approach have now been appreciated for some time, and it is known, for example, that the introduction of sociologically interdependent preferences[8] may seriously affect important theorems in both normative and positive economics. On the side of production, however, discussion of the implications of 'broad' behaviour is still more or less rudimentary. Apart from the work of the behaviourist school, such discussion as there has been of economic motivation among salaried executives has been vitiated by the influence of a utilitarian tradition which grossly over-simplifies the character of the pleasures and pains associated with 'work'. In classical economics,[9] there were two sorts of people: entrepreneurs concerned exclusively with profits, and workers concerned only to maximize the difference between the pleasures derived from income and the pains derived from labouring. Work was always unpleasant, always axiomatically a source of disutility. We now know that, even for manual employees, this simplification can lead to serious errors, especially when applied, for example, to incentive schemes. When applied to the kind of 'worker' supposedly represented in management, the errors are even greater and their economic implication more far-reaching. The orthodox approach regarded both the modern manager and the traditional entrepreneur as, like the manual worker, little more than crude machines, delivering output in a one-for-one dire relationship to the associated monetary reward. The possibility of deriving considerable positive satisfaction from the function was thus ignored. Several writers, including Norman Buchanan and Chester Barnard[10] began questioning the orthodox view as long ago as the late 1930s, but few of their pertinent observations were absorbed into the mainstream of economic theory.

The first comprehensive survey of the problem was undertaken in a classic study by R. A. Gordon in 1945,[11] who summarized the position as follows:

> The most important spurs to action by the businessman, other than the desire for goods for direct want-satisfaction, are probably the following: the urge for power, the desire for prestige and the related impulse of emulation, the creative urge, the propensity to identify oneself with a group and the related feeling of group loyalty, the desire for security, the urge for adventure and for 'playing the game' for its own sake, and the desire to serve others. ... These motives can be satisfied more or less through monetary rewards. They can also be satisfied in good part by other attractions which the large corporation offers its business leaders.[12]

He then went on to discuss the various motivational elements identified above at greater length. For example, of the desire for power, he said:

> One of the most important of the non-financial incentives offered by the large corporation is the opportunity to satisfy the urge for personal power. The corporation executive possesses power by virtue of his position of authority in a firm which is itself powerful. His power is a product of his position rather than of personal wealth. Power in this case means authority over subordinates, control of the disposal of vast resources, and great influence over persons and affairs outside the firm. The corporation is a vehicle through which power comes to be held and exercised. ... Power thus secured increases with the size of the firm. Here lies an important explanation of the tendency of many firms to become larger, even if sometimes the profitability of such expansion is open to serious question.[13]

And of the desire for security:

> As we have seen, the large corporation caters effectively to this desire for security. The executive's compensation is relatively stable, and he is likely to have a high degree of security of tenure. Wholesale purges of executive ranks are rare, and top management, usually securely in control of the proxy machinery, seldom has to worry about retaining its position.[14]

Gordon's conclusions have since become widely accepted, although it has to be admitted that none of the hypotheses have been tested by methods which sociologists would regard as rigorous. The author was relying considerably on secondary material and did not indicate clearly to what extent the conclusions were directly supported in the case studies on which his book as a whole was based. Nevertheless, it can hardly be denied that the arguments are persuasive, and many would no doubt accept them as self-evident or adequately supported by introspection. In what follows we shall accept them as being broadly correct.

We take as working assumptions, then, that in addition to 'narrow' economic rewards, such as salary, bonus, stock options, expense allowances, cars, call girls and the like, executives desire power, status, opportunity for creative satisfaction, opportunity for group-belonging, and security. What are the policy implications? In attempting an answer, it is essential to distinguish between collective and individual aspects of the problem. Some policy decisions affect overall managerial utility in a Paretian sense; others do not. Some factors entering individual utility do not affect collective utility and vice versa. As a matter of fact, the individual executive rarely has the opportunity to trade off between power, salary, security and so on, because these are usually offered to him in rather fixed proportions. For a number of reasons, some obvious, and some discussed later in the present chapter, a man's advance in the executive hierarchy is almost always associated with commensurate gains in salary, 'perks', power, status (both internal and external) and security (the last through the medium of service contracts and pension arrangements). Thus this package of utilities, seen from the viewpoint of the individual, is no more than a general measure of personal success, and tells us little directly about decision-taking. With the possible exception of departmental empire building, there is no obvious way in which an individual's policy decisions affect his relative chances of promotion. Furthermore, it is not until he has already reached a high position that he has much influence over policy in any case. It follows that the key to our problem is to be found, if anywhere, in the factors affecting collective utility alone.

There are clearly wide areas where policy choices affect the capacity of an organization to provide utility for its members as a whole, and for its top executives in particular. In some cases, the results come in combination, as, for example, when expansion increases the number of high-level posts available to be filled by internal promotion, and thus enhances the prospects of both power and salary for existing members – but in others they do not. The effect of expansion on security, for example, depends on the associated effect on the likelihood of collective dismissal, which depends in turn on the danger of take-over or financial failure. Unlike the civil servant, the industrialist's immediate livelihood depends intimately on the continuity of his own organization; if the organization is disbanded there is no residual institution available to guarantee him employment. And if a top executive is thrown on the market because his previous firm has failed, he will be tainted with the failure, and the demand for his services correspondingly affected. A large firm is more difficult to take over than a small firm, but a firm attempting to grow too fast may, as we have seen, incur serious risks. Thus if two firms growing at different rates happen to reach the same absolute size at a given moment, the faster grower may be less secure – although, if it survives it will eventually, of course, overtake the slower grower not only in size but also in security.

Similar arguments apply to security from financial failure. A large firm in crisis is able to find temporary assistance more easily than is a small firm, but the likelihood of crisis is itself considerably affected by leverage, which in turn reacts on both size and growth. It is therefore significant that the great majority of firms practise only moderate leverage: in the UK, for example, it has been found that over half the quoted companies pay out less than 10 per cent of their net profits in interest while, at the other extreme, only an insignificant fraction pay out more than 50 per cent: in the USA the ratio of debt to gross assets has typically been found to be less than 20 per cent.

So, when expressed in terms of effects on collective utility, the policy implications of the 'R. A. Gordon motives' prove both analyzable and important. They imply that power, salary, status and so on come as joint products on one dimension of a transformation function, while security from take-over and financial failure is a competing product on another. The rate of transformation between them depends on accounting practices and stock-market behaviour, a relationship which must be a fundamental feature of any well-developed theory of the managerial enterprise.

So far, however, the existence of a further link between power–salary–status and organizational growth is no more than a working hypothesis. Our next task, therefore, is to show a convincing argument why decisions leading to the expansion of a firm are likely to increase satisfaction for the men who make them.

For this purpose we propose to concentrate attention on the narrowest of all economic rewards, that is, the various financial elements incorporated in salary, bonus and stock-option profits. If is accepted that these almost always come jointly with power, status and so on, propositions established in relation to the one group of utilities will tend also to be valid for the other.

ECONOMIC MOTIVES (NARROW)

The empirical study of managers' incomes is largely confined to the USA; and even there, until fairly recently, the amount of material hardly did justice to the importance of the subject. In contrast to the volumes that have been published about the wages of manual workers, probably less than half a million words have been devoted to the factors determining the rewards of the small group of men who, at the heads of large corporations, determine the economic destinies of nations.

First, a few basic facts. In a typical firm, the total compensation of all corporate offices (presidents, vice-presidents, treasurers and secretaries) represents about 2 per cent of value added and about 5 per cent of profits, the inter-quartile ranges of these ratios running from 1 per cent to 3 per cent, and from 1 per cent to 10 per cent, respectively. Among corporate officers as a whole, bonuses (excluding stock-option profits) account for 30 per cent of the total remuneration, but for chief executives of giant corporations this figure may reach as high as 60 per cent, while for middle managers, not corporate officers, it is typically around 20 per cent. As to stock-option plans, it is thought that at the time of writing about three-quarters of all US quoted companies operate some form of plan, the great majority of these having been instituted since 1950, when capital gains from the exercise of options became liable to tax at the capital-gains rate, and no longer, as previously, at the more severe earned-income rate. Against this general background, we may now consider the analytical implications of the various forms of financial reward in more detail. For convenience, we first discuss bonus, then stock options, and finally basic compensation. Basic compensation or 'salary' is the most 'managerial' form, bonus schemes and stock option plans being regarded in many quarters, of course, as positive devices for inducing traditional motivation among the salariat, or at least for bringing the interests of managers and stockholders into closer accord.

AN ANALYSIS OF BONUS SCHEMES

Current bonuses may be related to the firm's aggregate gross profits, to aggregate net profits, or to net or gross profits after deducting a sum intended to provide a 'normal' return for shareholders. They may also be related, at least in principle, to the actual rate of return, or to dividends. In practice, schemes divide into groups: on the one hand those in which aggregate bonus is made to vary with both profitability and scale, and on the other, those where amount depends on profitability alone, and is therefore independent of scale. In the first group, bonuses may be increased by an expansion of the size of the firm, with a constant rate of return; in the second group, an increase in size will have no effect unless accompanied by a disproportionate increase in profits. The policy implications evidently differ considerably.

Managers subject to a scale-dependent formula are provided with an incentive to expand the size of the firm relative to the number of people with whom the total amount of bonus must be shared. In practice, this is just what happens when a firm grows: in the USA, for example, a 10 per cent increase in size is typically associated with a 2 per cent increase in the number of corporate officers. Therefore, scale-dependent schemes do, in fact, provide a considerable growth incentive, although some may appear to restrain the methods employed.

The implications of the scale-independent formulas are obviously rather different. It therefore of considerable significance that while some of the scale dependent formulae are adopted widely, few of these are. Why are scale-dependent schemes so popular? Dare we suggest that it is because managers, rather than shareholders, devise them? Some writers, indeed, have gone so far as to suggest that the true function of bonuses lies mainly in offering respectability for high levels of compensation which might otherwise be questioned by public opinion.[15]

STOCK-OPTION PLANS

Stock-option plans are another matter. In a typical arrangement the recipient is awarded by the company a right to buy, at a fixed price, a limited quantity of ordinary stock, which then become his absolute property to hold or sell as he pleases. Although he does not have to exercise the right immediately, the price is usually fixed at a small discount on the open-market quotation for the company's regular shares on the day of issue. He is therefore placed in a good position to realize a speculative profit.

The tax regulations, however, require that if the profits are to attract tax at the capital-gains rate alone, the option must be taken up within a relatively short time from the date of issue and the stock must be held for at least two years before selling. In other words, any capital profits must perforce be of the long-run kind, and the beneficiary is precluded from realizing large net gains on a 'quick turn'. But, provided the shares do not enter a period of secular decline after the option has been taken up, once the two years have elapsed it should not normally be difficult for senior executives, aided by inside information, to choose a good moment to sell, if that is what they want.

Provided the profits are not offered in lieu of a regular salary, the arrangements are obviously most attractive to the recipients. Professional people, however well paid, find that because their incomes rise gradually, rather than in jumps, sociodynamic factors inevitably cause expenditure to rise continuously in parallel; they therefore experience peculiar difficulty in saving and thus in accumulating those free assets so desirable for independence, security and a sense of belonging to the propertied class. Discontinuous increases in wealth, as provided in windfall capital gains, are therefore even more welcome than a comparison with the equivalent increase in time-discounted future salary would indicate. Furthermore, the benefit does not appear as a 'cost' in the company's accounts: the option discount (ratio of option price to market price on day of issue) is paid at the expense of regular shareholders in the form of dilution, and the effect, though certain, is difficult to observe. By contrast, if similar sums were paid as orthodox bonuses, they would appear in the accounts as profit-reducing expenses, and would not only attract tax at the full rate, but also, in all likelihood, public comment as well: they would be seen as profit-reducing, dividend-reducing or both. The stock-option method, therefore, represents a way of paying gratuities to managements which has the double advantage of ensuring that the whole cost falls on shareholders, while at the same time reducing the chance that the effect will be noticed. If shareholders, rather than managers, controlled methods of remuneration, they would serve their own interests better by providing incentives of the type offered in scale-independent bonus formulas. But, like bonus schemes, stock-option plans are devised, of course, by managers themselves, and in view of their real nature it is hardly a surprise that they are popular.

The implications are considerable. Whether the recipient finances the transaction from his own resources or employs a loan, he is immediately put in a 'bull' position in relation to his company, a position which, if he wants to avoid income tax, he must maintain for a substantial period. It is also likely that, when the statutory period expires, even though a rational arrangement of portfolio would suggest selling at least part of the issue, inertia and internal pressure to avoid becoming known as a man who sells his company short may lead him to hold on. It seems inevitable, therefore, that whatever the original intention behind the schemes, they will ultimately lead to a significant statistical increase in the proportion of his own company's stock held by the average manager. In fact, statistics relating to the stock proportions held by full-time directors do not yet show any marked trend, although nothing is known, of course, about holdings managers who are not directors. The holdings of the full-time members of a typical board still represent no more than 1 per cent of total stock, and it is possible that these men have be balancing their portfolios by selling old holdings to the equivalent of the amounts of the options taken up. If so, the effects of the movement would be largely confined to middle and upper-middle management, and the policy implications correspondingly reduced. None of these arguments, however, provides sufficient grounds dismissing the quantitative implications of stock options as trivial.

UPDATE ON BONUSES AND MANAGEMENT OWNERSHIP INCENTIVES

Six years later, in 1971, Wilbur Lewellen published a major study of the extent and nature of management stockholding in the United States (The

Ownership Income of Management, *New York: Columbia University Press for the National Bureau of Economic Research). For the period 1940 to 1963 he documented large increases in the value of holdings but falling physical quantities. The increase in value therefore appeared to be strongly associated with the general rise in stock market values of the 1950s and early 1960s. Reviewing the book in the* Journal of Economic Literature *(September 1972) I agreed that a substantial change in the motivational situation had potentially occurred, but argued that some aspects of the developments were ambiguous. For example, management-held shares had not, on average, bettered the market index. By the end of the century, the importance stock-holding in their own companies by top executives had undoubtedly further increased substantially. In 1985, the* Journal of Accounting and Economics *(Issues 3–9) published a major volume of studies under the general heading of 'Management Compensation and the Managerial Labour Market', whose results were summarized by Michael Jensen and Jerold Zimmerman as follows:*

The papers documented that: (1) executive compensation is positively related to share price performance; (2) poor firm performance is associated with increased executive turnover; (3) managers choose accounting methods that tend to increase their bonuses; (4) the adoption of new long term executive compensation plans are associated with positive share-price reactions; (5) the death of a firm's founder is associated with positive price reactions; (6) managers are less likely to make take-overs that lower their stock prices when they hold more stock in their firm. These findings generally support the view that executive compensation packages help align managers' and shareholders interests. (p. 4)

For a more complex picture, the contemporary reader may refer to the papers by Cubbin, Hall, Hill, Snell and Hunt, cited in the paper 'Managerial Theories of the Firm' reprinted from the International Encyclopedia of Business and Management *as Chapter 5 of the present edition of this book (p. 117). It is my opinion that the Jensen group gives the impression of being rather enthusiastic for the view that in contemporary capitalism (with just a small exception in the matter of bonus accounting) everything is for the best in the best of all possible worlds. A couple of critical comments concerning points (3) and (6) respectively may be in order.*

In the years following 1985 management bonuses *have become larger, more troublesome and more the subject of political comment. They have become a particularly hot topic in the financial sector where, because the performance of dealers and investment managers can in principle be clearly quantified, they have on the one hand spread down through the hierarchy and on the other led to a number of disasters. In the UK an ancient and highly respected merchant bank was made insolvent and one of the largest nationwide retail banks seriously damaged. The general cause has been the inadequate supervision of middle management by upper management. For example, a middle manager uses false accounting to convert losses into apparent profits, earning not only a potential bonus for him/herself, but even bigger bonuses (under the hierarchical principle) for the supervisors.*

In language classically created by Oliver Williamson (among many possible citations, see especially his 1975 book Markets and Hierarchies, *or his 1985 book* The Economic Institutions of Capitalism, *both New York: Free Press) I would say that once there is separation of ownership from control, the search for a perfect control contract between shareholders and managers is inevitably doomed. Of course, if the managers and share- holders are virtually the same body, there is no problem. The residual property rights and the decision-taking function lie with the same people. This is traditional, not managerial capitalism. But whenever and wher- ever there is a separation of these rights and powers, any control contract (such as a bonus or stock-option plan) is necesarily imperfect, and as Jensen and Zimmerman note at point (3), liable to be perverted.*

A STOCK-OPTION STORY

There is a convenient asymmetry in the argument deployed by food retailer Iceland in defending the rejigging of its share options arrangements.

As we report today, four directors graciously gave up a bundle of options that had virtually no chance of ever bringing any rewards. In their place, they were awarded options that only the most cata- strophic mismanagement could now render worthless.

And the excuse for this change? The management needed 'incen- tivising'. The old options set share price targets that were just too tough to achieve. Why? Because Iceland has been such a corporate disaster area for the last three years (and arguably for longer still) that the share price has collapsed.

Now consider what might have happened had Iceland been a company run with such flair and wisdom that the share price had doubled over the period, not halved. Would we then expect that the directors' old share options would have been scrapped and replaced

> with a new one setting higher, rather than lower exercise prices? I
> suspect not.
>   *Iceland says it granted the new options only after consultation with
> major shareholders. If so, shame on those shareholders for having
> been so compliant. Heads the directors win. Tails they certainly don't
> lose. (Ben Laurance,* Observer, London, *7 September, 1997)*

*Point (6), on mergers and take-overs, seems to me to have an very
important implication that its authors did not appear to notice. In the
update comment at the end of the section on take-overs in Chapter 1,
above, I referred to an overwhelming body of evidence that, because many
large acquiring firms do experience adverse share moments after the completion of take-overs, the net effect of mergers and take-overs on the total
wealth of the stockholding class appeared, on balance, to be negative.
This evidence, as surveyed and interpreted by Dennis Mueller[16] included a
major paper by Michael Jensen (with Richard Ruback) himself.[17] Taken
with the previous evidence the logical implication of Point (6), therefore,
is that management stockholding has not been sufficiently extensive to
prevent the negative result.*

BASIC COMPENSATION: A NEOCLASSICAL MODEL

Basic salary is the largest single source of income for all but the heads of
corporate giants. A modern business is inevitably partly 'bureaucratic',
and reward in the form of regular salary is an essential element in any
general characterization of bureaucracy. Increased salary often leads to
increased bonus, and almost always leads to increased status. Salary,
therefore, remains by far the best single indicator of overall managerial
ophelimity.[18]

   Who, or what, determines executives' salaries? The general answer, it
appears, is 'other executives'. This almost unique feature of corporate life
creates obvious problems of analysis; problems which, rather than being
solved, are merely suppressed by assuming that salaries are determined by
some person or body attempting to maximize the welfare of shareholders.
Nevertheless, it is possible that a form of 'neoclassical' approach may
provide a convenient stalking-horse with which to begin an attack on the
question. In Chapter 1 I suggested that the essence of managerial capitalism lay in the separation of organizational talent from supplies of finance:
a neoclassical system, I argued, would require that, although large-scale

organization was widely exploited, the separation did not occur. Organizers (managers) would need to be held to genuinely subordinate roles and virtually deprived of influence on policy except in a purely advisory capacity. Company policy would have to be determined by a quasi-entrepreneurial body – for example, a committee or board specifically charged and powerfully motivated to act for the shareholders alone. This body, among other functions, would control salaries and ensure that all concerned had the incentives necessary to induce desirable behaviour. Let our stalking-horse, then, be a theory of the firm in which just such an arrangement in fact existed.

Instead of electing a board of directors as we now know it, the company meeting would elect a committee of shareholders, which would in turn appoint a subsidiary body to carry out the detailed 'operational' functions now vested in boards. The superior committee would lay down the general lines of policy and keep control of all senior executive appointments and salaries, including all appointments to the subsidiary committee. The subsidiary committee would consist largely of full-time managers, none of whom would sit on the superior committee, and, in fact, no member of either committee could legally be a member of the other. Managers, therefore, would attend meetings of the policy-determining committee in the capacity of expert witnesses, and it would not be the practice for even the chief executive to be present throughout all deliberations. Things would be arranged so that membership of the shareholders' committee was not unduly onerous and need be only nominally remunerated. Whether, in real life, such a genuinely 'part-time' committee could succeed in its objects is doubtful, but we assume here that it could.

To add artistic verisimilitude to an otherwise unconvincing picture, we might additionally assume that the committee had the right to employ outside consultants whose fees would be paid from company funds, the consultants being allowed to require from the management on the committee's behalf any information they desired, and being generally permitted to snoop around the office. They would owe loyalty exclusively to the shareholders, and no ideas for 'the good of the company as a whole' should be supposed to colour their thinking.

Apart from these changes – the picture, surely, of an executive nightmare – the legal structure of the company would remain unchanged! The resulting institution would conform relatively closely to the corporate image projected in undergraduate schools of business. How, then, should the shareholders' committee determine salaries if the overriding criterion for all decisions were maximization of the current market value of the equity?

The quantity to be determined is the salary-bill of the whole top management team: that is, the aggregate salaries of those persons who effectively make the high-level decisions still left to management under the new arrangements. (The decisions could be 'big' but genuinely executive alone.) By definition, no firm has more than one such team. In large firms the number of members may be greater than in small firms, but however large the firm, the central group cannot exceed the maximum number of persons who can maintain regular intimate contact, safely share secrets and quickly make collective decisions. In the USA, where it is the practice to designate substantial numbers of senior executives as vice-presidents (who are then recorded as company officers), the total number of corporate officers is probably a fair indicator of the size of team, at least in manufacturing. Even though the two sets are necessarily identical, the size of the in-group is certainly unlikely to exceed the number of officers, and the ratio between in-group and officers is likely to diminish with the size of the firm.

Because, in our conception, the management team is unitary and indivisible, unlike other inputs, management cannot be subjected to ordinary quantitative variation. True, as the evidence mentioned above suggests, the optimum number of members may be a little greater in larger companies, but the team's capacity to earn profits cannot properly be thought of as a dependent function of its size. Instead, we may imagine the variation as being qualitative, quality being defined by reference to some convenient standard such as that of the ability of a team of optimum size to earn profit from a standard set of assets under standard conditions, a concept that should in principle be capable of measurement by the consultants. In effect, 'quality' would be analogous to intelligence in the individual, in the sense that whatever the method of measurement, the results were known to be highly correlated with specific types of performance; in this case, with ability to earn profits assets.

Indeed, we might even conceive of each team as possessing an 'ability quotient' (AQ), a number measurable by some method that did not involve observation of performance in the particular firm in which the subjects were employed.

Given the concept of AQ, for good neoclassical results we further require that teams and individuals are perfectly interchangeable in the sense that in a given firm – defined as a set of physical assets, an established labour force and 'goodwill' – any team of given AQ will with given policies obtain similar expected profits. There is no special relationship between teams and their firms, no tendency for a team's profit-earning capacity to be greater in the firm in which it grew up than in others. We also assume that there is a unique market-determined supply price (total salary-bill) for each ability level, and that to individual firms there is a perfectly elastic supply of teams of given abilities. In other words, although the firm will have to pay higher prices for superior teams, it can always obtain instantly at least one team of given ability at the appropriate price. The supply prices are determined entirely by factors external to the managerial market: managers of all ability levels face well-defined alternative occupations providing comparable net advantages, and the market is always in overall equilibrium; at any hint of disequilibrium, large numbers of managers immediately convert themselves into teachers, doctors, farmers, labour leaders and even politicians, or alternatively teachers, farmers, labour leaders and even a few doctors successfully offer themselves as managers, as the case may be. The task of the shareholders' committee, then, is to decide the optimum ability level for the team that is to manage their firm. In so doing, given the assumptions, they determine the salary-bill. In other words, they are deciding the optimum salary.

Since there is a one-to-one relationship between salary and AQ, we may treat salary as a regular input in the production function, and AQ need not feature directly at all. Given large-scale organization, the appropriate production function should display constant returns to scale: provided a team of appropriate ability is employed, we assume the firm has no optimum size: if, when the scale of output is doubled, salary and all other inputs are doubled, the rate of return is constant.

The next six pages[19] of the original book presented two alternative mathematical interpretations of the basic neoclassical idea (as far as is known, the first formal attempts, in economics, to model the role of management in a production function). In both, the left-hand side of the equation represented the profit, net of total management salary, of an individual firm, while the right-hand side included total capital and total management salary as explanatory variables. In the first model, however, capital and management were partly substitutable for each other; in the second they were required in fixed proportions. Thus, in very general terms, the first model said:

Net Output = F(Capital, Salary)
Profit = Net Output – Salary
Profit = F(Capital, Salary) – Salary.

Net Output is the value of sales less the cost of all current inputs including non-managerial labour. Salary represents both the 'quantity' (or input) of management and the cost of management. As input it contributes (in the first equation) to Net Output in collaboration with Capital. As a cost (in the second equation) it is a deduction from profit. Using calculus it is possible to find the optimum level of Total Salary – that is, input of management – in order to maximize the rate of return – that is, ratio of Profit to Capital. The model then predicts that if firms are in fact choosing this level of management input, a statistical sample of firms which vary both in the amount and quality of their capital (that is, vary both in size and intrinsic profitability) should exhibit a positive correlation between total salary and both observed size and observed rate of return. In a regression equation with the log of total management salary on the left-hand side and logs of measures of both size and profitability on the right-hand side, both coefficients should be significant. If a firm becomes larger, it should hire 'more': that is, better-quality, better-paid management. If, at given size, its profit opportunities improve, it should do likewise. Better quality capital is optimally served by better-quality management.

The second model revised the second equation to say that net output depended uniquely on capital, and added an equation saying that salary also depended on the size of the firm (as measured by capital) but in the special sense that, for any given size, there was a minimum 'required' amount (quality) of management. If that was not provided, no production would occur. If it was provided, there would be no benefit from further increase. Assuming that firms were, in fact, choosing exactly that amount of management, this model predicted that while obviously observed size and salary should be correlated robustly, there should not be a correlation between salary and rate of return.

Using a database created in a classic study by David Roberts,[20] we then presented an econometric study claiming to show that the second model was supported, but the first was not. The text continued as follows.

Thus the second model performs well predictively, and powerfully discriminates against other models. But it should be noted that it does not discriminate between the validity of alternative assumptions as to who or what in fact determines salaries. According to the model, any viable firm must conform to the minimum payment, and even in the presence of a shareholders' committee, the restraint on 'excess' payments is weak, particularly if we add a small dose of realism in the form of uncertainty. In other words, although the results strongly support the model's hypothesis as to the character of the managerial production function, it tells us little, so far, of implications for motivation. The observed results, and especially the error distribution, are consistent *both* with the hypothesis that the assumed production function is associated with salary determination by shareholders, and the hypothesis that it is associated with some other method.

There are further difficulties. Although the second model performs well predictively it is not intuitively convincing from a conventional economic point of view. In the first model, management is paid the value of its net marginal product, which in turn varies with aggregate profit-earning capacity of the assets; in the second model, management has no marginal product and is paid in unique proportion to the scale of the assets alone. To say that the optimum 'quantity' of management will vary closely with the scale of the job to be done is one thing, but to add that once a necessary minimum of this input is applied nothing will be gained by further increment is another. It is difficult to be convinced that, if a firm of given size and asset character fires a 'satisfactory' management and hires a more highly-paid 'superior' management, it can experience no gain at all in gross profits before salary. However, once we suggest that management does have a marginal product, we come up against the econometric contradictions: if management has a marginal product, this must vary, *inter alia*, with the profitability co-operant factors, therefore observed profitability should correlate; but, as we have seen, it does not.

So what happens if we apply the assumption of the existence of a shareholders' committee to the second model of the production function? Provided the committee employed the principle of profit maximization the altered production-function hypothesis would not, in fact, lead to greatly altered implications for managerial motivation. A management team which succeeded in biasing policy in such a way that their firm expanded would still be signing their own dismissal notices, for if, as the assumptions require, the team's measured ability is independent of both policy and the size of the firm in which they are currently employed, expansion must require that a new team of superior ability be brought in from outside. Conversely, if a team's AQ increased but the size of their firm did not, they should immediately seek, and would easily find, better-paid employment elsewhere. Finally, if both size and AQ happened to increase simultaneously and in the correct proportions, strictly speaking the incumbent team would merely compete on equal terms with other candidates for meeting the new requirement. Thus the manager has no incentive to attempt to bias policy in any direction; true, if the firm's size changes he must change employers, but he can always find other positions at the same wage, and costs of movement are ignored. He can advance in life only by improving his AQ rating, and this, it will be remembered, is unaffected by historical events in his firm.

Here, then, is the finally revised neoclassical model. It is consistent with certain econometric facts,[21] although not, of course, with other well-known facts of real life. What happens when we come down to earth?

THE SIMON THEORY

Down on earth there are no shareholders' committees, at least in our sense. Managers determine one anothers' salaries and are far from elastic in supply. They represent a non-competing group in relation to the rest of the population and are typically paid considerably more than would be necessary in the long run to discourage them from turning to alternative occupations. They are not good substitutes for one another, and when combined in teams are normally much more 'productive' in the firm where the team was developed than in any other firm of comparable size and character.

All these realisms have far-reaching implications for methods of compensation, for motivation, and for the behaviour of the system at large. But to say that managers, as a class, determine their remuneration does not necessarily imply that they can take any sums they care to name. They are not acting collectively or conspiratorially, and not necessarily even monopolistically. They are probably working within a system of rules developed from their own functional needs and based on their own norms. A managerially evolved system of executive compensation will be the sociological economic outcome of the whole office environment and not in a crude sense a mere conspiracy against the public. We are then presented with a considerable chicken-and-egg problem: the system of compensation is the result of the function, but must also, through motivation, affect the way the function is performed, i.e. must affect policy. Of course, we shall never be able to say which came first. Rather, we shall assume that managers have developed a system of incentives reflecting their own perceptions of their rôle and so, by observing the results, we shall hope to gain insight into the ultimate origins of their motives.

All societies tend to develop economic incentives that match sociological intent, and there is nothing very special about management in this respect. But in other walks of life the implications have already been analysed; so far, unlike traditional capitalism, where the 'profit motive' clearly matches a social ideal, managerial capitalism has escaped. (This is almost certainly the reason why the true implications of typical bonus schemes, for example, have been overlooked, for, as we have already suggested, these only begin to make sense when it is appreciated that instead of being designed by capitalists to induce managers to behave as capitalists think they ought, they are rather designed by managers as a self-inducement to what they believe their behaviour should be.) We seek, then, a reward system meeting the functional and social needs of a class of persons whose role is to provide the large-scale organization necessary for economic activity on the scale of modern industry. A major part of the answer can be found in a theory created by Herbert Simon.[22]

As a starting point we observe that all large organizations are compelled to adopt many of the characteristics of ideal bureaucracy in the sense originally described and employed by Max Weber.[23] In order to function efficiently they must be to some extent hierarchical, must to some extent define offices independently of persons, and must to some extent employ well-defined chains of command. In practice, particularly in business, it is difficult to avoid some semblance of the conventional pyramidal structure in which members are arranged in ascending levels of authority, the number of occupants declining as the level rises. This stems from the needs of co-ordination. To co-ordinate is to resolve disputes and inconsistencies, and if two or more people occupy a given level of authority there must be at least one above them to perform this function. In practice, few business organizations are compelled to adhere to the principle rigidly: 'line and staff' methods cut across vertical boundaries, and disputes can be resolved by committees. Nevertheless, a pyramid of sorts inevitably underlies almost all administrative structures, and can hardly be avoided if essential delegation is to be achieved without anarchy. In fact, the greater the degree of delegation, the greater the need for authority. Committees may be, and are, widely employed as a partial substitute, but when these, as they must, fail to agree, some superior authority is compelled to act. (Informal committees such as exist widely in modern business firms are observed to achieve remarkably consistent apparent unanimity, a result which is almost certainly due in part to collective appreciation of the dangers of disunity, but also in part to the presence of chairmen who are senior to most of the other members and whose view is usually deferred to in the last resort: the committee system works precisely because it is backed up by the hierarchy.) When an organization is described as 'flexible', what is usually meant is that it is not as rigidly hierarchical as some others. Outside such relatively cloistered areas as intradepartmental administration in universities, probably the only viable 'democratic' organizations operating anywhere in the world today are the co-operative settlements in Israel, and there, significantly, because the output is mainly agricultural, the administrative task, though not insignificant, is relatively small. Partly democratic institutions have been tried in agriculture by both

Russia and China, but all have more or less failed. In manufacturing, democracy in the sense of government by all is unknown. The only alternative to government by all is government by pyramid, and it has everywhere prevailed.

Once it is accepted that pyramids are inevitable, it is difficult to escape a corresponding salary structure. For it has been forcibly argued (and this is the starting point of the Simon theory) that the belief that a man must be paid more than his subordinates is virtually universal – a social law which has no conventional economic rationalization, because, since middle-class males typically enjoy the psychic satisfactions of responsibility, the 'net advantages' approach would suggest that higher posts be paid less than lower posts, rather than the other way about. There are, of course, dozens of reasons why this does not happen, of which we need mention only three, each sufficient in itself to produce familiar result. First, in any society where income and status are closely associated (which means almost any modern society where incomes are unequal) it is difficult, if not impossible, for authority either to be exercised or accepted in reverse order to income, or, more precisely, this is impossible wherever the persons concerned are in close contact. Authority may be accepted (up to a point) from a lower-paid policeman or other public official, but not from a lower-paid 'boss'; and where, as occasionally happens, such inversion is attempted, pathological tensions and suspicions almost inevitably arise. Secondly, position in bureaucratic hierarchies tends to be closely associated with age and experience, and, unlike the working classes, the middle classes 'expect' their incomes to rise over the life cycle, a distinction which remains as valid in the USA, where there are supposed to be no classes, as anywhere else. Third, in a system where the salaries of individual managers are decided by other managers, the salaries of subordinates are naturally decided by seniors, and are unlikely to be settled in such a way that determinors are paid less than determinees.

Therefore, the world over, Presidents are paid more than Vice-Presidents, Commissars more than Deputy-Commissars, Admirals more than Rear-Admirals, Peoples' Chiefs of Police more than Deputy Peoples' Chiefs of Police, and middle managers more than junior managers. This law, however, is internal to organization and applies to whole societies only by aggregation. There is little apparent similarity in either the salaries paid at given levels in organizations of different types, or in the scale of gradation. In the USSR, top 'intellectuals' (academics, writers and the like) receive more than non-top-intellectuals, but both, it seems, do better than corresponding administrators or industrial organizers, a position which, unfortunately for Western intellectuals, is elsewhere reversed.

Once established sociologically, the law or convention spreads. Individuals may feel compelled to refuse high positions unless the salary is commensurate, even though, on narrow economic grounds, they would have been happy to accept a lower figure. So we have an economic supply relationship. Firms will see salaries as organizational status symbols, and within organizations of similar types both seniors and subordinates will come to expect and accept a conventional rate of gradation; if this is not obeyed, authority may break down. Thus observance becomes a functional necessity.

It is also worth noting how exceptions typically are dealt with. When, as indeed often happens, middle or junior managers, supported by better offers from other employers, succeed in negotiating increased personal salaries, the change is often legitimized by some real or simulated increase in responsibility. Indeed, in Western countries, 'responsibility' seems to be the key ideology. In these countries, the law in question may be stated as a widespread belief in one-to-one relationship between income and responsibility, an essentially aristocratic convention of possibly feudal origin. This may explain the relative downgrading of otherwise worthy people who are notably free of responsibility. In Communist countries, on the other hand, there is some evidence that power and responsibility are regarded as their own rewards, while artists and such are provided with relatively high incomes in the hope of keeping them out of politics. Be that as it may, if we can find an appropriate measure of relative responsibility under managerial capitalism, we may have a considerable clue to the salary system.

Let us define the 'responsibility' of an individual at a given point in a hierarchical pyramid as the number of people at the bottom level who, directly or indirectly, report through him. (Thus the responsibility of the person at the top of the pyramid – that is, the chief executive – is all the occupants of the bottom levels). If, then, there is to be a behaviour relationship between responsibility and salary, there must be a corresponding relationship between an individual's 'span of control' (the number of his immediate subordinates) and his rate of salary gradation (the proportionate amount by which his salary exceeds those of his immediate subordinates). On these assumptions, the algebra comes out rather nicely.

The original text then developed a mathematical model of salary structure based on the assumption that the sensitivity of salary gradation to span of control was constant through the hierarchy. It then follows that, given the salary at the lowest level, there is a unique relationship between the level of a person's salary and his or her responsibility. And, since the responsibility of the chief executive is by definition equal to the total number of people at the bottom levels, this salary depends uniquely on two factors: the size of the organization (as measured by bottom-level numbers); and the gradation sensitivity. Given the latter, it is fundamentally the case that the larger the organization measured in this way, the more the chief executive must be paid. The text then continued as follows.

This, then, is the 'bureaucratic' theory of salaries. As already explained, it is not to be regarded as a rival to the economic theory but rather as an (unconventional) explanation of it. The number of people at a given level, say the lowest, can be taken to vary with productive capacity, and the theory states that the greater the desired productive capacity, the greater the number of required administrators of given responsibility, or the greater the average responsibility, of a given number of administrators. The 'required' salary-bill for the top management varies directly and uniquely with size. If these salaries were not paid the firm would fail through socio-organizational misfunctioning: if, for sociological reasons, the task of production cannot be carried out without a particular income distribution, the social law becomes an economic one. Rather than 'bureaucratic', therefore, we might give the theory some name which combines both origins, and, for want of a better, we try 'bureconic'.

Staring me in the face was an economic theory of earnings differentials that has since been elucidated by David Grubb and Sherwin Rosen, and later further discussed by me in a more recent publication.[24] The reason why people with responsibility are highly paid is that their efficiency affects the productivity of other people (that is what they are there to do). The greater the responsibility, the greater the effect. In an organization of 100 employees at the bottom level, with span of control of five, there are three levels above the lowest, with individual responsibility at each level ascending in the series 5, 25, 100. Of course, the chief executive, with responsibility 100, is by no means the sole engine of productivity in all these people; much is contributed by themselves and much by the intermediate managers. But the statement that a person's 'responsibility' is so much, is an indicator of the spread of their indirect influence. As will be seen, in the example, this multiplies by a factor of four with each increase in level. Grubb shows this means that if ability and responsibility are correlated and people are paid according to both factors (as at least they should be), there will be a numerical interaction between the two factors causing proportionate salary differentials to increase in the upper reaches of the hierarchy. The prediction is statistically confirmed. The distribution of earnings in society is therefore much more dispersed than the distribution of ability. I suspect that in the 1960s I was not alone in under-

*emphasizing the economic value of the supervising role of management –
their role, that is, in enhancing general productivity by restraining
bureaucratic inefficiency. Since then I have been impressed by the theoretical and empirical literature on the topic, as cited for example in my paper
'Managerial Theories of the Firm', included as Chapter 5 in the present
volume.*

It has further characteristics we have not yet mentioned. From its
bureaucratic parent it inherits the character that individuals' salaries represent less their personal qualities than their offices; true, to reach high
office one should display ability, but the system as such merely lays down
a set of relativities, and there is no indication that the absolute income of
a person of given ability must take on any particular value. Consequently,
the general level of corporate salaries, like that of most other incomes,
remains indeterminate. This leads to a point of more immediate importance. In the 'neoclassical' economic model, payment of salaries in excess
of the minimum was prevented, or at least restrained, by the imaginary
shareholders' committee attempting to maximize profits. In the present
theory, no such restraint is obvious. We have seen that frequency distribution of salaries predicted by size is positively skewed; but what, in fact,
prevents compensation from taking on any value above the minimum?
We already hinted at one answer: subordinates may become discontented,
and hence function badly, if they observe that immediate seniors are paid
an unconventional differential. This factor is likely to be important wherever subordinates and seniors are in close daily contact and can observe
both each others' work and each others' standard of living. There is more
than fear of internal misfunction, however, to deter senior executives
from awarding each other grossly excessive salaries. The prevailing gradation sensitivity is as much a valid social norm as any other. If they
offend, others may accuse them of 'milking' the business, and they, in
turn, may feel their own 'Wright Mills' loyalties come into play.
However, unlike the case of investment and finance policy, these factors
are not reinforced by any very powerful external agency, because, with
the magnitudes currently prevailing, the effect of salary variation on rate
of return is relatively slight: characteristically, an average excess payment
of the order of 100 per cent reduces the rate of return by no more than
twentieth (that is, a 10 per cent rate of return would be reduced to half a
point only). Hence, from a cynical view, we should not expect these supposed restraints to be as strong as they might be. All in all, therefore, we
feel justified in basing our main motivational analysis on the assumption
that the 'bureconic' theory, as we have described it, is reasonably valid.

POLICY IMPLICATIONS OF A 'BURECONIC' THEORY

The organization of modern business combines features that the man in the street would describe as 'bureaucratic', in the sense of 'like the civil service', with features he would describe as 'commercial', in a sense perhaps implying more flexibility. Now armed with the bureconic theory of salaries, we shall continue the analysis by attempting to isolate these two sorts of feature, beginning with a model representing an extreme form of bureaucracy, and gradually relaxing or modifying the assumptions until we have something more like a real-life, profit-making corporation. By this means we hope to be able to establish motivational theorems that are both more rigorous and less dependent on intuitive reasoning than has been possible so far. In particular, we shall hope to provide a more solid, logical basis for the motive of growth, a motive whose existence the reader has so far been asked to accept only as a working hypothesis.

Imagine a Weberian and socialistic nightmare in which all production is organized on strict civil service lines, 'firms' representing no more than subordinate departments with carefully defined and limited spheres of activity, no freedom as to internal organization, and no control over salaries or appointments. Some central body would lay down internal structures, set spans of control, determine salaries of new entrants and, more importantly, fix the gradation sensitivity. Departments could differ in size (measured by occupants of the bottom level), but this would be decided by the central body alone and could not be influenced by members. The heads of the larger departments would therefore be paid more than the heads of the smaller ones, because the larger would represent taller pyramids. Promotion would be based partly on merit and partly on seniority, and inter-firm transfers at all levels would be encouraged freely. Indeed, whenever any vacancy occurred, the central appointments board would consider candidates from throughout the system and would try to avoid any bias in favour of internal promotion. Thus the average rate of promotion would be independent of size, and a man with high ambitions could, in principle, as well start in a small department as in a large one. In fact, the system would be not dissimilar to that adopted by government bureaucracies the world over: in such systems, personal advancement is supposed to depend exclusively on merit; the organizations being static and transfers easy there should be little room for any form of built-in policy bias and none whatever for the growth motive.

But now suppose that, with otherwise unchanged arrangements, the policy on transfers is reversed: unless they are hopelessly incompetent, 'inside' candidates are always given absolute priority. Since vacancies arise from natural wastage alone, the rate of promotion and 'prospects' generally will then be inferior in small departments to those in large, and a man reaching the head of small department would have little chance of moving to a post in a large department and would have to sit out his position until retirement.

If initial appointments were made by centrally decided postings over which the subject had no influence, and if the total supply of new entrants to the system as a whole was normally equal to requirements, the main effect of a prohibition on transfers would be discontent in the small departments. A man's prospects in life would depend on the accident of his initial posting, a type of situation which, while acceptable to working-class fatalism, violates almost every principle of middle-class individualism. Malfunctioning would be almost inevitable; the smaller departments would tend to lose their best men to employers outside the system and to become inefficient, strings would be pulled to influence postings, and so on. If the central body, aware of the dangers, sought remedies other than a change in transfer policy, it could adjust either starting salary or gradation sensitivity in the smaller organizations, so that, in partial compensation for their bad luck the members would be paid higher salaries for given responsibility than their opposite numbers in large organizations. (Socioeconomic tension might well continue, however, because so long as society continued to expect income to be closely matched to responsibility, the relative positions of the heads of small and large organizations might be regarded as anomalous.) Little is changed if we assume a free market in new entrants. If new entrants could choose their own initial postings, the same adjustments would be necessary to avoid a chronic imbalance between supply and requirements in departments of different sizes. Motivation would remain unaffected.

At last we are ready for Hamlet. He is brought on by removing the assumption that the departments are static. We know that the most fundamental difference between business firms and government departments lies in the capacity of the former for autonomous growth. Once an otherwise bureaucratic organization is permitted to grow, while high-level mobility continues to be inhibited (as is empirically the case in firms), the policy implications are considerable. In the bureconic model, if initial salary and rate of gradation are the same for all organizations, people occupying given levels, numbered from the bottom, are everywhere paid the same salaries, the essential difference between large and small firms being that the former are 'taller' and therefore provide more posts at any given salary; in the large organizations there are high posts which in the small do not exist at all. In other words, the large firms provide better 'opportunities' for personal advancement. If transfers were not restricted, this, we have seen, would represent a purely abstract state of affairs devoid of personal implications, but with transfers restricted (and expansion permitted) it provides a powerful motive for senior officials to attempt to induce expansion and thus create higher vacancies into which they themselves are surely most likely to be appointed. There can be no doubt at all that this fundamental characteristic of the interaction between salary system, organizational structure and poor transfer market provides a real and powerful motive for inducing internal expansion in every modern business. As a managing director who held not a penny of stock in his firm once told me, 'the reason, quite frankly, why I want growth is so that I and my colleagues can all have more money' (meaning higher salaries).

GENERALIZATION OF THE GROWTH MOTIVE

Here, then, is how the typical manager has the power to affect himself by affecting his environment. The effect is reinforced when we also drop the assumption that ability is judged independently performance *in situ*. When a man takes decisions leading to successful expansion, he not only creates new openings but also recommends himself and his colleagues as particularly suitable candidates to fill them (and his colleagues, recognizing this, will gladly allow him a generous share of the utility proceeds). He has demonstrated his powers as a manager and deserves his reward. So personal ability also becomes judged by achieved growth, and encouragement of growth becomes a motive for not only collective but also individual advancement, thus reinforcing the basic connection. True, if personal promotion were, in fact, decided by shareholders' committees, ability (in the absence of AQ tests) might be judged by achieved profits, but when, as is in fact the case, the individual manager's rate of advance is determined exclusively by peers and superiors, it is more likely to be governed by criteria derived from the collective situation of the managerial class, which, as we have now seen, means favouring expansion. This does not that a man's profit-earning ability will necessarily be ignored. Profits are required for growth, and minimum profit is necessary to avoid a take-over. But it does mean that a man is unlikely to be judged by his ability as a profit *maximizer*. By contrast, he may well be judged by his ability to maximize, or at least promote, organizational growth.

The association between personal responsibility and achieved expansion resolves the disequilibrium in the supply of recruits between organizations with different prospects. Without this association, recruits would still be faced with a nice problem in assessing relative prospects in large, comparatively static firms as compared to smaller, faster-growing firms. On occasion, in real life, such choices have to be made, but the effect is damped by the probability that unless an individual has had some respons- ibility for expansion he is not necessarily so much favoured over outsiders of comparable ability for the new middle-level vacancies.

We are chiefly concerned with conditions at the tops of pyramids; and by this we mean conditions among given levels numbered down from the highest: that is, the levels in or adjacent to those defined as 'the manage- ment'. If the reader visualizes the population of firms as a set of disembod- ied pyramid tops, he will then see that, with transfers inhibited, management members can improve their position only by expansion, which, as it were, pushes them up from below: the summit rests on a struc- ture of middle and junior managers whose 'lift' increases whenever the organization expands, an effect that is quite independent of where the new subordinates are recruited.

In fact, most of our theorems can be obtained from a single assumption about recruitment, to wit that whenever and wherever a vacancy occurs, the *probability* of its being filled by internal promotion increases with the *level* at which it occurs. With this assumption, policy theorems become independent of the level chosen for defining the management. For example, we can say that both an individual's policy influence and his motive for promoting expansion will increase with his level, and thus the theorem that the system must produce bias in favour of growth is made general. The same applies to other collective policy motives – for example, that of secu- rity. The policy bias of an organization as a whole can be thought of as resulting from the preferences of its individual members, weighted by their relative influence position. Wherever there is a reason to expect correlation between a particular type of individual bias and his relative weight in the collective decision-making function, we shall expect a corresponding bias in collective policy. We have now discovered a general source of such cor- relations: that is, the association of both bias and influence with a 'third factor', hierarchical level. Obviously, the correlation between level and influence must always be strong; therefore, wherever there is a further cor- relation between level and some particular type of policy bias, that type of bias will become collective. In the case of security, it is clear that the per- sonal consequences of financial failure or take-over will be more serious for senior executives than for junior.

It is important to appreciate that, unlike some bolder spirits, we are not implying a whole new system of social relationships. With characteristic elan, J. K. Galbraith once wrote:

The income of a business-man is no longer a measure of his achievement: it has become a datum of secondary interest. Business prestige, as a moment's reflection will suggest, is overwhelmingly associated with the size of the concern which the individual heads. American business has evolved a system of precedence hardly less rigid than that of Victorian England. It is based almost exclusively on corporate assets.[25]

This picture leads to a final point of central importance. If he and the reader will forgive us, his picture could be likened to one of a range of corporate mountains, log-normally distributed as to height, with the summits inhabited by gods who battle across the intervening valleys. These gods have a status order based exclusively on altitude: to acquire kudos it is necessary to struggle to the top of, and sit firmly upon, one of the higher peaks; a game, in other words, that is played in a largely static environment. This is not the picture that emerges from our analysis of the internal mechanism of managerial motivation in general. For how, knowing that inter-peak transfer is difficult, if not impossible, would one explain absence of battles at the *feet* of the larger mountains? In other words, although it is true that in general more utility is obtained from *being* at the head of a large firm than of a small one, the most effective means of obtaining this pleasure is by encouraging one's own firm to grow. Furthermore, to the extent that transfers are possible, personal ability is likely to be judged by performance in previous firms, and internal prestige is similarly generated. In short, we argue, this motivation is inescapably dynamic, and the relevant variate in the actual or proximate utility function is not size but rather change in size: that is, rate of growth.

A MANAGERIAL UTILITY SYSTEM

A consumer attaches utility to the growth of his income because it implies potentially rising consumption; as he normally has to pay for this by current abstinence we conventionally apply a rate of time discount to the problem. A manager, on the other hand, is not usually required to sacrifice personal consumption to induce his firm to grow; 'his' saving is here done by others. But there are important possibilities for trading off between the firm's growth rate and variables on other dimensions of managerial utility. Growth may be traded for security and a similar, though not identical, effect arises if direct utility is obtained from the stock market quotation as such.

For the rest of the work we shall concentrate on the two managerial utility dimensions, growth and security, representing the former by the growth rate of gross assets and the latter by a standardized measure of the firm's stock-market value, which we call the valuation ratio. It is the ratio of the market value of the equity to the 'book value' (that is, accounting value, or replacement cost net of depreciation) of all the tangible assets, including cash, owned by the firm. The growth rate acts as an indicator of the several satisfactions associated with scale (salary, power and prestige), and the valuation ratio as a proxy for both security and the more positive utilities connected with the market quotation.

To the extent that the valuation ratio is also an indicator of the extent to which shareholders are getting value for money from their holdings, this measure can also be seen as the indicator to be maximized if a firm is to be managed strictly in their interests. Given the past history of a firm, including the assets and environment it has accumulated, to maximize the valuation ratio is equivalent to 'long-term profit maximization'.[26]

MAXIMIZING, SATISFICING AND BEHAVIOURISM

There remains one last question. Are we justified in assuming that anything is *maximized* at all?

We have already mentioned the 'behaviouristic' approach to economic analysis. As many readers will be aware, this school has mainly developed under the influence of Professor Herbert Simon, and is associated in most people's minds with the concept of 'satisficing': that is, a form of behaviour in which the subject, faced with a difficult problem to solve, sacrifices some of the rewards of the optimum solution in order to reduce the pains incurred in searching for it. Rather than maximize, he chooses to 'satisfice' – to accept some solution that is 'good enough' in relation to various criteria such as survival, aspiration or avoidance of shame. The significance of the approach lies in possibility that the satisfactory or 'satisficing' levels of reward are determined by dynamic processes that have no particular relation to the optimum solution. The subject is endowed with various adjustment reactions (for example, a rate at which aspiration increases over time relative to the time rate of growth of achievement) which yield a system of differential equations, the solution to which, if stable, represents an equilibrium from which he has no necessary tendency to depart and to which the optimum solution relates only coincidentally.

Closely allied to these concepts is the concept of 'organizational slack',[27] representing a belief that the decision-making and general efficiency of most organizations is often for long periods well below potential, particularly if no new talent is imported. In all organizations, it is argued, being prone to slack, socks will be pulled up in response to definite stimuli, such as the stimulus of observed performance. Firms which in some sense have recently done badly may be expected to do better, while firms which have done well may be expected to become slack. Such behaviour sets up oscillatory processes difficult to reconcile with the orthodox concept of maximizing.

These ideas are clearly suggestive. They seem particularly likely to be useful where the corresponding maximizing problem is already well-defined and the analyst is now mainly concerned with empirical testing. Where, however, the task in hand is that of defining some problem afresh, 'satisficing' qualifications may import more complexity than understanding. It is of little use to consider the implications of satisficing behaviour if one does know what is to be satisficed – if one has not yet decided, for example, what is meant by 'doing badly'.

The general procedure we adopt in the present work is to begin with the assumption of maximizing behaviour, in the process identifying objectives, and then consider the powerful alternative of satisficing.[28]

3 Concepts and Methods

Having, as I hope, set our stage, I now attempt to characterize the players. We must also explain the language they are to speak and the meaning of some of their clothes. We have discussed at length the economico-institutional environment of the modern corporation and the possible motives of the managers. Both require to be dressed for operationality. We have suggested that managers may derive utility from growth, but what does this in measurable economic terms? And if 'the firm' is no longer regarded as a chattel of proprietors, how *is* it to be regarded?

The present chapter, therefore, represents a bridge-passage intended to lead the reader from ideas expressed in the first chapters towards the models developed in those that follow. I consider first the character of the firm and the nature of the processes of growth. I then sketch in my view of the general economic environment. Finally, I discuss definitions, concepts and methods of analysis.

CHARACTERIZATION OF THE FIRM

In orthodox economic theory, the firm was either no more an abstraction hypothesized for a particular role in theories of price formation and resource allocation, or, where recognized as an institution, the form assumed was essentially traditional. One can hardly blame Alfred Marshall for ignoring the implications of the joint-stock company in his otherwise realistic and homely descriptions; one can be more censorious, however, of subsequent theorists. But until the relatively recent contributions of Downie and Baumol,[1] the firm continued to be regarded mainly as an organ for maximizing profits and allocating resources. In the mid-1970s, however, there began to be developed in the USA the new academic discipline that came to be known as Organization Theory. Largely resulting, one suspects, from a desire for academic legitimacy among the staff of business schools, the new subject at first seemed likely to have an immediate impact on economics, for it indicated numerous ways in which productive organizations may develop independent *raisons d'être* merely by virtue of their internal functional character and requirements.[2] In the event, while a number of interesting developments occurred, things did not work out quite as might have been hoped. It was soon widely recognized that firms should be seen as administrative organizations, that as such they were of considerable intrinsic interest, and that their behaviour might well deviate from consistency with so-called 'higher' objectives. Significant normative studies of optimal administrative structures also appeared in due course.[3] But from the point of view of economic theory, 'the organization' remained the tool – albeit unreliable – of those for whom the higher objectives had been set, and the objectives themselves were almost always traditional or neoclassical.

To all the foregoing, there are two major exceptions: two works by economists who have specifically considered the relationship between their subject and the other. We refer to *The Theory of the Growth of the Firm* by Edith Penrose, and *Economic Theory and Organizational Analysis* by Harvey Leibenstein.[4] The second work is concerned with the general interaction of the two approaches and, while it has influenced the present author considerably, it is not of the same specific relevance as the first, which is concerned with precisely our own problem, or, in other words, with the ways which corporate organizations may develop quasi-higher objectives of their own, and the means by which they pursue them. Penrose, as the title of her book implies, is essentially concerned with the motives and means associated with growth. The present chapter is based considerably on her work, although in places the interpretation may perhaps be rather free.

In the language of organization theory, the previous chapters of this book were attempting to reconstruct higher objectives. In the usual conception, the organization is set up to achieve certain definable ends. These it is intended to serve faithfully, but the results may be otherwise; such deviations, however, are rarely thought of as purposive. Yet we have seen that, in the corporate system, far-reaching, high-level purposive objectives may pursued by people who are organization members; that is, are other than those whose interests the organization was formally set up to serve. Organization is required to exploit the advantages of scale, and people capable of providing this acquire considerable bargaining power. In the resulting balance, it is impossible to confine the senior executives to a purely immanent role; indeed, it might almost seem as if the institutions of managerial capitalism were developed to serve this class, as much as any other. Managers are people with the ability to organize. In order to excercise their talents they require appropriate instruments and institutions: in other words, they require organizations. The joint-stock company might well be regarded as *their* creation, and its shareholders merely one of several co-operating elements (of which, another example would be the non-managerial labour force). On such an interpretation it is not clear that even a normative approach would not recognize valid 'higher' objectives in managerial motivation. So the productive function in a modern economy is carried on by autonomous administrative organizations with minds and capacities of their own. From an extreme view, the 'higher' arrangements become details, and any economic system – capitalist, socialist or *dirigiste* – may be seen as a collection of competing and co-operating organizations. Consistent with this, economists also defined 'the firm' in relation to the specifically technical function of operating transformation processes. The firm is the ultimate allocator of resources, or the ultimate cell of the input–output system. For this type of usage it is necessary to specify the relevant activity-set with some precision; the firm is thus usually supposed to exist to select from limited lists the commodities it will produce, the techniques to be used, and the prices and scales of output. Once the data have been specified, together with some appropriate objective function, little remains but to solve the mathematical problem. This, in essence, is the approach of activity analysis. As soon, however, as we recognize the firm as a transcendent organization with a will of its own, the concept of the limited specification, except in a purely proximate sense, becomes rather fuzzy. The firm has the power to mould the environment, and to add new possibilities to its own information; we must then consider the limits on its power to change its limits.

It is here that the influence of Penrose becomes so important. She sees the firm as an administrative and social organization, capable, in principle, of entering almost any field of material activity. The firm is not necessarily limited to particular markets, industries or countries; indeed, there is no theoretical reason why firms should not venture anywhere in the universe. In practice, of course, they find advantages in specialization, but this represents a deliberate choice whose direction and degree may be varied at will. Every firm, at any given moment, inherits a degree and direction of specialization from its own past, and this is represented in the knowledge and talents of the existing members and the sphere of technical and commercial activity with which they are familiar (as well as, of course, in the nature of the physical assets). But new members and new assets can always be recruited; the firm is a changeable bundle of human and professional resources, linked through the corporate constitution to a corresponding bundle of material and financial assets. The matching between the humans, *inter se*, and between the humans on the one hand and the machines on the other is a unique result of the historical process by which all have been built up. The result may be far from ideal, but in non-pathological cases is at least viable.[5]

Thus individual firms are not only unique, but they also possess the capacity for biological growth. In the traditional theory, the size or growth of one firm was no more than the indirect result of performance of the profit-maximizing function. And size could be determinate only in the presence of diseconomies of scale. (*Rates* of growth were rarely discussed.) Significantly, these diseconomies were usually attributed to problems of organization. If the administrative problem could be solved, it was usually admitted that growth was, in principle, ultimately unlimited.

But the managerial-capitalist corporation possesses the unique capacity to initiate its own growth: members may be recruited, demand induced to expand, profits retained, and suppliers of capital persuaded to provide the wherewithal. But in commercial organizations such growth must be based on past success, and the rate is therefore subject to considerable dynamic restraint. However, the growth of administrative organizations is also limited by factors that are not directly economic, and we now discuss these.

THE INTERNAL RESTRAINT ON THE GROWTH RATE

Almost by definition, the planning and execution of expansion is the least routine of administrative acts: organization must be created where none existed before, recruits must be found, tasks undertaken, and new delegation-patterns developed. It is axiomatic that such planning can only be undertaken by existing members. If an organization is to remain efficient, it cannot possibly expand at an indefinitely rapid rate merely by infinitely rapid recruitment.

Why, in fact, should not a firm at a certain time recruit large numbers of highly qualified managers (representing, say, doubling of the size of the relevant echelons) and then expect to be able to employ these men to bring about a very large increase in activity in due course? The answer is as follows. The new member of an existing going concern, however highly qualified, can almost never become fully efficient as a non-routine decision-maker the instant he is recruited. He may have been fully efficient in his previous post, but he now requires time to learn his new colleagues' ways, and they to learn his. He also requires time to acquire the experience necessary for the exercise of good judgement in the new context. Whether he be an imported president, vice-president, chairman, managing director or relatively junior subordinate, he has to be 'trained' in his new position, and the process inevitably requires time. The length of the period may vary considerably according to the circumstances, but is never insignificant.

The need for 'training', however, is not itself sufficient to set up a dynamic restraint on growth. There is still no reason, apparently, why the firm should not take on large numbers of recruits, await the completion of their training, and then expand rapidly. Provided the training period is independent, the average growth rate could always be stepped up merely by raising the numbers initially hired. Everyone knows that this is not realistic, but, as far as I am aware, formal explanations have so far been lacking. They must arise from the nature of the training process: its length is not, evidently, independent of the attempted expansion rate. The average time required to train one new member must vary with the numbers recruited.

The existence of such a 'saturation' effect seems extremely plausible, and is confirmed, of course, by everyday administrative experience. The recruits are 'taught' by peers, superiors and subordinates. At high level, they must find out the nature of the human and material jigsaw puzzle represented in the organization, and in particular must find out the shapes into which new pieces will have to be fitted if further expansion is contemplated. They cannot learn these things from one another. They must learn them on the job by personal contact with old members, and the capacity of these 'teachers' is necessarily limited. For example, if the teacher is a superior, the necessity to keep things going will limit the amount he can delegate to inexperienced people requiring close supervision: if provided with too many such, he will probably concentrate his attention on a limited number, leaving the others with only trivial responsibilities until he has more time for them. If the 'teacher' is a subordinate, similar effects are produced by processes which may be less obvious, but none the less real. And once they are admitted, the theorem is as good as established.

Suppose we represent the average decision-taking efficiency of a management team at any one time as being composed of two ratios, the ratio of the efficiency of the average recruit to that of the average old hand, and the ratio of the total number of recruits to total membership. Then, if the former varies with the latter, average efficiency varies with the attempted expansion rate as indicated by the latter. If efficiency declines with the attempted expansion rate, and actual expansion depends on efficiency, expansion is dynamically restricted.

The foregoing could be generalized by assuming that the efficiency or usefulness of individual members varies directly and continuously with length of service. Average length of service evidently varies with the rate of growth of the number of members, therefore average efficiency would vary continuously indirectly with the growth rate of the firm.

But in gaining generality in this way we would almost certainly sim-
plify. It is most unlikely that efficiency – especially in relation to the planning of further expansion – varies with length of service in quite so crude
a fashion. For length of service is likely to be strongly correlated with age,
and it is probable that, for any given managerial task, there is an optimum
age: if average age passes the average optimum, a counter-effect on
efficiency sets in. And apart from the question of age, there is that of stale-
ness. Outside recruits may import new ideas transcending mere expertise,
and their freshness may be vital to expansion. In other words, there is a
sense in which attempts by organizations to expand breed the capacity to
expand. What recruits lack in immediate ability to co-ordinate, they may
make up in drive and vision.

In other words, it may well be the case that, at low rates of growth,
acceleration, rather than affecting efficiency adversely, has precisely the
opposite effect. This does more than merely demonstrate the organization's efficiency by its ability to accelerate. It means that accelerations of
the recruitment rate – as indicated by permanent decreases in average
length of service – may well have beneficial effects on the quality of a
wide range of decisions that are connected with expansion only indirectly.
Resource allocation, sales management and production costs, for example,
may all be affected. However, the range of this effect cannot be unlimited.
As growth is increasingly accelerated, the adverse effects previously
described must, eventually, take over. Otherwise we would in the limit
reach the absurdity of an organization attempting to expand at an infinite
rate, whose members, their average length of service being infinitesimal,
would not even know each others' names.[6] So the continuous relationship
between some measure of the attempted growth rate and some measure of
decision-taking efficiency may well be non-monotonic: with efficiency as
the dependent variable, at low growth rates the relationship may be direct,
but at high growth rates it is always inverse. Once the peak is passed, the
organization must become liable to suffer in the way described by a corporation president who told Professor Mason Haire: 'We just got too big *too
soon* and began to lose money. We had to trim back to a reasonable size'
[italics added].[7]

These ideas may be thought of as representing a dynamization of the old
conception of diseconomies of scale. A non-growing firm may be subject
to positive economies of scale in the sense that it would be more efficient
at a larger absolute size than at a smaller. But once these static economies
are exhausted, the existence of corporate organization creates the pre-
sumption that returns to scale are thereafter constant. The ultimate size of
the firm is therefore unlimited. We say, however, that the ultimate size is

then meaningless, and turn our attention to the rate of change. In place of a relationship between efficiency and absolute size we substitute a relationship between efficiency and growth rate.

THE CONCEPT OF BALANCED OR SUSTAINABLE GROWTH

Throughout all that has gone so far we have spoken recurrently of growth, of motives to grow, and of restraints on growth rates as if 'growth' was, in the context, a concept both universally understood and clearly defined. We have made no attempt to provide a precise definition of growth; nor have we much discussed the means by which growth is to be achieved. If size is to be measured by output, for example, growth requires sales expansion. If it is to be defined by gross assets, then capital must be absorbed. Which of these, and many other possible definitions, should be used?

There is no real problem here. We are concerned with what we have described as 'sustainable' growth: that is to say, with growth that is consistent with the firm's continuing on a financial basis such that the same rate can be maintained indefinitely, or at least until there is some change in the data. In this condition, most of the alternative measures of size are required to expand in balance. For example, if capacity in terms of gross were to expand more rapidly than the volume of saleable output, average capacity utilization must gradually decline, and with it the rate of return. But a steadily declining rate of return cannot normally be reconciled with a constant growth rate; 'unbalanced' growth in this sense cannot be sustainable.

We therefore confine the analysis largely to conditions where growth is balanced in the sense that the long-run growth of demand and of capacity are equal, and we shall frequently use the adjectives 'balanced' and 'sustainable' synonymously. Furthermore, we shall typically consider situations in which balanced growth rates are associated not only with constant rates of return, but also with constant overall profit margins and capital–output ratios. In such conditions almost all measures of size (including, for example, aggregate profits and aggregate turnover) march together; so to maximize the growth rate of one is to maximize that of most of the others.

THE ROLE OF DIVERSIFICATION

So much for definitions of growth; but what of the means? How may a firm deliberately cause variation of demand growth: that is, how may demand be made subject to policy? In earlier theory, the firm faced a statically conceived demand-curve, whose trend – or rate shift over time – if any, was entirely exogenous. In the Marshallian arrangement, price was then the only decision-variable capable of influencing quantity sold; post-classical writers added others, such as advertising expenditure or quality variation, but none such could conceivably be employed for sustainable growth. If demand were to be increased continuously by price reduction, rising unit selling expenditure, or both, profitability would be declining continuously, and the growth, therefore, inevitably non-sustainable. Continuous sustainable volume increase could result only from residual trend in the demand-curve, and this, as already indicated was by definition something incapable of influence by policy.

These conclusions, which seemed so inconsistent with evident fact that most business executives appeared to believe the contrary – that the influencing of demand was one of their important functions – arose because the orthodox analysis supposed that before the demand-curve was drawn up, a number of important policy decisions had already been taken. We refer, of course, to decisions determining what goods should be produced – what demand-curves, in effect, should be created. For a firm that is going to produce only a single product, this decision is likely to be far more important to its destiny than subsequent price and volume decisions, and one sometimes wonders why economic theory has previously taken so little interest in the subject. Be that as it may, we know that, ever since the Industrial Revolution, firms have been able to grow by the successive marketing of products they had not previously offered, thus enabling themselves to progress by 'jumps' to appropriate situations among an ever-growing family of otherwise static demand-curves. That businessmen have become increasingly aware of this since the 1930s is apparent from only a cursory glance at the literature.[8]

It is Edith Penrose again who appears as the leading contemporary writer to emphasize the role of continuous diversification in the normal process of growth. She points out that by this means many firms have continued to grow over very long periods, such as fifty or even seventy-five years, although there is, apparently, evidence of a tendency for the rates of growth themselves to decline over time.[9] The planning of diversification is *par excellence* a typical function of high management. Characteristically, it has been found, these decisions are taken at higher levels within the management hierarchy than are, for example, pricing decisions. We may therefore define a distinct decision-variable, to be known as *the rate of diversification,* intended to summarize the implication of the series of individual decisions that lead up to the marketing of new products. Many new products, of course, fail to succeed in the sense that their sales prove to be so small that their contribution to overall growth is insubstantial.

The rate of diversification, however, is to be taken as referring to both successes and failures: it may be defined as the ratio of the number of new items added to the catalogue during a given period to the number already catalogued at the beginning of the period. We realise that this still leaves the definition 'fuzzy', in the sense that we do not know how to distinguish strictly between new products and/or variants of old ones, but we believe that it should not in practice be difficult to develop appropriate conventions for converting the diversification rate into an observable variable. For the time being the reader can best visualize the concept as measuring the rate at which the firm is attempting to increase the number of independent demand-curves relating to products it is actually producing.

Clearly, if a 'new' product is expected and intended largely to kill the demand for a product the firm is already selling, as in the case of new fashions in clothes and road vehicles, it does not represent meaningful diversification, although, evidently, deliberately induced increases in the rate of obsolescence may offer a method of fostering growth in an otherwise saturated market for consumer durables. But as the US automobile industry has learned, this is yet another method that cannot easily be made continuous. Diversification may involve marketing products that are close substitutes for those of other firms, but they must not be substitutes for products already marketed by the diversifying firm.

Diversification, as usually understood, is not, of course, the only method of fostering demand-growth. There may be occasions where substantial increases in the sales of an existing line can be induced without necessarily involving a severe reduction of profitability. A technical improvement in consumer-appeal for example, may permit the achievement of a major increase in a firm's share of an old-established market, perhaps at the expense of an old-established rival. These events, however, must also be regarded as discontinuous. In any one product, for example, growth potential is exhausted when all rivals have been eliminated. Continuous growth requires such actions to be successive – that is, taken in relation to first one product, then another, and so on. At each successful attempt a discontinuous increase in demand is achieved; when this is completed, attention must at least be turned elsewhere.

THE ROLE OF THE MERGER

There is another important method of growth to be considered, namely the 'growth' involved in mergers. This does not fit into the conceptual scheme very easily. In Chapter 1 we investigated 'take-overs'; these, although often leading to the union of two organizations, are in one sense clearly distinguishable from 'voluntary' mergers: that is, unions welcomed by both managements. But while the take-over raid performs a mainly punitive or restraining function from the point of view of the raided firm, the act is 'voluntary' from the point of view of the raider, and can thus be regarded as a means of his growth.[10] This is a particularly relevant course in the case of the inter-managerial raid. So all forms of merger, from one point of view, are part of a growth process. Evidently the method is adopted because it permits faster growth than would be permitted by others. But, like others, it is also subject to dynamic restraints, and cannot be made to yield growth at unlimited rates.

When a firm is diversifying by internal expansion only, demand, capital and administrative capacity must all be extended in balance. But the expansion rates on each dimension are variously restricted and constrained. By taking over a going concern, on the other hand, it is possible that some of these restrictions may be weakened considerably. True, the merger itself requires organization and presents new problems in coordination, but these are evidently often less serious than the corresponding difficulties that arise in internal expansion. The firm taken over may be modified or improved, and may, indeed, eventually be so absorbed as to lose all vestige of identity. Alternatively, much of the original identity may be deliberately preserved, and the process be seen as part of a programme of growth by decentralization in the central firm. In either case, the result is, from our point of view, the same; growth can occur at a faster rate for given efficiency and the administrative restraint is weakened.

Like all other methods, however, this one in turn must be subject to dynamic limits. The digestive capacity of the absorber is limited, so also is the number of suitable 'victims' available at any one time. Thus the potentialities of merger do not eliminate the administrative restraint on growth, but rather they modify it; the effect is quantitative rather than qualitative. For this reason, through most of what follows I shall write as if internal expansion were the only method of growth.

THE ECONOMIC ENVIRONMENT

We have now characterized the firm as an autonomous organization capable of growth (subject to the rules of the game) at a limited rate in a pliable environment. This growth may occur mainly at the expense of other firms in general, or of a small handful of firms in particular, or it may mainly reflect expansion of the economic system as a whole. Where growth occurs through diversification that is innovatory in the full Schumpeterian sense, developments in consumption tastes and production may go hand-in-hand. A firm marketing a product that is new to itself and the economy may soon be required to create a significant amount of new technology. In other cases most of the technology may be absorbed from the national stock of knowledge, and necessary, suitably qualified specialists may be recruited (a common explanation of merger is 'to acquire a going team of specialists'). Evidently, then, for our theory to have any bite firms must be living in an environment where these things are possible.

They must be living in an environment where both consumer and producer techniques are capable of responding to continual development and change. Both consumption and production functions must be capable of organic extension, and in a sociological sense the society must be neither primitive nor traditional. Modern developed economics are known to be pliable, are known to progress both by increasing production and consumption of 'necessities', and by the constant development of new wants and new products. Although, strictly speaking, the theory that follows could be applied formally in a static economy, it would not be of much interest there. Firms could grow only by 'imitative' diversification, and this would always be at the expense of others. In the absence of diseconomies of scale, production should eventually be concentrated in a giant monopoly or, alternatively, an extremely rigid oligopolistic stability might develop. In either case comparative statics, possibly modified by a stochastic model of perturbations) would be the most appropriate method of analysis. In fact, while technical dynamism is intimately associated with industrial concentration, it may also be partly responsible for the fact that concentration does not go further. The reader may take it, therefore, that we are assuming a 'dynamic' economy.

Typically, then, we envisage an environment with continual change and new product creation, in which new products, both final and intermediate, are responsible for the lion's share of incremental output and demand.

METHODS OF ANALYSIS

Here followed a passage describing the analytical method called 'comparative dynamics'. Basically, this consists of making assumptions that permit constant proportionate rates of change of variables relating to size, in a model where these conditions are consistent with constant levels of other variables, normally ratios, such as the ratio of profit to assets, the proportion of profit retained for reinvestment ('retention ratio') or the ratio of total stock market value to assets ('valuation ratio'). Alternative growth paths, with different growth rates and accordingly different values of the 'state' variables, are then compared, without investigation of the problem of transferring from one path to another. Again, we have to concede, that since the IT revolution at the end of the twentieth century, there have been numerous examples of such amazing and explosive growth of individual firms, that the concept of 'steady' growth also appears dated. Of course, firms always grew in an irregular fashion, but in the first three-quarters of the century, it seemed reasonable to interpret the data as if the typical firm did have a long-term growth path, albeit subject to significant chance disturbance in any given short or medium period.

The remaining text of the original chapter follows.

Our general method is as follows. We first consider some vector of decision-variables that is capable of being shown to be consistent with some stable, sustainable condition of growth, in the sense that once the growth rate is established, neither it, the decision-variables nor any other endogenous variables will change so long as the exogenous data remain constant. (All such conditions, of course, require that the growth be balanced.) Then we consider alternative equilibrium vectors against the same exogenous data, or alternative data values against the original vector, and compare the characteristics of the various equilibrium states. If the fact of changing the vector would in reality induce disturbances, our gaze is averted until such time as things have settled down again, and we assume, of course, that the firm is in a position to ensure that things always will settle down, eventually. This implies that whenever any particular position is analyzed it is implicitly assumed that all relevant variables have been constant for some time past and will be constant for some time into the future. For example, only if the gearing ratio has been for some time constant is it true that marginal and average gearing are the same, a condition that is also required for steady equilibrium. The reader will therefore appreciate that the concept of balanced growth, explained earlier, is closely associated with this methodology. The method also carries the implication that choices between fast growth in the immediate future and slower growth later have never to be made. We consider only equilibrium states in which the growth rate is constant over the whole theoretical future. Since the firm is a continuing organization with a changing management, the approach seems not unreasonable. But we do not deny, of course, that the history of many firms has much of the appearance of an S-shaped growth-curve: our assumptions are merely intended to represent a convenient analytical simplification.

Finally, we conclude the section by reminding the reader that most of the operation represents an exercise in partial equilibrium analysis. This means that, in general, when policies and conditions vary within the single firm that is being analyzed, all relevant aspects of the environment are assumed to remain constant. 'All relevant aspects' will usually include general economic variables, such as factor supply prices and the general level of product prices; they will also include the magnitudes of the policy variables set by other firms. Other individual prices, however, will not always be constant, because in the theory of demand we do take account of anticipated oligopolistic reactions.

4 'Demand'

We have seen that, in order to sustain growth, a firm must either create new products, enter existing markets it has previously ignored, or merge. The first two methods are called 'growth by diversification', and the third, 'growth by merger'. These, as we have seen, are related, 'growth by merger' often representing no more than a means of overcoming dynamic organizational restraints on growth by diversification. In this chapter we are concerned with the dynamics of growth by diversification. We are concerned, that is, with the relationship between the rate of growth of the productive capacity required if there is to be no trend (in either direction) in the level of capacity utilization. In essence, the problem is one of policy; we are asking how certain variables within the control of the firm, such as price policy, diversification policy, research and development expenditure, and selling expenditure, react on the endogenous variables that feature in the conditions for sustainable growth. How do the policy variables affect the growth rate of the quantum of demand for the firm's products; and how do they react on such factors as rate of return, which govern the growth rate of the firm's supply of capital?

In microeconomics, we may consider 'demand' either from the point of view of the firm or from the point of view of the consumer. In the latter case, the theory should relate to items of consumer' need – to such entities as 'potatoes', 'private motoring' or 'refrigerators'. But a firm may sell in a number of such classes; for example, a firm may produce both cars and refrigerators. A theory of the growth of demand for the products of a firm as a whole will stem from, but must go beyond, the ordinary theory of consumer demand and, as we shall see, it is certainly wrong to treat the forces controlling 'demand for the firm' as being nothing more than some simple compound of the forces controlling consumers' demand for the products the firm happens to manufacture. In what follows we develop a theory we believe to be appropriate to the problem of the individual firm; to be appropriate to the conditions of a dynamic managerial economy (or, if preferred, of an 'affluent society'); and, going beyond the analytical convenience, to represent a considerable advance in realism.

As already indicated, growth by diversification may be 'differentiated' in character, 'imitative', or both. In all cases the products marketed are 'new' to the firm, in the sense that it has not produced or marketed products of this type before, but in the 'differentiated' case, they are also

73

largely new to the public. More precisely, the effects of the diversion of consumer expenditure involved in the growth of demand for a successful differentiated product are, by definition, spread thinly over demand for products in the economy at large, and are not perceptible to the producers of any one existing product or narrowly defined group of products. By contrast, the growth of sales of a product which is 'new' to one firm, in the sense defined above, but nevertheless 'imitative', is only at the expense of the sales of the product or products of a relatively small number of other firms, and, if the imitation is successful, these other firms will experience a noticeable reduction of demand in relation to the sales they could have expected had the imitation not been marketed. Many products, of course, will contain both imitative and differentiated elements. For example, suppose the growth rate of demand in the economy as a whole is 2 per cent per annum, and this rate precisely is being experienced by a group of producers of a product, X. A firm under analysis then markets a product X'. During the period immediately after it is first marketed, sales of X' grow at 10 per cent per annum, in consequence of which, sales of X, instead of growing at 2 per cent, grow more slowly, or even decline. When X' has ceased its rapid phase of growth, both it and X resume the 2 per cent rate, but the absolute level of sales of X, of course, will now be lower at all future points of time than would have been the case had X' never appeared. Then we say that X' is only 'partly' imitative if X experienced only part of the total divertive effect, the growth rate of demand for all other products in the economy at large having also been slightly (but imperceptibly) reduced during the same period; the potential sales of X' are 'large' in relation to those of X, but small in relation to the economy at large. Had the whole effect been spread over the economy at large, X' would have been defined as fully differentiated; had none been so spread, as fully imitative.

In the first part of the present chapter we concentrate analysis first on the case where the firm diversifies through the medium of products, all of which are as 'differentiated' as the definition allows; and then on the case where all are fully imitative; and finally we attempt to combine the results in a model that not only takes account of partly imitative products but also of the need for policy decisions between them.

THE CONSUMER AND HIS BRAIN

Economists are notorious for bias in favour of behaviouristic inductions that fit conveniently with favoured analytical methods. Thus the

'Marshallian' static demand-curve was the convenient concept for the method of comparative statics. This, one often suspects, at least partly explains why the associated static theories of utility and consumer preference – essentially philosophical and axiomatic – have gripped the subject for so long.

By a static demand-curve we mean a stable, reversible and, in general, monotonic and fully differentiable functional relationship in which quantity demanded depends on prices, income and so on. This conception remains 'static' as much when the function is allowed to 'drift' over time as when it is not. To accept that quantity demanded can exhibit residual variation which may be treated as a statistical trend does no more than introduce slow change into a set of basically statically-conceived relationships; reversible dependence on price and income remains the dominant feature of the system. The practical weaknesses of the conception stem from two implicit assumptions. The first is the assumption that the consumer's brain incorporates a relatively stable and comprehensive preference system analogous in character to a computing machine governed by a definite exogenous programme. The second is the assumption that the preference systems of individuals are independent; more precisely, that the effects of the decisions of individual brains on the decision-taking functions of others are, in this field, sufficiently unimportant to be ignored.

In affluent societies, neither assumption is plausible. Both were first identified and attacked by James Duesenberry. In *Income, Saving and the Theory of Consumer Behaviour*[1] published in 1949, Duesenberry outflanked the stable reversible preference system and destroyed the assumption of independence. But at that time his main concern was to construct a new macroeconomic theory of the relationship between income, consumption and saving, rather than to develop the microeconomic implications; consequently, the third section of the sixth chapter of his book, which provided an original model of the growth of demand for individual new products, remained somewhat isolated from the rest; the macro theory did not depend on this particular piece of micro theory. In the present work, although we do not adopt his particular theory, the influence of Duesenberry will be obvious. Once the standard of living has bettered 'subsistence', the static reversible preference system becomes particularly implausible. The brain probably possesses a virtually infinite capacity for recording experiences, and its state – an electrochemical condition – is the product of everything that it has felt and done during the whole of its history. Each experience, however trivial, makes a permanent alteration. But while the present state of the brain is the product of all that has gone before, it is also the sole determinant of how it will react to stimuli received now. Hence, while the act of consuming a certain quantity of a certain commodity (a consequence of a decision of the brain) may represent a response to current stimuli such as price, income, advertising and the behaviour of other consumers, it is also an act that permanently alters the actor. Therefore there is no presumption what ever that repetition of a particular constellation of prices and income will induce approximately the same consumption decisions as before; one price movement may be needed to induce a man to consume a new product, another to make him give it up, yet another to revert, and so on. The preference 'system' existing in the mind of a single consumer at a particular instant of time is the product of past experience, and is therefore continually developing. This fact, which no one seriously denies, invalidates both the assumptions of stability and of reversibility in the demand curve. It has also, incidentally, interesting implications in welfare economics. For the primary biological goal of the organism (the brain) is as likely to be development as the achievement of static equilibrium. 'Maximization of consumer welfare' might be better defined as consisting in the maximization of the rate of refinement of preferences than in the achievement of a stable state within a given system. In other words, as we often say that the general goals of human endeavour lie primarily in the development of new capacities rather than in the exploitation of existing ones, so we might define the primary economic goal as the refinement of new wants rather than the satisfaction of existing ones. The last argument, however, is superfluous to the immediate purpose, for which we need consider only objective behaviour.

THE PROCESS OF WANT CREATION[2]

It is not difficult to identify primary elements in the mental processes leading up to a consumption decision. In the first place, the brain contains a store of memories of previous consumption experiences, and these form the framework against which current decisions are taken. The most common reason for purchasing a product is the fact of having consumed it before and found it to be satisfactory or (to use more dangerous language) 'satisfying'. More precisely, the previous experience, whether repeated or isolated, has in some sense gratified a psychological motive – has provided pleasurable sensations, prevented pain, or met a social requirement. 'Wants' therefore are largely the product of experience. But the relevant experience need not always be direct; wants can also result from vicarious experience, such as is provided by the reports of other consumers or the blandishments of advertising. Furthermore, it is clear that in addition to this apparatus (which can very loosely be described as 'habit') most human brains are also constantly scanning for possible new experiences. In many people the scanning mechanism may be so weak as to be practically non-existent, but the achievements of the human race as a whole bear witness to its strength in others. It is clearly of vital importance in the struggle between new products and old. Finally, there remains the fact that the same mental forces that encourage the consumption of one commodity also encourage the consumption of others, and the results do not automatically harmonize. The force of the scanning effect, for example, encouraging a decision to sample a particular new product, has to battle with a similar force encouraging the choice of a different new product, or with the force of habit asking for old products. By some means a decision is taken, and, with limited income, the decision-taking process must involve some weighing of relative sacrifices, and hence a consideration of prices.

How does a typical consumer come to decide to buy a product he has never bought before? He evidently requires stimulation; he requires, in fact, to be made for the first time strongly aware of the potentialities of the product. Advertisements can provide this stimulus, but their obvious bias makes many people resist them to at least some extent. There is considerable sociological evidence that[3] the most effective stimulus remains that of contact with other existing consumers – more conversions are made by previous converts than by priests. We can illustrate this argument with two examples, one a new consumer 'durable', and the other a traditional perishable. Suppose, for the first time, an effective dishwashing machine is put on the market. No one believes the advertiser's claims that the machine eliminates practically all the labour of washing dishes; most, however, will accept that the labour is probably reduced in volume, or at least favourably changed in character. But, for the average family, these potentialities must seem very uncertain. How many person-hours of work will, in fact, be eliminated? How far will the change in the nature of the task lighten the psychological burden? Will a new machine in the kitchen encourage the household to help more often? Will they, in their turn, feel a worthwhile reduction of guilt? These questions can only be answered after extended practical experience of using the machine. Alternatively, if the members of another family who have already bought such a machine are consulted, their views will be of value only if, as a family, they are sociologically similar. And, in practice, of course, it is usually contact with a sociologically similar family already using a similar machine that puts the idea of buying into the first family's collective head.

Our second example relates to meat. Suppose a family with a specified income has been in the habit of buying only low-quality beef. Their real income rises. Among other things on which they might spend the increment is beef of better quality. But at first, never having tasted anything better, they do not believe the commodity could yield them any 'utility'; they continue to regard such things as pointless luxuries, and in consequence a large proportion of their marginal income is saved. Then, one day, they eat with friends who for one reason or another are already consuming good meat. The gastronomic experience is a revelation to them; from now on they will find it difficult to eat cheap beef again. This is not a process of emulation, but of stimulation. The behaviour is not simple conformism, but the development of acquired tastes. The habit-forming commodity is not the exception: it is, and always has been, the rule.

Once, therefore, a person has been stimulated to buy a new commodity, he possesses a 'want' or 'need' where he had none before; stimulation, in this sense, is a process of want creation.

In fact, we may distinguish between needs and wants. A product meets a need if it provides the consumer with sensible advantages in the achievement of specific socioeconomic aims. But consumers cannot 'want' the product until they have experienced it in action: until, in fact, it has been created and is in use. When they do come to want it, they also need it. Before this, the need can be described as latent. There is a being latent need for a product if, were it created, it would become wanted. The commercial process consists of sensing the existence of latent needs and exploiting them – that is, converting them into conscious wants by marketing and advertising appropriate products. It is sometimes argued that wants can be created from nothing, without the existence of objective latent needs. If this were generally true, nothing would limit the rate of growth of capacity required by the individual firm, and relative growth among firms would depend on factors other than demand. But it is not true. Consider two case histories, neither of them relating to 'durables'.

After the Second World War, American manufacturers of 'cola'-type drinks made a considerable attempt to expand further into world markets. Among the countries they attacked was Great Britain. 'Cola' drinks are to some extent habit-forming in the ordinary sense of the term, but, despite being consumed in both winter and summer, the 'craving' can only be sustained effectively in continental climates with regular long, dry summers, and winters sufficiently cold that interior space heating significantly dries the domestic atmosphere. In the UK these conditions are absent and the drinks have not really caught on; they have achieved a modest steady sale, but their position in the consumption pattern cannot be compared with their corresponding position in the USA and many other countries. Notice a difficulty in separating cause and effect: one might well argue that the relative failure of these drinks in the UK stemmed from failure to develop distribution methods in the characteristic American manner. But this only leaves the basic question unanswered; we must still explain the explanation. Cola drinks must be served cold: in the UK they rarely are. And, once bottled they are bulky. Hence success depends on a wide distribution of large-capacity refrigerating plant in retail outlets. But despite all attempts to induce them to behave otherwise, potential British retailers of this type of commodity have by and large refused to invest in the necessary machinery, although no difficulty was experienced in persuading food retailers to invest in deep freezes. The answer, surely, lies in the mildness of a climate that makes the cold drink, though often desirable, rarely essential. The retailer, therefore, invests elsewhere.[4]

Consider now a famous British product 'Babycham'. This is an alcoholic beverage made from pears and possessing some of the more superficial characteristics of champagne: it is fizzy and straw-coloured, and capable of inducing a fairly 'light' variety of intoxication. It is also rather sweet and in general not very attractive to the sophisticated palate. For the unsophisticated, who like it, it is not overwhelmingly improved by chilling, and is generally served at room temperature. This drink was marketed with spectacular success in British inns in the 1950s, following a large-scale advertising campaign. The success flew in the face of the virtual failure of all earlier attempts to create a mass market for products derived from the cider and perry family, and was due to a new, sociologically-created latent need, acutely observed by the manufacturers. British pubs had been becoming more respectable, more bourgeois and more feminine. But the new female customers found a deficiency in the products traditionally offered: they did not drink often; they wanted to get intoxicated without appearing to want to do so; they disliked beer; and were more than dubious about hard liquor. Gin, the traditional drink of women, had severe drawbacks, and the American cocktail was impossible to serve properly in the average pub because there was never enough ice (and there was never enough ice for the reasons given above). To cut a long story short, Babycham proved to be the answer to a maiden's prayer.

The first point of this second story is that before the product's introduction, the maidens' prayers were quite inaudible. A latent need is latent, and the consumer himself is hardly aware of it. Ordinary processes of questioning would have been unlikely to have revealed the potential market for 'Babycham'; 'market research', with samples, operates after a product has been invented. The second point is to draw attention to genuine objective conditions favouring the product, without which it could not have succeeded. And, as a postscript, it might be added that the invention also represented a considerable technical achievement. The drink is less cloying than anything of this type made before, and, in particular, provides a major improvement in the character of the intoxication produced by beverages fermented from pears or apples. Thus not only is it the case that wants cannot be created without latent needs, but one cannot normally exploit a newly discovered latent need without technical innovation – more precisely, given the technology of a certain time, even should there exist an unlimited number of latent needs awaiting exploitation, only a limited number could be exploited by any one innovator at the time; and, in general, a firm is likely to find that the greater the number of new products it markets in a period, the lower the technical efficiency of production.

THE PIONEERING CONSUMER

In the dynamic theory of demand, then, instead of adjustment to price changes among established commodities, we emphasize the process of interpersonal stimulation and want creation. How does it originate? If no consumer ever bought a new product until stimulated by an existing consumer, new products would never get started. There must be some 'pioneers' among consumers – individuals or families who decide on new purchases without benefit of stimulus from others. We must therefore make a formal distinction between these pioneers and the general run of consumers, or 'sheep'. Pioneers may, but not necessarily, represent a distinct psychological type, and different people may at different times pioneer different products. For our purposes, therefore, the concept of the pioneer need only be defined in relation to a 'given' product. But this does not mean we can get away with assuming nothing about pioneers beyond that they exist. For one thing, we must assume that each pioneer is sufficiently in touch with the rest of the community that, although himself able to act without stimulus, he can stimulate others; otherwise, his behaviour is of little interest. But the biological machine in the skull of the pioneer is basically the same as in the skull of the 'sheep'. Just as with the 'sheep', so the pioneer's new consumption experience can create want where none existed before; and as a result of the experience, his brain is permanently altered. The only essential difference is that, unlike the 'sheep', the pioneer for one reason or another chooses to undergo the experience without social stimulus. One might say that, in both pioneers and 'sheep', wants are established by consumption experience, but with 'sheep' they must first be planted in the mind by another person. Unusual ability to perceive one's own latent needs, unusual adventurousness or unusual susceptibility to advertising might all explain pioneering decisions. Alternatively, as we shall more generally assume, in relation to any given new product they are stochastic events distributed among the whole population of 'sheep'.

The total number of new pioneers acquired by a product in a given period will therefore be a function of its intrinsic qualities, of the money and skill devoted to advertising and other forms of sales promotion, of its price, and of the social and economic characteristics of the population. In general we assume that, unless special steps are taken to arrange things otherwise, a given number of pioneers will be randomly distributed in a given population, in the sense that in the absence of special knowledge about a consumer (such as that he has a special disposition to pioneering) he has the same probability of being a pioneer as every other consumer. The act of becoming a pioneer, however, merely represents a decision to become a buyer, it does not determine the quantity bought except in the case of commodities where only one unit is taken. We can well assume that, having decided to become a pioneer, a consumer then behaves according to a perfectly orthodox demand function, but, and it is a very important but, the behaviour function controlling the total number of pioneers cannot normally be derived directly from the characteristics of the post-pioneering demand functions of the individuals. The 'pioneering function' is inherently 'macro' in character, derives from 'macro' social and economic variates, and cannot, in general, be obtained by mere aggregation. For example, many firms believe this function to be rather insensitive to price,[5] and there is some evidence that they are right, but this does not necessarily imply that the 'pioneering' function that determines the quantity bought by a person who has already decided to pioneer will also be inelastic. For example, a product might be marketed at a high price and acquire a certain number of pioneers, each of whom, on account of the price, took only a small quantity. A reduction in price might significantly increase their *per capita* consumption but not greatly influence their number, and vice versa. Or the situation might be reversed. When firms say that the demand for new products is inelastic, they sometimes mean the one thing, sometimes the other, and sometimes both; we shall find the distinction important. The case most easily analyzed is, needless to say, the one where both the pioneering and the pioneer's functions are inelastic.

Evidently, the foregoing ideas *could* be expressed in orthodox terms – for example, by assuming suitable peculiarly-shaped individual demand-curves, and building by aggregation a model based on an analysis of the elasticities around the points where these curves cut their origins, but the result would not be convincing. The act of becoming a pioneer is different in kind from that of moving along an established demand-curve. Pioneering consists of becoming aware of the product, of incorporating it into the preference system – the very act, in fact, of establishing the demand-curve itself. Pioneering is thus irreversible: before the act no curve exists, consumption is zero at all prices and incomes; after the act, zero consumption happens only if prices are above a definite (positive) level.

Precisely the same applies to 'sheep'. When a 'sheep' is stimulated to become a consumer as a result of contact with other existing consumers, a process we call *activation,* he is irreversibly changed. Before, he had no demand-curve; now he has. Its form, however, may be of many varieties, and indeed we need not necessarily assume that he actually buys any positive quantities. Activation might be defined as a change of state indicating merely that now, if the price were low enough, the consumer would buy some positive quantity, whereas before he would have bought none at any price. Many firms say that, as compared with the pioneering phase in a product's development, it may often prove rather sensitive to price[6] in the rapidly expanding or saturated stage, although we do not know whether by this is meant that in such circumstances it has usually acquired competitors, or that 'sheep' are naturally more price-sensitive bodies than pioneers.

The point is important because it is vitally involved in the mechanism by which the demand for new products grows. We have described the process of activation as that of receiving stimulus from other consumers with whom a person is in socioeconomic contact. In the 'opinion leader' concept of the process,[7] certain particular members of the population are endowed with the quality of being able to activate other members of their primary groups, but not the other way about. For demand to grow, therefore, it is necessary that pioneers be concentrated among these people, and the resulting process, involving carefully planned selective selling, is not properly cumulative. In our view, any active consumer should be regarded as, in principle, potentially capable of stimulating others, irrespective of whether he was himself originally a pioneer or an 'activated' 'sheep'. By this means (and we believe the picture to be more generally realistic), chain reactions are obtained. It therefore becomes important to know whether or not a 'sheep', having been activated in the sense of now possessing a demand-curve for the product, finds himself so placed on this curve as to indicate some significant positive consumption; because, if he does not, he cannot pass on the effect to others. In order to ease the analysis, therefore, we shall assume that pioneers' demand functions, once established, are in general of some form implying significant positive consumption even at high prices; in effect, this is a part of the definition of a pioneer. In the case of 'sheep', we define the concept of a *market population*, this being the population of all consumers who, if activated (or if pioneers), would, at a given price, consume sufficient positive quantities to be capable of stimulating others. The size of a market population is therefore a function of price, of other characteristics of the product and, of course, of characteristics of the population.

THE CHAIN REACTION

The characteristic early history of a new commodity in a society where the standard of living of a large number of people is well above subsistence is therefore as follows. When it is introduced, the number of immediate consumers is small, because pioneering is a minority activity. As time passes, pioneering purchases increase, but in the absence of other influences would probably eventually flatten out. If the pioneers give their contacts a good account of the product, they may stimulate them into purchasing it, and these 'sheep' may in turn stimulate others. In this way a chain reaction may spread consumption far beyond the pioneering frontier. The idea would be trivial unless the beginning of the reaction could be shown to depend on the number of pioneers reaching some definite critical size: to put the point another way – if the 'critical' number were no greater than one consumer (the first) – we might just as well ignore the chain reaction and concentrate attention, as in orthodox analysis, on the situation existing after it is finished. The evidence, however, is otherwise.

The process of stimulation and penetration is inevitably stochastic in character, because the chances of life determine who stimulates whom, or (to parody the words of an unprintable limerick) who does what, when and to whom. *Criticality,* therefore, is defined as a condition where the probability of a continuing chain reaction tends to unity. In a limiting case, where a product is so appealing that almost the whole market population can be activated with the minimum of stimulation, criticality in this sense occurs almost the instant the product appears and after only a very small number of pioneers has been obtained. In the meantime, we concentrate on the conditions for criticality in the more general case where the number of pioneers required represents a significant proportion of the (market) population as a whole.

In order to stimulate one another, consumers must be in a state we shall define as 'socioeconomic contact'. One is stimulated by one's friends, and sometimes by one's neighbours. But not everyone with whom one is in social contact, in the sense of 'knowing', living next door to, meeting at work, or meeting at play, is a socioeconomic contact. The tautological definition of a socioeconomic contact is a contact with a person who is capable of inducing one to consume a new commodity, and to this end it is necessary that one shares at least some of the contact's tastes and values. Evidently, therefore, socioeconomic contacts will tend to be concentrated among social contacts within one's own social class. Reports of a new commodity from a person whose values in general one does not share are unlikely to have much effect. This may be a matter of snobbery, but may also represent a quite reasonable appreciation that his pattern of living is so different from one's own that a commodity which discovers a genuine latent need in his life may be valueless to oneself. If one belongs to a social class where a mother-in-law spends much of her time in the daughter's home and gives substantial help with the housework, a dishwashing machine may be more trouble than use, but with an upper-middle-class mother-in-law who merely creates work, the same machine may be a godsend. To someone belonging to a social class in which wine is drunk regularly, nothing can make 'Babycham' acceptable. In other words, as Katz and Lazarsfeld more soberly put it, 'Seeking out a woman of like status for advice means seeking out a woman with similar budgetary problems and limitations.'[8]

The correlation between social class and socioeconomic contact is, of course, reinforced by the correlation of the two with income. The theory we are propounding by no means purports to eliminate the hard reality of income from consumption decisions. Many new commodities are quite out of the range of certain income groups, and no amount of social stimulation can alter the fact. 'Not being able to afford it' remains the most important reason for not consuming most things. Nevertheless, 'affording' is a relative term, and becomes increasingly so as affluence increases. Suppose, after meeting his so-called 'subsistence' needs, a manual worker has half of his income left over for so-called 'luxuries'. There is nothing in principle to prevent him from devoting the whole of the margin to one item normally regarded as a preserve of the much better off; but normally he is dissuaded from doing so by competing temptations from other 'luxuries'.

We cannot say for certain that either shared social class or shared income class is an exclusive ingredient in a socioeconomic contact. The lady who comes to help with the cleaning in my house belongs to a family with a net income after tax of about a third of mine. Some of the things she sees consumed in my house are ruled out in her own by the 'cannot afford' argument, and others by virtue of an entirely different set of social values. But some of the things she sees in my house, she persuades her husband to buy for her. Conversely, some of the ideas about new types of 'do-it-yourself' equipment gleaned from her husband's workshop are effectively communicated to me. So we are driven back on the tautological definition of social contact; we can, however, lay down the required conditions more precisely. A socioeconomic contact is a person with whom one has a relationship such that his consumption behaviour is capable of influencing one's own. The socioeconomic contacts of an individual are therefore limited to those people with whom he is in general contact (sees and speaks to fairly regularly), and, among them, to those with whom he shares enough relevant values for the contact to be economic as well as social.

We define a single stimulus as the automatic consequence of a socioeconomic contact with one existing consumer of a product during a given period of time. Thus if, during a given period, I am in contact with one existing consumer, I have experienced one stimulus. If during the next period I am in contact with another existing consumer, or my contact with the first is repeated, I have experienced two stimuli. Thus the number of my stimuli in any given finite time period is the product of the number of separate sources of contact with separate individual existing consumers, and the average number of times I have been in contact with each during the period. It is probable that, in order to be induced to consume a commodity that is new to them, most people need more than one stimulus. It is also likely that they need stimuli from more than one source: the forces of emulation and conformism, though not the only factors in the chain, are by no means negligible, and, evidently, to any extent that conformism is, in fact, important, the greater the number of separate sources of stimulus, the greater the chance of activation. Indeed, in cases where conformism is really the dominant factor, evidence from a single contact only, unless subsequently reinforced by evidence from others, may lead to the suspicion that the original individual was a crank; it is known, for example, that the 'Organization Man' who buys a car one grade more expensive than that of his neighbours, far from inducing them to follow suit, may instead find himself ostracized.[9]

SOCIOECONOMIC STRUCTURE

A society of consumers thus consists of a large number of individual units, each of whom is in socioeconomic contact with a limited number of others. Some of these contacts will represent relationships with consumers

who are themselves interconnected; and others not. Within any large population, therefore, we can also identify a (large) number of *primary
groups*: that is, groups of consumers, all of whom are in socioeconomic
contact with each other. Such groups may, and in general probably will,
intersect, in the sense that an individual may belong to more than one: for
example A may be in contact with B and C, who are in contact with one
another, and also with B′ and C′, who are similarly related, but neither B′
nor C′ need be in contact with either B *or* C. *A pair of groups whose intersection contains at least one element can be said to be 'linked' and if the
intersection contains at least* n *elements we shall describe them as 'linked
in degree* n*'.*

This conception of a primary group is of considerable importance. If,
within one group, there exists the minimum number of active consumers
required to activate one 'sheep', because every member is in contact with
every other member, every member must in due course become activated.
Furthermore, if the 'threshold' number of separate contacts is m, then any
other group with which the first group is m-degree linked will also, eventually, be saturated (that is, all its members become active), and in turn
these will activate and saturate all other groups with whom they are similarly linked, and so on. The reaction, in fact, will continue until every
group that is linked either directly or indirectly with the original group is
saturated. It follows that the chance of obtaining a chain reaction depends
intimately on the structure of the system of groups and links.

To assist the analysis, let us clear the decks by eliminating 'redundant'
primary groups, (that is, all those that are subsets of others). If *A, B, C* and
D form a primary group, there is little point in separately identifying the
subsets *A, B* and *C, D,* since anything of significance that can be said
about the one set can also be said about the other – a condition that by no
means applies to pairs of groups which, though linked, are not inclusive.
For example, if m is the threshold and *A, B, C* and *D* form a primary group
with subsets *A, B* and *C, D,* in order to saturate both *A, B* and *C, D* it is
necessary only that there occur m pioneers located in any arrangement
among the group *A, B, C, D;* for example, if m were 2, one pioneer could
be *A* and another *D*. By contrast, if two groups, although intersecting, are
not inclusive (that is, one is not a subset of the other), then in order to saturate both it is necessary to obtain m active consumers located either
entirely within the one or entirely within the other. Redundant groups,
therefore, are of little interest and we may 'rationalize' our structure by
ignoring them. A 'rationalized population' is then defined as the set of all
possible primary groups derivable from a given market population other
than those which, if included, would prove to be proper subsets of others.

In what follows, unless otherwise indicated, all populations considered are implicitly assumed to be rationalized. Consequently, every consumer in the market population is included in at least one of the elements of the rationalized population, but not every element in the rationalized population necessarily contains more than one consumer.

What determines the size, shape and linkage of typical primary groups? Socioeconomic structure is often conditioned by such economically trivial factors as housing layout, but in other cases, particularly those of older societies, the arrangement of contacts in geographical space is more the result than the cause of sociological phenomena. Alternatively, among classes able to afford the custom of frequent distant visiting, contact systems may represent spacial networks that are both many-dimensional and non-geographical. In the crudest example of patterns caused, or at least occasioned, by elementary geographical factors, the linear suburb, it is often customary to maintain contact with immediate neighbours to right and left, with the family immediately opposite and with their immediate neighbours, but not with any of the families beyond the backyard fence. In some types of older British semi slums, almost the opposite situation was sometimes found, and in 'ribbon' developments along congested highways, contacts may literally be confined to immediate neighbours only. In high-class, non-linear suburbs, the network may prove to be almost identical with the system of blocks and courts. Thus, writing of his famous subject, the Chicago suburb of Park Forest, William Whyte said:

It is the group that determines when a luxury becomes a necessity. This takes place when there comes together a sort of critical mass. In the early stages, when only a few of the housewives have, say, an automatic dryer, the word-of-mouth praise of its indispensability is restricted. But then as time goes on and the adjacent housewives follow suit, in mounting ratio others are exposed to more and more talk about its benefits.[10]

Whyte was discussing a new and mobile society. It must be emphasized that in older societies, if families are established long enough to develop contacts on deeper anthropological, psychological and sociological bases, these geographical analogies of socioeconomic structure become less valid. In such societies, definite structures exist, of course, but they require a more sophisticated mathematical representation.

Geography must nevertheless always remain important. A well-defined system of primary groups requires more than that people merely have contacts; it requires the existence of some factor tending to encourage the probability that among all those with whom a typical consumer is in contact, a certain number will also be interconnected. If I am in contact with only B, C, D and E, and if I am to belong to a reasonable-sized primary group, there must be some factor tending to make the probability of occurrence of contacts between these persons considerably greater than chance; if not, either primary groups will be very small or the average number of contacts per person must be unrealistically large. Many non-geographical social and economic phenomena may help perform this role: in old rural societies, the village; in urban societies the family; and in modern suburban societies, the club and the church. But in all societies, new or old, until the day when travel becomes free, effortless and infinitely convenient, geography will remain the predominant de-randomiser among all but the richest or most sophisticated classes. Simple geographical examples of socioeconomic structure, though inaccurate, are therefore unlikely to be grossly misleading.

The simplest example of all, as previously mentioned, is the linear suburb. Each family, without exception, is supposed to be in contact only with neighbours to the left and right and the three nearest families opposite. Each has therefore five contacts and belongs to two primary groups, but the primary groups themselves each contain only four elements. Each, however, has two 2-unit intersections (that is, links) with adjacent groups, and the population of the drive as a whole forms a set of groups all of which are linked in the second degree.

What happens when there are also contacts over backyard fences? Each family now has three additional contacts, making eight in all, and each primary group acquires two more links (we are assuming the system extends indefinitely). The size of the groups remains the same, but the number of links per group is doubled.

The change of pattern is of considerable significance, for while the size of the primary groups is unchanged, the increase in the degree of 'compactness' alters the size of the rationalized population relative to that of the market population. In other words, in the more 'compact' pattern, more non-redundant primary groups are derivable from a population of given size.

It follows that if the total number of consumers is large, the number of primary groups in the first example is approximately, $\dfrac{N}{g-n}$ in the second example $\dfrac{2N}{g-n}$, where N is the total population and g the membership per group and n the degree of linkedness. More generally,

$$G_n \to \frac{N}{g-n} \cdot \frac{L_n}{2} \quad \text{as } N \text{ becomes large,} \tag{4.1}$$

where

$N =$ the total number of consumers;
$G_n =$ the number of non-redundant primary groups that are linked in degree n;
$L_n =$ the number of links per group; and
$g =$ number of consumers per group.

(*Clarification: We were speaking of a body of* N *consumers, arranged in a number of primary groups (that is, groups in which every member is in contact with every other), each group containing* g *members, linked in a network of intersecting contacts. A group may have an intersection with more than one other group;* n *signifies the number of elements (consumers) in one intersection;* L_n *the number of intersections (links) per primary group.*)

The above formula applies to a regular structure in which L_n and g are constant over all groups, and all intersections contain precisely n consumers; it may, however, be used as an approximation in irregular cases also. Evidently, the 'chainlike' arrangement of the linear suburb where L_n is 2 represents the minimum degree of compactness consistent with a chain of any length. Thus $L_n = 2$ also represents the minimum condition for a significant chain reaction; in fact, the very definition of a chain, of course, requires that each element is linked to at least two others.

It will also be seen that the number of consumers with whom each consumer is in contact is related to both g, the size of the primary groups, and to L_n, the number of links per group. The character of this relationship depends, however, on the pattern of the structure; all we can say is that contacts per capita must tend to vary directly with both g and L_n, an increase in either with the other held constant necessarily increasing the contacts, and vice versa.

SOCIAL BARRIERS AND SOCIAL BARS

So far we have been arguing as if patterns were not only regular but also unbroken. If a pattern permits a family to be in contact with their neighbours, then, we have assumed, every consumer is in neighbourly contact. Obviously this is unrealistic. If someone does not like a neighbour, or if they merely belong to different age groups, contact may be avoided; other friends may be found outside the prescribed pattern, or the person may simply have fewer than the specified number of contacts. More generally, if we redefine the concept of a pattern as a system of possible contacts, actual contacts will be fewer and quasi-randomly distributed among the possible. The 'missing' connections could be described as social bars. If social bars are present in significant numbers, actual primary groups will be irregularly shaped and variable in size, and the chains of linked groups extensively interrupted. Some of these interruptions will be of little economic importance, because, being relatively trivial, they will usually be consistent with the presence of other routes by which chain reactions starting from given sources can pass through the population. Others will be more significant. In a very crude example, a housing location might be bounded by congested highways which discourage the inhabitants from venturing further afield. This does not mean that they may not have numbers of contacts all over town whom they regularly visit by car, but it does mean that these 'out' contacts are less likely to represent elements of intersections of primary groups. In other words, even in a relatively homogeneous population it is extremely unlikely that the largest set of linked groups will contain a substantial proportion of a total market population, except in the case of products where the market population is small and in some appropriate sense highly localized. In consequence of both random and non-random interruptions in the chains of contacts, any given rationalized market population will be divided into a considerable number of distinct linked sets which we may conveniently describe as 'secondary' groups. More precisely, we call any unbroken chain of n-degree linked primary groups 'a secondary group of degree n', and we refer to the consumers contained in such a group as a 'secondary population'. And when a rationalized population has been arranged in the minimum number of secondary groups of degree n permitted by its structure, we shall say it has been 'stratified in degree n'.

Highways, random interruptions and other similar factors are, of course, far from being the only causes of stratification. In all but the most classless societies there will be important areas in social space where the bars are both non-random and dense. For while, as we have seen, for some products, cross-class contacts are possible, income and class barriers are inevitably powerful inhibitors.

'Barriers' operate on a different plane from the more trivial 'bars'. In new development areas barriers may be superimposed on, but consistent with, a basically geographical system, in the sense that in such areas most neighbourhoods are, for familiar reasons, rather homogeneous as to class. In old urban centres, on the other hand, large populations of different classes can live in close proximity without ever exchanging a word, let alone a contact. In effect, then, for a product of given type marketed at a given price, these broader social strata define the market populations: a manufacturer can, in theory, activate any homogeneous population, however much stratified, provided only that he can achieve a chain reaction in each of its secondary groups, but when he has exhausted these, he cannot necessarily repeat the process by moving in on another homogeneous population unless that population also has sufficient income to belong to the product's market population. For example, if he has saturated all the secondary groups of a primary population whose members have incomes greater than the minimum income required for positive consumption in the 'sheeplike' demand function, he can expand sales no further until either the income of the non-saturated groups rises, or he is able to lower his price. But notice that where a product is within the means of all but the poorest members of the population, so that the market population contains several socioeconomic strata, the presence of these less economically significant barriers to contact has no more significance than the interruptions that occur for other reasons already described within a homogeneous population. From the manufacturer's point of view, both phenomena present him with more-or-less the same problem: that he must get a chain reaction going on each side of the break if he is to achieve total saturation.

Clearly, the number of secondary groups into which a population is divided depends not only on the causal factors responsible for interruptions, but also on the specified degree of stratification, that is, on the value of n – the size of the specified intersections: obviously, a particular intersection is less likely to be missing if it is only required to contain one consumer, say, than if it is required to contain two. It is therefore convenient to represent the underlying stratification by means of some index simplifying the relationships between the various aspects of stratification: that is, in some index defined in such a way as to combine the effect of degree and of division into secondary groups. Since we should expect the n-sensitivity of the number of secondary groups to be considerable, we may reasonably write:

$$\lambda = \sqrt[n]{S_n} \quad = \text{index of stratification.} \tag{4.2}$$

Given this definition, we suppose that, other things being equal, the lower the index, the easier it is to saturate a given market population with a given new product.

CHAIN REACTIONS IN INTERMEDIATE PRODUCTS

So far, we have only considered final consumer goods, largely of the manufactured variety. A similar theory clearly applies to producers' goods also. If technology were fixed, in the sense that the economy was governed by a never-changing matrix of Leontief coefficients, changes in the demand for producers' goods would depend entirely on the effects of explosions occurring among consumers' goods. But technology is not fixed; new methods of production are invented, new intermediate products are substituted for old, new machinery is introduced. Inevitably there is inertia. The effect of inertia is greatest in the production of saturated products, where, since output is not expanding, new equipment need not so often be considered, and control is probably in the hands of the more routine-minded among the average firm's salariat. Planning the production and marketing of new products will usually be concentrated among the more enterprising members of the staff; they not only 'invent' the product but also, to some extent, the methods of production to go with it. Even here, however, there is room for conservatism. The methods employed to produce something that has never been made before inevitably borrow much from existing technology, and a firm contemplating the introduction of a specified new product will often be faced with a choice between several distinct manufacturing processes. If, for simplicity, we imagine the alternatives are only two: one in which the basic operation is done by the prevailing technique for operations of that type; and the other involving a new and as yet untried technique, then the cautious will adopt the one, the adventurous the other.

It is well known that the rate at which machinery is scrapped is very variable. If equipment is scrapped before it wears out or becomes uneconomic to repair, the reason must be a desire to substitute new machinery of an improved type. We may suppose that management requires stimulus to introduce new machinery, in the similar sense that the consumer requires stimulus to undertake new wants. What is the character of the stimulus here? Managers may be stimulated to innovate; in two ways: by personal contact with other managers who have already innovated, or by feeling the effects of others' innovations through competition in the product market. In the first case, each manager will have a limited number of contacts with managers in other firms specializing in the same field of technology, and the process of stimulation, activation and propagation is directly analogous to the process described among final consumers, the only major difference being, perhaps, that it has greater economic rationality. Social space becomes managerial social space; and the society of the lunch club replaces the society of the parlour. In the second case, in the characteristic 'competitive' situation, each firm faces a relatively small circle of close competitors and is largely insensitive to the actions of firms outside it. As among consumers, the circles are not exclusive; they form an interlocking network, interrupted by various kinds of barrier and bar, spreading through the whole of industry. The type of system we employed in the consumer example is, therefore, equally appropriate to describe this network of competition, or 'commercial space'. When, say, three out of a firm's close competitors have adopted an innovation, the quantitative effect on the firm's trade is likely to be such as to force it to follow suit. And once this firm has made the change, it may in turn contribute to creating a similar situation for a rival who is also a rival of some, but not all, of the original three innovators; so the chain reaction spreads. The starting point of the process, as with consumer goods, is the appearance of a sufficiently large number of pioneers (who innovate without the stimulus of managerial social contact or commercial competition) to create criticality; and the end comes when the innovation has spread through all firms for whom it is appropriate: that is, when the reaction is halted by an industrial barrier.

A MATHEMATICAL MODEL FOR THE CRITICAL RATIO

In the original book there now followed twenty-five pages which presented a mathematical model designed to support an analysis of the process of profitable growth supported by a strategy of successive launches of new products. This is presented below, very heavily shortened, with new equation numbering.

The strategy was based on obtaining a critical number of pioneers for each product sufficient to create a chain reaction (that is, explosion) in demand. There is thus a 'critical ratio' of pioneers to the total market population of potential ultimate consumers. If we can calculate this ratio for a typical secondary group, it will be approximately the same as the average ratio for the whole market population. Therefore, we defined:

p = *the proportion of pioneers in a secondary population; and*
$\hat{p}$ = *'critical ratio'* = *value of* p, *which, if achieved, will cause explosive growth in demand for a new product.*

Relying on the assumption that $\hat{p}$ *will generally be small – that is, number of the order of less 5 per cent, we were able to derive the following expression for the probability of explosion, for any given value of* p, *for a particular product:*

$$P(p) \cong \binom{g}{m}(p)^m G_m, \tag{4.3}$$

where

P(p) = *the probability of explosion conditional on obtaining* p;

m = *threshold for the product; that is, the number of other consumers with whom a latent consumer must be in contact in order to become active;*

$\begin{pmatrix} g \\ m \end{pmatrix}$ = *the binomial coefficient for* m *successes in* g *trials; and*

G_m = *the number of primary groups in the secondary population when the latter is defined in degree m.*

That equation was then solved for the case of P(p) = *1, arriving at the following result:*

$$\hat{p} \cong \sqrt[m]{2S_m (g-m)/N \begin{pmatrix} g \\ m \end{pmatrix} L_m} \qquad (4.4)$$

where, in addition to the symbols already defined:

L_m = *the number of links (m-unit intersections) per group.*

It was then found that if the ratio of g *to* m *lay in the range from 2 to 4 the expression* $2(g-m)/\begin{pmatrix} g \\ m \end{pmatrix}$ *can, with an error of no more than 10 per cent, be approximated by the number 3. Bearing in mind the definition we gave of the index of stratification in Equation (4.2), namely* $\lambda = \sqrt[n]{S_n}$. *This could also be substituted into the formula, finally giving us:*

$$\hat{p} = \frac{1}{\sqrt[m]{(N \cdot L_m)} \cdot \sqrt[3]{g/m}} \qquad (4.5)$$

The interpretation is as follows:

(i) *The greater the stratification (λ), the higher the critical ratio and the less easy it is to 'explode' a market of given size;*

(ii) *Similarly, the higher the threshold (m);*

(iii) *Given these factors, criticality is easier if the size of primary groups (g) is larger; and (iv)* There are economies of scale. The absolute number of pioneers required for criticality increases less than in proportion to market size; (d *log* p̂N/d *log* N = $1- \frac{1}{m}$).

Examples are as follows:

(i) If g were 4, L_m, 4, m, 2, N *(the 'market population, that is, total number of potential consumers) a million, and* λ, *10 (implying 400 secondary groups of 2500 members each) the critical ratio* (p̂) *would work out at 0.0008, just under 1 per cent. Ten thousand pioneers would be required for criticality.*

(ii) If λ *and* m *were 1 and* g *was 2, representing the smallest meaningful values of each, the absolute number of pioneers required for criticality* (p̂N) *would be 1. There is a perfect unbroken chain of linked primary groups running through the market population. If one goes, they all go.*

(iii) If m *were zero, the critical ratio* (p̂) *would also be zero. The product is one for which consumers are obtained without any stimulation from other consumers, that is, a product lying outside this theory.*

Given the critical ratio, it was possible for the firm to calculate the cost of marketing a new product with a high expectation of take-off and eventual saturation. After saturation, the firm has a partial monopoly of the product and may look forward to long-term net profits, which represent an absolute addition to the organization's permanent profit-earning capacity. The cost of obtaining criticality is a cost of growth. By incurring these costs, long-term, sustainable and profitable growth may be maintained.

In reality, of course, despite Equation (4.5), it is impossible for a firm to undertake actions that will create absolute certainty of criticality for any given new project. Even if the equation were fully understood, the various factors appearing on the right-hand side could only be perceived uncertainly. Consequently, in reality, the diversifying growth strategy in fact consists of marketing successive new products with a given probability of success. Some will fail. The cost of failures are also part of the costs of growth.

The original text then continued as follows.

GROWTH BY IMITATION

We have now completed our account of the demand-growth process for a
firm expanding by means of differentiated strategy. The reader will recognize that the analysis has involved a considerable excursion to the frontiers
of economic theory, most previous writers having, for good reason,
regarded the area as one where angels should fear to tread. Imitative activity, on the other hand, looks much more like familiar stuff. An imitative
product is a 'competitive' product, whose vendors perforce must play
games that have been the subject of economic study for more than a
century past. Admittedly, except on the implausible and often inconsistent
assumptions of 'perfect' competition, the results have to date been somewhat inconclusive, but this has been caused mainly by the dffficulty of the
problem rather than faults in the investigators; it may well be the case that
the reason why the earliest discoveries in the field (such as those of
August Cournot) have held their positions for so long is that there are few
others to be made. However, it is now clear that the approach by way of
game theory, or at least by the kinds of argument which – if not strictly
game-theoretic according to an acceptable mathematical definition, nevertheless owe much to this source – is at last beginning to bear fruit.
'Competition', variously defined, is now widely recognized as a special
case of oligopoly, and oligopoly is clearly a game of conflict; the only
problem is to find useful and solvable formulations.

There is one case, however, of considerable importance (to us, at least),
which has received almost no analytical attention whatever: the case of
oligopolistic entry into a market that is in the process of exploding. The
advantages are virtually self-evident: the job of starting the chain reaction
is already done; much of the uncertainty of the outcome is removed; and
no act of innovation is required. As compared with the situation in a static
market, the tension between competitors is likely to be less severe, and co-
operative – but not necessarily collusive – solutions are therefore especially plausible. Consequently, it is not surprising that the tactic appears
empirically to be one of the most popular methods of growth. We shall
call it 'bandwagoning'.

Bandwagoning is particularly appropriate for a loose, game-descriptive,
but not strictly game-theoretic type of analysis. The other types of imitative
growth are not. In static markets the conflict situation is necessarily intense,
and the whole gamut of oligopoly theory (and, for that matter, of competition theory) may well have to be run in dealing with them. The most suggestive contribution, at least since the appearance of The *Theory of Games and
Economic Behaviour*,[11] comes from Martin Shubik, whose book *Strategy*

and Market Structure,[12] first published in 1960, gradually but surely began to make itself felt. Below, after dealing with bandwagoning, we do little more than attempt to derive from Shubik's work a few generalizations appropriate for consideration of restraints and constraints on policies involving successive entry into static markets, or in deliberate, discontinuous increases in shares held in static markets already previously entered.

THE BANDWAGON STRATEGY

If there were no such thing as commercial retaliation, dynamic, fully imitative strategies would correspond to static perfect competition: if the price of any of the imitations were set slightly below that of the corresponding rival, sales would grow rapidly until the rival had been driven out altogether; after that, if the market were still exploding, sales would grow at the market explosion rate, or, if the market were saturated, they would stagnate. The larger the proportion of successful unsaturated imitations in a firm's catalogue, the faster would be the rate of growth in terms of capacity required. But the larger this proportion, the lower, on average, would have to be its prices, and so also, of course, the rate of return.

In reality, if one firm grows noticeably at the expense of another, the second is likely to retaliate. Retaliation may consist in either price reduction or intensified selling effort; in what follows, for simplicity, we assume that the former method predominates. An imitator must therefore assume that he will meet retaliatory price reduction, and should take account of this in his calculations; in such a set-up, the effective sensitivity of growth rate with respect to rate of return must usually be smaller than might at first appear.

A firm contemplating an imitative attack on a particular existing product must attempt to assess the lowest possible level to which its opponents could, in the process of retaliation and counter-retaliation, reduce their prices. It may treat this estimated enemy's 'sticking price' as a datum. Presumably it will declare war only if it can see its way to cutting its own price at least to that level. If it believes it can undercut the enemy sticking price, it can start a war to the death, and an overall strategy for a number of products could, in principle, be constructed of a series of such wars. But, in practice, total war is not common. Rivals' sticking prices are uncertain; the strategy is risky, unpopular and psychologically unrewarding. Business communities, like many animal societies, develop many ethical restraints against fighting to the death, transgression of which may invite the costs of commercial ostracism.

In an exploding market, however, close imitation is not synonymous with war to the death. Suppose i imitates the exploding product of j, charging a price noticeably lower than j's, then i's share of the market will begin to rise, and j's to fall. But in contrast to the assumptions of competitive statics, we do not assume that adjustment occurs instantaneously. We assume that it takes time; more precisely, we assume that the greater the difference in the prices charged by the two firms, the faster the rate of change of their respective shares in total sales. With a given price differential, therefore, so long as the market is exploding, j's sales are subject to opposing tendencies: they represent a falling proportion of a rising total. In the early stages, when i's sales (representing a rising proportion of the rising total) are still of little weight, the unfavourable tendency for j will be more than offset by the favourable. Later, the position will be reversed. From the moment of i's entry, therefore, j's sales curve will flatten – that is, continue to rise but at a diminishing rate. Eventually, if the price differential continues, the curve will reach a peak and go into decline.

For example, suppose that, as a result of a price differential, i in each period gains x per cent of the total customers of j in the previous period. In addition, i's entry into the market means that an increasing proportion of the new consumers of the product recruited in any period will have been stimulated by existing customers of i, rather than of j, and hence will themselves be likely to buy from i. Even in the absence of customers who shift from j to i, therefore, i's sales are likely to grow at least at the same rate as the explosion rate of the market as a whole: i experiences a 'normal' chain reaction of growth, whose speed is determined by the same factors as those governing the explosion rate for the whole market; but i obtains his 'pioneer' customers by piracy from j rather than by the normal method. The growth of demand experienced by i, therefore, for any given price differential over any given short time period, will consist of the sum of direct gains from j, plus the effect of i's share in the explosion. Thus, let j start with 100 customers, exploding at 10 per cent per period, and let i enter when j has reached 110, and then make direct gains of 5 per cent of j's existing customers per period; this, plus the fact that i must be assumed to acquire customers who are new to the product altogether, at the rate of 10 per cent of his own existing customers in each period, will create conditions in which j's rate of growth will be reduced to zero in ten periods from the starting point. At that point, i will have 40 per cent of the total number of customers.

During the early phases of the process j will not be strongly stimulated to retaliate; he may well be uncertain as to how fast the total market is expanding, and his own sales charts will not tell him how his *proportion-*

ate share is behaving. But he knows for certain that his absolute sales are still expanding, and at a price he finds profitable. He may be concerned about the competitive activities of *i*, but before reaching for his gun he has to consider the possibility that *i*'s price policy may soon get *i* into financial difficulties, difficulties that he, *j*, would also meet if he copied the policy. In other words, the problem of competition from *i* may solve itself, either by *i*'s raising his price or by retiring altogether; *j* is therefore very likely to pursue a policy of wait and see. Only if *i* maintains his position and *j*'s sales curve begins to look seriously unhealthy is *j* forced to take action. If he retaliates with a price cut, open war breaks out, and retaliation will be followed by counter-retaliation; *i* is now established in the market and *j*'s most likely, if limited, objective will be to prevent any further change in their relative shares. Depending on how aggressive *i* still feels (which, in turn, will depend on the volume of sales he has already achieved), the war may be long and severe, or short and mild. It will normally end in the establishment of a 'peace' in which the proportionate shares are stabilized. For convenience we shall define the whole period from the entry of the imitator to the establishment of peace as a period of 'war', and divide the latter into two subsidiary periods – the period of incipient war, when retaliation is not occurring, and the period of open war, when it is. Peace requires peaceful prices, or, for short, 'peace prices'. These may or may not be collusively arrived at in the sense of resulting from direct parleys, and they need not be the same for each firm. Each firm's peace price is the price which, taken in relation to the price charged by the other, will keep market shares constant; when both are charging peace prices, the proportionate rate of growth of each firm's sales is identical with that of the market as a whole. Evidently, in the case of close imitations, the two peace prices are unlikely to differ more than slightly, because of the high cross-elasticities. Thus a peace price for a single product contains two elements – a differential against the price charged by the rival, and an absolute level. The differential depends on the character and closeness of the imitation, and is therefore 'given' in this context. The absolute level depends on the absolute level of the price being charged by the rival. Hence, although the required differential can be defined independently, the absolute level cannot. The absolute levels of peace prices can only be determined in conjunction with one another; they can only be defined in pairs, and established jointly. A single firm's peace price is thus an aspect of a pair.

Before the peace is established, the precise moment at which retaliation occurs will depend on the character of, and the information available to, the defenders. In some cases, retaliation may never be necessary. The imitator, once he has established a reasonable share in the market, may anticipate retaliation and raise his price before it happens: peace breaks out before incipient war becomes open. Before saturation is reached, therefore, any highly imitative product has a determinate prospect of growth at virtually one price – the ultimate peace price for that product. At a significantly higher price, the probable growth of demand is very small, if not zero, but, because of retaliation, a lower price makes little difference. A more accurate way of describing the position is to say that there is a determinate path of growth for the product, together with an associated path of prices. The paths contain two phases; in the first, price is any price markedly below the enemy price and sales are growing very rapidly; in the second phase, price is the peace price and sales grow at the explosion rate of the market as a whole; eventually, they saturate when the market saturates. In circumstances where the first phase is short relative to the second, the rate of growth in the second (that is, the market explosion rate) can be regarded as characteristic of bandwaggon growth; otherwise, it is necessary to consider some average of the rates experienced in the two phases together. *En-tous-cas*, a strategy relating to a group of successive imitations of exploding products offers a firm a determinate prospect of average overall growth (of demand) at a specifiable constellation of prices. Given the strategy, there is at any moment a narrowly-limited range of 'right' prices for each of the close imitations it comprises; in this sense, the firm does not have much freedom of action in respect to prices. But, of course, it can vary average profitability by varying the strategy, since profitability will depend, *inter alia*, on the proportion of very imitative products in the catalogue as a whole, because with less imitative products the prices consistent with growth are evidently less circumscribed.

STATIC MARKETS

Any firm attempting to enter a static market already dominated by a relatively small number of established producers faces considerable problems. If the product-type is one that is inherently 'differentiable' (in the subjective consumer sense), there may in principle be room for a new partial imitation, but, as Joe Bain has shown in his classic study,[13] the very same conditions are likely to present particularly high barriers to entry because of consumer loyalty to established brands: the greater the extent to which consumers can be persuaded to see differences in brands, the greater the tendency to brand loyalty. The reason for this phenomenon, familiar to 'hidden persuaders', is that the greater the consumer's uncertainty and misinformation about a product, the more likely he or she is to hold desperately to brands known to perform reasonably satisfactorily. Thus the housewife, unable to conduct controlled experiments, has not the faintest idea whether one brand of washing powder is better than another, and so this particular market is notoriously susceptible to the blandishments of advertisements or the opinion leaders of the Katz-and-Lazarsfeld type (that is, of people whose opinions are followed less because of their rationality than of some quality in the holder).[14] At the other extreme, among producers' goods, not only is non-informative advertising less effective, but (irrational) brand loyalty is also less prevalent. Where brand loyalty prevails, the potential entrant must face the prospect of having to accept for a substantial period a significantly lower rate of return than that enjoyed by incumbents, even though his product is, by any objective test, quite as good as theirs. The resulting loss of profit would be analogous to the marketing expenses in non-imitative diversification. Alternatively, if the product-type is one that is easy to imitate, in the sense that brand loyalty is weak, the potential entrant faces all the problems of retaliation, for the more easily he is able to damage incumbents by conventional methods, the greater their incentive to fight him off. In other words, the better his chances of success with the customers, the greater the likelihood of 'trouble' from the producers. In fact, since the potentialities of retaliation are also closely related to concentration, easy prospects from this strategy are likely to be generally confined to areas where, for some reason, concentration is still relatively moderate.

The problem may be characterized by an actual or potential game of 'economic survival'.[15] In this type of game the players make a series of moves, representing combinations of product quality, price and advertising policies set and adhered to for short tactical planning periods, the outcomes of which are uncertain. That is to say, at the beginning of each period, all players decide their tactics for the period according to hunches as to how both consumers and the opponents are likely to act, and at the end of the period each experiences various outcomes in terms of profits, volume and so on. Some find they have gained in one or both dimensions, others have lost, and the objective observer can do no more than specify the probabilities of any particular result. If an individual player finds he has not done well, he may decide to try again, hoping next time to do better. If he succeeds, all well and good; if he fails, he may try yet again. The process continues until either he, or one or all of his opponents, have experienced such losses that they are forced, or prefer, to retire, leaving the victor(s) in sole possession of the market. In other words, if a potential entrant desires to establish a reasonable share of a static market, he may be compelled to fight a war in which one (or more) producer(s) is/are driven out to make room for him, and this means entering a game of chance which may result not only in failure to achieve the objective, but also to substantial financial losses through wasted investment in specific equipment and non-recoverable development expenditure. To lose such a game is equivalent to a failure to explode in differentiated diversification.

The most conveniently analyzed models of games of economic survival are two-person, zero-sum gambling games, such as 'gambler's ruin'. The results can then be shown to depend intimately not only on the chances-in-play (the probability of either player winning at each round), which may be thought of as analogous to relative commercial advantage, but also on the maximum amounts each player is able, or prepared, to lose before retiring; the latter, called 'initial resources', may be considered as analogous to financial strength. Thus in 'gambler's ruin' the players successively match pennies, the loser at each round paying the winner one unit. The chances-in-play, with unbiased pennies, are 0.5. Each player starts with a limited stock of pennies, and the game ends with an ultimate win for one when the coffers of the other are exhausted. If the initial resources are equal, the chances of ultimate victory are, of course, also equal – that is, 0.5. But if the initial resources are unequal, the chance of ultimate win for a given player is $1/(1 + r)$, where r is the ratio of opponent's initial resources to his own. When the game is played against a casino, r is very high, and the probability of breaking the bank is very low. Shubik has shown how this type of game may well be adapted to correspond to the characteristic conditions of economic conflict, including those of entry.

We should add that, in economic applications, initial resources are appropriately defined as the total resources available to the firm – for example, the total amount it is prepared to lose on all projects, and this need not be confined to sums supposedly earmarked to support particular attacks. If a policy of earmarking is adopted (as is evidently the case in some real-life firms), significant advantages are thrown away. Imagine a gambler entering a casino where, in contrast to the usual situation, he is faced with a number of tables, each of which has a bank equal to his own resources, but none being allowed to borrow or lend funds to others. Suppose he is then permitted to play gambler's ruin against each table simultaneously, transferring resources at will: in effect, the usual roles of casino and gambler are reversed. He plays until either his own funds or those of all his opponents are exhausted; if one opponent is defeated in the course of play, he continues to the death against the survivors. It can then be shown that his monopoly of the power to switch resources from tables where he is doing well to tables where he is doing badly gives him considerable actuarial advantages. For example, if he plays two opponents in a game in which chances-in-play are even, the probability of ultimate victory is precisely the same (that is, 0.5) as if he had played one table only. But since in playing two opponents the value of an ultimate win is doubled (because he then takes the total resources of two players), while the cost of losing is the same, the mathematical expectation of profit or 'value of the game' is doubled. The author once heard the owner of a famous Las Vegas establishment tell a television interviewer that, rather than biased chances-in-play, this phenomenon (in reverse, of course) was the source of the greater part of a typical casino's profits.

We could suggest, as a loose economic generalization, that a firm prepared to diversify by taking on a number of games of economic survival simultaneously will be in a stronger position than its opponents, even if their average resources are equal to its own, provided, of course, that they themselves are wedded to single-product strategies. If its typical opponents are similar to itself, however, the presumption vanishes. We may therefore suppose that at any moment of time a firm under analysis will perhaps be presented with a *limited* number of opportunities where, even though its commercial strength does not greatly exceed that of incumbents (that is, chances-in-play may be even), its initial-resource position is such that, if it attacks all simultaneously, it may expect a reasonable proportion of successes associated with a reasonable level of financial return. That is to say, if it plays a limited number of survival games simultaneously, it may expect to drive out opponents and achieve a good market share in a sufficient proportion of cases, so that the losses suffered on the failures do not depress average profitability by more than is tolerable. Its 'marketing expenses' are the failures' losses, and its gains are the increases in volume and relatively assured future profit streams resulting from successes. Then, because the opportunities are limited in time, the usual dynamic restraints must come into operation, and we can assume that if it attempts to accelerate growth further by this means, at least beyond a certain point, despite the advantages of resource switching, it will increasingly encounter cases where the initial-resource position is less favourable, and the failure rate will rise correspondingly. The rate of return will decline, and the rate of growth fail to increase in proportion to the rate of diversification.

Another type of market suitable for attack by warlike methods is that in which, although the initial-resource position is more or less the same as the opponent's, the chances-in-play are not. Obviously, if gambler's ruin is played with loaded dice, the players' chances of ultimate victory are affected irrespective of resource position. The inventive resources of the attacking firm have been deployed successfully in the development of a product that is *likely*, but not certain, to prove more attractive to consumers than the existing variants, so that at each round of play, however skilfully the defender chooses his strategies, he has less than a 50 per cent chance of winning (unless, of course, he can in turn imitate the new variant, which is what, in fact, he usually does try to do). Even when the chances-in-play are only equal, a firm may be prepared to attempt a set of attacks simultaneously, hoping that the losses on the failures will be worth the gains in both volume and profit on the successes. More precisely, maximum sustainable growth might be obtained with a policy of moderately rapid diversification into market situations with only even chances of success, because the net overall profits at each round would still, on average, be sufficient to support the capital expansion required for the next round. Again, of course, the policy is restricted by the dynamic limits on the number of cases with at least reasonable odds discoverable at any one time.

However, it is of course by no means certain that the game of survival will in fact have to be played. An alternative approach to the problem of entry is by way of the concept of 'threat'. 'Threat', in game theory, is the capacity to inflict damage on one's opponent even at the cost of damaging oneself (nuclear deterrents being a case in point). For example, a defender may have to incur considerable losses in warding off an attack, even when he is ultimately successful. And inasmuch as he has also to face the possibility that in the event the effort will prove to have been of no avail, the mere advent of an attack implies for the defender the certainty of definite loss (in the sense that profits will be less than would otherwise have been the case). Rather than face this, he may prefer to seek a co-operative solution: that is, in the manner of the bandwaggon case, seek a 'peace' in which the interloper is conceded a definite, but limited, market. The defender then takes a certainty of some loss of volume (and probably of profits as well), instead of an uncertainty of more serious penalties. He may well in fact adopt this course even in cases where successful defence would be costless, because his Neumann–Morgenstern utility of a certainty of keeping a reduced share may exceed that of a risk of losing all.

Various methods of reaching co-operative solutions have been studied in the literature, and most are analogous to the gestures exchanged by animals preparing to fight over territory: each participant is trying to tell the other how vicious he is able and willing to be, and thus build up the mutual information necessary for both sides to realize that a co-operative solution along given lines will maximize utility for each. In situations of this type, the equilibrium division of spoils will probably be related to relative strengths of threats,[16] with these, strictly defined, being measured by the relationship between the utility losses likely to be suffered by each side if one threat is enforced. With some temerity, we may stretch the concept by suggesting that the threat in many cases is, in fact, the threat of playing a sub-game of survival. Because it is in the essence of that game that provided resources on both sides are limited, and any one player can always force the opponent to participate. If a player persistently enforces his most vicious strategy, and ignores all co-operative gestures, the opponent is willy-nilly involved in a game of survival whether he likes it or not. That is to say, co-operative solutions require co-operation. Then we may suggest that the likelihood of a prospective entrant being co-operatively permitted to absorb a given market share after appropriate signalling depends on the probability of his winning, in the event that he had enforced war to the death. Thus the general conditions governing growth through actual games of survival also govern the cases where the eventual outcome is more peaceful, and the features of the potential game of survival have similar policy implications to those of actual games of survival. Growth by successive efforts intended to end in co-operative outcomes is therefore restricted as to pace for almost precisely the same reasons: the number of cases where the potential threat position is adequately powerful will be limited in time, and excessive acceleration of a diversification programme designed on these lines will therefore encounter the usual penalties. In particular, as acceleration involves declining average threat-strength, the average size of market share obtained in actual solutions will also be declining, so that attempted and actual growth will separate in a manner similar to that obtaining from a rising failure rate in differentiated diversification. The only way growth by threat of war would appear to differ significantly from growth by actual war is that, in the former, the costs of battle are avoided and the main analytical effect is felt in a declining success rate (as diversification rate increases) for given average profitability. But this is not a very realistic qualification. As already mentioned, in order to make a threat appear convincing it is almost always necessary to offer at least some hostile gestures (for example, at least get a product variant into production); only rarely will defenders concede a reasonable share merely on receiving a threatening letter. These gestures evidently cost money and the outcomes remain uncertain. It is always possible that, as a result of the information exchanged during the display period, the defenders will decide to play for survival, and the entrant will eventually lose.

Hence the cases of growth by actual war and growth by threat of war are not really distinct, and a characteristic programme will contain an uncertain mixture of both results. Therefore, as in the case of differentiated growth, we may set up two alternative models – one in which it is assumed that the firm always expends sufficient resources on research and development, and that in the cases where imitative entry is in fact attempted, a reasonably successful outcome (either warlike or co-operative) is virtually certain; and the other in which it is accepted that it might be a better policy to admit a certain proportion of failures.

GENERAL IMPLICATIONS OF IMITATIVE STRATEGY

It should now be apparent that, taking the whole range of imitative strategies, including bandwaggoning, the implications for the costs of growth are similar to those of differentiated strategies. It follows that the firm is faced not only with policy decisions within the types of two strategies, but also with a decision as to how much emphasis to place on each. For example, a firm which for historical reasons is relatively weak in imagination, but clever in production, would find comparative advantage (in terms of sustainable growth) by emphasizing imitation, and vice versa. Except where otherwise stated, we shall henceforth assume that firms under analysis always attempt to make this decision in such a way that the growth rate experienced is maximized for all given rates of return, and rates of return maximized for all given growth rates.

NON-DIVERSIFYING GROWTH

In Chapter 3[17] we suggested that the ultimate limiting example of 'imitative' growth was represented in the case where the firm achieved a discontinuous increase in its share of a market for a product it was already producing. Such developments evidently could not generate sustainable growth unless repeated successively over a number of such markets. Now, in the light of the more recent discussion, we can describe the process better. The share held of an existing market will depend, we have seen, on the various elements, such as threat strength, which characterize the particular game-situation in question. If one of these elements is quantitatively changed, the quantitative characteristics of the 'peaceful' solution are likely to change also. For example, an increase in relative threat strength may lead, after a short outbreak of demonstrative hostilities, to a permanent revision of market shares in favour of the gainer. If, therefore, a firm can successively improve its threat-competitive position in market after existing market, it can achieve by this means a form of continuous growth.

Such improvements must require definite innovation. Costs of production may be reduced, or consumer appeal increased, in such a way that, whether prices are in fact reduced or not, competitors realise that the chances of this firm winning a war of survival are increased and/or its probable relative losses in total attrition reduced. But the capacity for making innovations of this kind is evidently limited in much the same way as the capacity to differentiate or imitate. Hence the whole process is subject to precisely analogous dynamic restraints, and requires no special analysis. We assume that, in optimizing the balance between imitation and differentiation, the firm also makes optimal decisions in relation to the balance between this limiting case of imitation and the more general case. (Empirically, the limiting case is obviously quite important.)

EMPIRICAL SUPPORT

To a considerable extent the whole of the foregoing 'theory of demand' may be regarded as an explanation of a body of facts that have been known for some time: we know that new products follow growth-curves; and we know that oligopolistic imitation accompanied by price-stability is a general phenomenon. The reader will also remember that I have supported my arguments with references to a considerable body of existing material relating to the way price and diversification decisions are taken within firms.[18] Articles in business periodicals generally lend support to the view that our concepts and assumptions are well represented in the language of the business world; indeed, I would claim that the theory presented above is better-related to the relevant problems of real concern to businessmen in this area than any predecessor.

5 Managerial Theories of the Firm

In the original book, Chapter 5 was called 'Supply', Chapter 6, 'Complete Micro Models', and Chapter 7, 'Behaviour and Evidence'. The first two of these, taken together, closed the model based on the general assumptions described in the preceding chapters. The third was concerned with empirical testing and also with the question of maximizing versus satisficing behaviour, or what would now be called the debate over bounded rationality.

It is now easy to see that the theoretical model was unnecessarily complicated, if not obscure. In addition, the empirical discussion has been overtaken by subsequent research. The discussion of satisficing and bounded rationality, however, deserves reproduction. Although a very large literature and a richly deserved Nobel Prize for Herbert Simon have occurred since, it is my subjective opinion that my original discussion of this topic in the explicit context of the theory of the growth of the firm still stands up.

I have therefore replaced the three original chapters with three new ones consisting of, first, a reprinting of my contribution on 'managerial' theories of the firm to the recently published International Encyclopedia of Business and Management;[1] *second, a new simplified account of the original theoretical model; and third, a lightly edited version of the old section (from the old Chapter 7) on satisficing.*

The reasons for using the encyclopedia article are that it gave a convenient verbal summary of the theoretical model, preceded by a general account of various theories (of which mine was only one) that emerged from 1960 onwards, based on the fact of the existence of managerial 'discretion' (a term first used by Oliver Williamson, whose very important book, The Economics of Discretionary Behaviour *was first published in the same year (1964) as* Managerial Capitalism*), and followed by a survey of the empirical testing that has been done during the ensuing years on all the theories.*

Subject only to the deletion of the first paragraph, here follows[2] the full text of the encyclopedia article including the Further Reading list given at the end.

BACKGROUND

The twentieth century saw the emergence of business organizations – in the form of quoted public companies – that were on the one hand very large and on the other marked by a considerable degree of separation of ownership from management. Shareholdings were often widely dispersed, reducing the potency of voting rights in most circumstances other than those of a take-over bid. Boards of directors came to be dominantly composed of full-time senior executives who nominated new members and initiated decisions concerning high management appointments and remuneration. High management effectively became responsible not only for operating the organization but also for strategic decisions concerning investment, finance, internal growth and diversification, profit retention and acquisitions. Business corporations displayed a capacity for persistent, if irregular, long-term growth in size and, in consequence, in a typical advanced industrialized country, the share of the largest 100 corporations in total industrial value-added, which was less than 10 per cent in 1900, will, by the year 2000, range from 30 per cent to 50 per cent. The value added by the largest US corporations exceeded the gross national product (GNP) of some small countries. These concentrating phenomena are not inconsistent with coexistence of the 'other half' of the modern economy, where traditional capitalist modes (markets containing large numbers of small, owner-managed businesses) effectively persist. In addition, towards the end of the twentieth century, technological developments, such as personal computers, which increased the comparative efficiency of small administrative units, and new institutional developments, such as corporate divestitures and management buy-outs, may be reducing or reversing the previous concentrating tendencies.

The 'powers' of the managerial 'new class' are, of course, by no means unconstrained. On the one hand, they are constrained by the stock market through the threat of 'involuntary' (meaning undesired by management, and not shareholders) take-over, and by the debt market through threat of capital starvation; and on the other, they are constrained by the ever-present force of competition in product markets. The world of 'managerial' capitalism is a jungle of competition among giants where no laws prevent the invasion of one giant's territory by another. The problem for the science of economics was and is that this twentieth-century industrial system, whatever its advantages and disadvantages to society, is extremely different from the model of the competitive economy that is not only universal in elementary economics text books but also underlies the prevalent research paradigm. In that paradigm, product markets are assumed to be supplied by large numbers of small, single-product, owner-managed, price-taking firms with limited capacities for growth.

THE THEORIES

Economists began to respond to the problem in the mid-1950s, with first results being published in the following decade (strictly, from 1958 to 1972). The responses can be placed in three groups which may be called, respectively, *Discretionary*, *Growth-orientated* and *Bureaucratic* theories. The original authors in the Discretionary group were William Baumol and Oliver Williamson (Baumol, 1959; Williamson, 1964, 1970); in the Growth-orientated group, Edith Penrose, Robin Marris and Dennis Mueller (Penrose, 1958; Marris, 1964; Mueller, 1969 and 1972); and, finally, in the Bureaucratic group, Joseph Monsen and Anthony Downs (Monsen and Downs, 1965). Taken together, the three groups have provoked a literature that is fifty to a hundred times larger than the Further Reading listed below. A bibliography can be found in Marris and Mueller (1980).

THE DISCRETIONARY THEORIES

These theories are based on the model of a firm with given assets, a given high management and a given external market environment that is, in economists' language, monopolistic, oligopolistic or imperfectly competitive. The management does not have a significant stake in the ownership, and is also free of both operational and strategic supervision by owners. There exist well-defined demand curves for the firm's products. They can be shifted by means of marketing expenditure, which may be internally financed and organized, externally contracted, or both. Internally-organized marketing expenditure is broadly defined to include any activity that might be considered to improve sales at a given price, including such activities as expanding the number of managerial subordinates with general functions. Simplifying somewhat, management is effectively responsible for three decisions: namely, price, marketing expenditure, and their own remuneration. The question is, on what basis will these decisions be taken?

A convenient way to consider the answer is to combine marketing and management remuneration into a portmanteau item called 'expense'; then assume that, as expense, thus defined, is increased, sales, at given prices, also increase, but with diminishing effect. Define current profit as gross sales revenue, less expense and less all other current operating costs. The decision problem then resolves into choice of only two variables: price and expense level.

The problem is assumed to have a traditional maximum-profit solution. The Discretionary theory assumes that the owners have neither sufficient power nor knowledge to impose on management the profit-maximizing policy; they do, however, have power in crisis, more specifically if reported profits become low. Managers know this, and base their decisions, whatever they may be, on a minimum reported-profit constraint. (The level of this constraint is exogenous to the model, flowing from the general financial environment; consequently, it appears that the Discretionary models effectively relate to individual firms of this type operating in a sea of traditional firms. In an environment where the dominant type of firm was the discretionary type, it is not clear where the minimum level of profit would come from.)

Managers are endowed with an objective function that differs, in the direction of their own interests, from the profit-maximizing objective function. In William Baumol's version (Baumol, 1959) subject to the constraint, the objective is gross sales value. One may envisage a graph with sales on the horizontal axis and profits on the vertical: profits are plotted against sales. Starting from the origin, as sales expand, so do profits, but at a diminishing rate, so that in due course the profit–sales curve reaches a maximum and declines. The maximum indicates the profit-maximizing level of sales; the contrasting 'managerial' solution is found by drawing a horizontal line at the level of the minimum-profit constraint and finding the intersection with the expense–profit curve. Provided minimum profit is below maximum profit, the solution must involve 'excessive' sales relative to the profit-maximizing optimum. If, for some exogenous reason, the minimum profit level is increased (so the horizontal line shifts upwards) the intersection moves to the left and the managerially optimal level of sales is reduced.

The excess of maximum profit level over minimum profit level is a quantitative measure of managerial discretion. The greater it is, the greater the predicted managerially-selected sales level. When managerial discretion is zero (minimum profit equals maximum), managers must, according to prediction, choose the sales level that is optimal for owners.

In the Oliver Williamson version (Williamson 1964), managers' motives and satisfactions were directly derived from expense as such. As well as managers' own emoluments, expense also contained benefits to high managers in hierarchical organizations from increasing the number of their own subordinates as well as their perquisites of office. Thus managers displayed 'expense-preference'. (Williamson, in fact, kept emoluments and expense separate; their combination in this exposition is for simplification.) The resulting model is at heart similar to, but more complex than, the Baumol model. At heart there is a similar diagram, but the horizontal axis now represents expense, with a result profits–expense curve yielding similar predictions.

Willliamson, however, brilliantly applied the analysis to the problem of testing the model. A typical commercial crisis for an individual firm would be represented in a sharp fall in demand, resulting, in effect, in a vertical decline in the profits–expense curve. It is possible to show that the predicted response involves a disproportionate reduction of expense as compared to other operating outlays. By careful case studies Williamson was able to confirm that firms in crisis did just this. By contrast, the profit-maximizing model tends to predict that, in crisis, expense will be reduced more or less proportionately with other outlays. Consequently, the case studies confirmed the actual existence and practice of managerial expense-preference in the real-life economy.

In important later work, which led in turn to his subsequent work in so-called transactions-cost economics Williamson (1970) argued that expense preference was particularly likely in 'U-form' firms organized in functional divisions. The divisional outputs not being commensurable, the comparative performance of division chiefs could not easily be evaluated, making them prone to empire building. In the mid-twentieth century, however, the U-form was being replaced by the 'M-form', where divisions were product-orientated, making for easier evaluation and freeing the head office for strategic functions. The M-form is more 'efficient' than the U-form because the latter, in propagating expense in excess of the profit-maximizing level, inflates the cost to owners of producing a given output. (Because marketing expenditure affects consumer tastes, and because expense-preference affects corporate employment and payroll, the total effect on society is less clear. Intuitively, it seems likely that 'excess' resources absorbed by expense preference would be better employed elsewhere, but no proof of this proposition has been published.)

THE GROWTH-ORIENTATED THEORIES

The Growth-orientated theories formally start from the same point as the Discretionary theories – that management has power over a distinct objective function – but differ in being more complex, dynamic rather than static, and more grandiose. By the last adjective is meant that the Growth-orientated theorists (especially Marris and Mueller) see their model as being pervasive among mature large corporations, setting the norms for high management behaviour in respect of internal growth, acquisition and own remuneration decisions among the general population of such corporations. Marris, indeed, first described the resulting economic system as one of 'Managerial Capitalism' (Marris, 1964), a term that was subsequently adopted by other writers. The Growth-orientated theories can therefore be said to be the most distinctively 'managerialist' of the managerial theories.

In the Growth-orientated theories, the various possible candidates for inclusion in a managerial objective function are collapsed into the single motive of desire for sustainable long-run growth in the size (measured by assets, employment or real output) of the whole organization. This motive can be pursued by means of policies which, at a cost, open diverse new opportunities for sustainable expansion. As in the Discretionary theories, pursuit of managerial desires is not unbridled but is subject to a degree of constraint arising from the existence of external owners, explicitly shareholders. Managers have the power to pursue a long-term growth-rate faster than the one that would be optimal for shareholders, but the further they go, the more they are in danger of depressing the market value of the firm to the point where there is a serious risk of involuntary take-over, the latter being feared because it means loss of office.

Marris's version contains various distinctive features that combine together into a closed model quantitatively determining the planned long-run growth-rate of the firm. Some of the elements come from outside Marris's own work (for example, Penrose, 1958) and, in turn, some incomplete aspects of the model formed the basis of major further developments (for example, Mueller, 1969, 1972). The starting point is, in fact, the highly original work of Edith Penrose (1958). In that book the author characterizes the firm as an administrative organization capable of indefinite expansion. The *rate* of expansion is constrained by a limit on the rate at which new members of the management team can effectively be absorbed; new members require familiarization by the experience of working with old members; consequently, the current absolute absorptive capacity for new management depends on the current absolute size of the existing team – a proposition that inevitably implies a constraint on the proportionate effective growth-rate of the team through time. Marris generalized this 'Penrose theorem' to argue (without great influence) that the economics profession should turn away from attempting to base models on the concept of an optimum absolute size of the firm, but rather on the corresponding (proportionate) rate of change of size. The concept of 'diminishing returns to scale' should be replaced by a concept of diminishing returns to the growth-rate, meaning that as the growth-rate was accelerated past a certain point, for various reasons, such as the Penrose theorem, *current* costs would tend to increase.

The full Marris model may be summarized as follows. First, sustainable long-run growth requires market growth; and this can be achieved, at a cost, by search, research and development. In turn, new markets must be supported by new productive capacity. The combined costs of the Penrose effect, R&D and new capacity may be called the 'costs of growth'. They require cash flow. Cash flow may be obtained from retained profits, new share issues and new debt. The amount of the last, in any given period, is constrained on the one hand by the unwillingness of lenders to offer unrestricted sums relative to the firm's existing scale, and, on the other, by managers' fears of the risks, to them, of excessive leverage. The financial effect of new issues is similar to that of retentions and for this reason (and also because it is in practice a small source of finance) may for simplicity be ignored. Hence, for simplicity, the problem may be posed as if the only source of finance for accelerating growth were retentions.

Suppose that the operating profit rate on existing assets from existing markets is given. By retaining cash (and thus lowering current dividends) in expectation of future growth of markets, profits and hence *future* dividends, management effectively throws the path of future dividends into the future; the accelerated path substitutes the prospect of higher future for lower current rewards for stockholders. Allowing for equivalence, before tax, of dividends and capital gains, such a change may, over a range, be welcomed by shareholders and tend to raise the market value of the firm on the stock market. Beyond a certain point, however, the effect must go the other way, as shareholders are increasingly 'stuffed' with more jam tomorrow, relative to jam today, than they would desire.

It follows that the management can pursue a growth rate (implying specific costs of growth and profit retention ratio) that would maximize the firms's 'valuation ratio' (the name given by Marris to the ratio of market value to underlying assets, subsequently renamed 'q' by economics Nobel Laureate, James Tobin). Alternatively, the management may pursue a faster growth-rate at the price of reducing the valuation ratio to below its maximum; this may be called an expression of 'growth-preference', paralleling Williamson's 'expense-preference'.

Marris then added two propositions: (i) management desires both growth and security from take-over; and (ii) the risk of take-over will vary inversely with the valuation ratio. (A robust empirical relationship between low valuation ratio and statistically-observed probability of take-over has, in fact, been found – see, for example, Bartley and Boardman, 1986.) If managers have growth-preference, the model closes, with a unique management-desired growth-rate. Thus the factors that encourage 'managerial' behaviour encourage faster growth of firms, more expenditure on R&D and marketing expenditure, and hence possibly faster growth for the economy. In the pursuit of the goal of growth, managers have full incentive to make the firm's current operations as efficient as possible (operational inefficiency detracts from cash flow) and managerial behaviour is 'inefficient' only if it can be shown that the faster growth (as compared with that which would otherwise be the case) is in some way excessive from the point of view of society.

Dennis Mueller contributed major additions to these theories in two distinct ways. The first was a managerial theory of conglomerate merger seen from the point of view of the *acquiring* firm (Mueller, 1969) and the second was a life-cycle interpretation of firm growth (Mueller, 1972). If managers desired growth but were limited by internal constraints, they could to some extent free themselves (again, not without constraint) by successive acquisitions of other going concerns. Thus, in the jungle, any firm may be a predator and any firm a victim. The typical potential predator to fear, from the point of view of the managerial firm, is another managerial firm. However, because of managerial firms' concern with their own security from take-over, acquirers would be unlikely to push their activity so far as dilute the market value of their own shares sufficiently to create the reverse risk of take-over of themselves. Hence the hypothesis implicity predicts that over the broad range of mergers and take-overs, the net gains to acquiring firms shareholders will be either slightly negative or not significantly different from zero.

Mueller's life-cycle was a major qualification of Marris's linear characterization of the growth-path of a firm. A firm is 'young' when it succeeds in finding or creating an unusually profitable group of new markets. The costs of growth at this time are low and, in consequence, the value-maximizing growth-rate is comparatively high. Management can enjoy fast growth while also benefiting shareholders; their retained money is being better spent than if they had invested it elsewhere. Eventually the new markets saturate and, unless others, similarly profitable, are found, the firm becomes mature. The shareholders might well benefit if it were wound up, or at least, if significant profit retentions and attempted growth ceased. But now a Marris-like situation occurs. The management does not wish to cease growing and retains an increasing proportion of more modest profits to finance heavier growth-costs. Growth slows, but does not cease, and remains faster than it would have been in the absence of effective managerial growth-preference. Mueller was able to reinterpret existing stock-market studies to show that they were convincingly consistent with this story.

THE BUREAUCRATIC THEORIES

Monsen and Downs (1965) started from the same general background, but developed a qualitatively different approach that especially contrasted with that of Marris. The main differences concerned (i) the definition of the managerial firm; (ii) the authors' emphasis on the significance of internal organization; and (iii) the nature of managerial motivation concerning growth. In (i), Monsen and Downs defined a managerial firm as a firm with diffused shareholdings; a firm with concentrated shareholdings, whether or not in fact owner-managed, was defined as 'owner controlled'. Marris, by contrast, implicitly defined any firm not full-time managed by its controlling owners as managerial.

In (ii), Monsen and Downs, antedating Williamson's later work on the same lines (Williamson, 1970), pointed out that (a) managerial firms were necessarily large and therefore necessarily organized in pyramidal hierarchies, where the length of the chain of command (the height of the pyramid) increases with the size of the base – that is, with the number of people at the lowest level, a rough measure of the operating scale of the organization; and (b) because the salary and promotion prospects of subordinates depends on pleasing their superiors, information-transfer through the chain of command will be cumulatively biased. The two effects together mean that large firms, especially large non-concentrated-ownership firms, are inherently inefficient; their high managers lose control of them. (Later, in Marris and Mueller (1980), Marris argued that, because mathematically the height of the pyramid varies only as the log of the width of the base, the inefficiency-effect of scale is weak and diminishing, and easily offset by administrative scale economies and monitoring systems – an argument that is not generally accepted in the economics profession, especially in the USA.)

In (iii), Monsen and Downs argued that managers of managerial firms would be more risk-averse than those of owner-controlled firms, because they expected to be blamed for failures but inadequately rewarded by the profits of success, which latter largely accrue to the shareholders. More specifically, these managers would tend to try to offer shareholders steady capital gains and earnings increases, in contrast to possibly more fluctuating but on average more lucrative possibilities. They would also tend to favour less risky types of R&D – an argument that has been interpreted for research purposes as a general aversion to R&D.

TESTING THE THEORIES

It is desirable to distinguish between evidence that tests the broad hypothesis that managerial motivation in the modern corporation exists and is widely exercised, from results that attempt to discriminate between significantly different predictions of the three sub-groups of theories. Particularly significant are stark qualitative differences between the original Marris version of the Growth-orientated theory (Marris, 1964) and the other two groups, differences that are clearest when Marris (1964) is compared with Monsen and Downs (1965), the first predicting that managerial firms will favour fast growth and comparatively high R&D, and the latter predicting almost precisely the opposite. The contrast is less clear-cut when the convincing Mueller life-cycle argument (Mueller, 1972), is accepted, because the evolution of managerial control in the sense of dispersed shareholdings is co-variant with the managerial phase of the cycle.

Testing may also be divided into direct and indirect. Direct testing looks for evidence of relationships between ownership structure and relevant aspects of organizational behaviour, such as productivity, diversification, growth, and R&D. Indirect testing looks for indirect evidence, such as merger and executive-compensation behaviour, offering logical strong support for this or that main hypothesis. In the case of executive compensation, all the theories, Discretionary, Growth-orientated and Bureaucratic, imply that, in managerial firms, compensation will be more closely related to firm size than executive performance. Growth-orientated theories also carry the implication that executive compensation will reward rate of change of size.

Hunt (1986) comprehensively surveys literature appropriate to direct testing of the Bureaucratic theories and tabulates the relevant conclusions of some twenty previous quantitative studies. Hill and Snell (1989) use econometric path-analysis to test a final model which, subject to the life-cycle qualification (with neither firm 'age' nor size being controlled for) appears directly to confront the Bureaucratic models with Marris. Cubbin and Leech (1986) test Marris directly with a simultaneous-equations econometric model specifically based on the detailed elements of the original (1964) model. (This work provides the only example, throughout the literature, of the direct testing of a fully-specified original model rather than a reduced-form model.) Mueller and Reardon (1993) directly test the Growth-orientated-theory prediction of comparatively low returns to retained profits.

Bartley and Boardman (1986) and Scherer (1988) indirectly test and/or survey tests of the Growth-orientated theories (in effect, in confrontation with the Bureaucratic theories) by observations and surveys on merger/take-over data. Cubbin and Hall (1983) and Gomez-Mejia *et al.* (1987) do similarly with executive compensation.

RESULTS OF THE TESTS

Hunt (1986) found that about half the studies he surveyed confirmed the proposition that overall economic performance of managerially-controlled (MC) firms was inferior to that of shareholder-controlled ('control' being measured by share distribution). He also found some support for the idea that MC firms offer a more risk-averse time path of shareholder returns. Hill and Snell (1989) found that MC firms did more diversification, which supports Marris, but undertook less R&D, which does quite the opposite; they were also notably less productive as measured by value-added per head. Unlike Hill and Snell, Cubbin and Leech (1986) control for firm age, and at the end of an analysis that cannot be fully described in a short space, concluded, 'These results are consistent with all managements' being wealth maximizers or growth-maximizers or a random combination of the two.' On the other side of the argument, Mueller and Reardon (1993) found that the returns to retained profits are indeed pervasively low, a result that in logic can only imply that retained profits are used to support faster growth rates than would be observed if firms were managed entirely in the interests of external shareholders.

With indirect testing, the results surveyed by Scherer (1988) give overwhelming support to the Mueller (1969) conglomerate–merger hypothesis and thus support the Growth-orientated theories generally. As it was to be ten years before the beginning of the spectacular take-over boom that provided the greatest confirmation, this is a remarkable example of successful theoretical prediction in the literal sense of the word. In the case of executive compensation, in what is again the most sophisticated theoretical–empirical analysis to be found in the relevant literature, Cubbin and Hall (1963) point to numerous logical traps in distinguishing traditional- (that is, 'neoclassical-') supporting results from results which support the managerial theories as a whole or discriminate between the three groups of them. At the end of a complex discussion they conclude that both the Discretionary theories and the Growth-orientated theories are well supported, while the neoclassical alternative is not. In the data they studied (80 UK quoted public companies, 1969–75), they also found that high management was especially strongly rewarded for achieving growth by acquisitions, thus further reinforcing support for the Mueller (1969) hypothesis. Gomez-Mejia *et al.* (1987) (who unfortunately missed seeing the Cubbin and Hall paper) reach comparable conclusions in support of the broad managerial hypothesis.

CONCLUSION

The managerial theories, in opposition to positive neoclassical theories implying that management-managed firms not only ought to be, but effectively *are*, strategically directed largely in the sole interests of their shareholders, are theoretically convincing and very strongly empirically supported: in this respect they dominate empirical Agency theory in so far as the latter tends to claim that the effects of separation of ownership from management are in practice negligible. In practice, managerial behaviour appears as a mixture of the behaviours associated with all three theoretical sub-groups: Discretionary, Growth-orientated and Bureaucratic. A broad interpretation of the Mueller (1972) hypothesis that the blend varies through the life-cycle is also well supported.

Managerial firms do apparently tend to have both expense-preference and bureaucratic inefficiency. When these handicaps are present they imply loss of potential to grow. With given capacity to grow, however, managerial firms exercise growth-preference by attempting to, and to a degree succeeding in, growing faster than the rate that would, in given circumstances (including life-cycle phase), be in the interests of their shareholders. Hiro Odagiri (Odagiri, 1992) has applied these conclusions dramatically in partial explanation of the Japanese economic miracle.

Further Reading

Bartley, J. and C. Boardman (1986) 'Replacement-cost-adjusted Valuation Ratio as a Discriminator Among Take-over Target and Nontarget Firms', *Journal of Economics and Business*, vol. 38, pp. 41–55. (The definitive study of the hypothesis that the primary determinant of a firm's liability to take-over is the ratio of stock market value to underlying assets.)

Baumol, W. (1959) *Business Behavior, Value and Growth* (New York: Macmillan). (The first theoretical economic model of a managerial strategy that maximizes gross sales subject to earning adequate profit.)

Cubbin, J. and G. Hall (1983) 'Directors' Remuneration in the Theory of the Firm C Specification and Testing of the Null Hypothesis', *European Economic Review*, vol. 20, no. 1–3, pp. 333–48. (Outstanding theoretical and empirical analysis of executive compensation and managerial versus neo-classical theories of the firm; needs intermediate economics; uses calculus.)

Cubbin, J. and D. Leech (1986) 'Growth versus Profit-maximization: A Simultaneous-equations Approach to Testing the Marris Model', *Managerial and Decision Economics*, vol. 7, no. 2, 123–31. (Impressive uses of advanced econometric techniques to test the several elements of the theory.)

Gomez-Mejia, L., H. Tosi, and T. Hinkin (1987) 'Managerial Control, Performance and Executive Compensation', *Academy of Management Journal*, vol. 30, no. 1, March, pp. 51–70. (The most comprehensive study in a large literature on the subject of executive compensation.)

Hill, C. and S. Snell (1989) 'Effects of Ownership Structure and Control on Corporate Productivity', *Academy of Management Journal*, vol. 32, no. 1, March, pp. 25–46. (Definitive testing of managerial theories of the firm based on cross-sectional hierarchical regression analysis of over 100 Fortune-500 firms.)

Hunt, H. (1986) 'The Separation of Ownership from Control: Theory, Evidence and Implications', *Journal of Accounting Literature*, vol. 5, pp. 85–124. (Important survey of previous studies on the predictions of and results from managerial theories of the firm.)

Marris, R. (1964) *The Economic Theory of 'Managerial' Capitalism* (London: Macmillan). (Core contribution to Growth-orientated managerial theories; lively text peppered with equations.)

Marris, R. and D. Mueller (1980) 'The Corporation and Competition', *Journal of Economic Literature*, vol. 18, March, pp. 32–63. (Essay-cum-survey on neo-classical and managerial theories of the firm and non-price competition in the twentieth century.)

Monsen, R. and A. Downs (1965) 'A Theory of Large Managerial Firms', *Journal of Political Economy*, vol. 73, no. 3, June, pp. 221–36. (Lucid structured verbal argument, based on internal organization, that large corporations necessarily suffer bureaucratic inefficiency.)

Mueller, D. (1969) 'A Theory of Conglomerate Mergers', *Quarterly Journal of Economics*, vol. 83, November, pp. 643–60. (The first theory of merger and take-over from the point of view of acquiring firms.)

Mueller, D. (1972) 'A Life Cycle Theory of the Firm', *Journal of Industrial Economics*, vol. 20, no. 3, July, pp. 199–219. (The original statement and first testing of the important life-cycle hypothesis.)

Mueller, D. and E. Reardon (1993) *Rates of Return on Corporate Investment* (Washington DC: Anti-trust Division, Dept of Justice). (Strong findings that internal returns are generally lower than returns that could have been earned if retained profits had been distributed.)

Odagiri, H. (1992) *Growth Through Competition and Competition Through Growth: Strategic Management and the Economy in Japan* (Oxford: Clarendon Press). (Explains the Japanese economic miracle with the aid of the managerial theory.)

Penrose, E. (1958) *The Theory of the Growth of the Firm* (Oxford: Basil Blackwell; New York: John Wiley). (The foundation work on the idea of the persistently growing firm; highly original non-mathematical account of the internal administrative forces that encourage and restrain the growth-rate.)

Scherer, M. (1988) 'Corporate Takeovers: The Efficiency Arguments', *Journal of Economic Perspectives*, vol. no. 2, 1, Winter, pp. 69–82. (Comprehensive and detached theoretical, empirical and historical survey of the apparent motives for, and efficiency-effects of, take-overs.)

Williamson, O. (1964) *The Economics of Discretionary Behavior: Managerial Objectives in a Theory of the Firm* (Englewood Cliffs, NJ: Prentice-Hall). (The author's prize-winning Ph.D. dissertation; the classic exposition of his original model of managerial expense preference with important empirical support.)

Williamson, O. (1970) *Corporate Control and Business Behavior* (Englewood Cliffs, NJ: Prentice-Hall). (Lucid discussion of how exigencies of internal organization affect actual behaviour of managerial firms.)

6 The Completed Micro Model

BACKGROUND TO THE NEW CHAPTER

In order to grow, a firm must have finance. To increase demand for its products and services it must finance the costs of growth as they were described in Chapters 3 and 4. To undertake increased production to meet the increased demands that it has created, it must have new capacity: that is, investment. The original Chapter 5 was therefore titled 'Supply', because it was essentially concerned with the supply of finance. The original Chapter 6, which brought 'Demand' and 'Supply' together – in the sense of balancing the profitable growth of demand with the financable growth of capacity – was called 'Complete Micro Models', but the plural was a mistake: there was basically only one model. In this new chapter I set out the bare bones of that model, removing unncessary complexities, but maintaining the basic economic assumptions.

I have kept some, but only some, of the old terminology.

DEFINITIONS

Since we are concerned with the growth of the size of organizations, our first definition must be size. This was taken as the constant-price depreciated book value of underlying real assets, including cash. With regard to debt, in order to reflect the concept of capacity, only short-term debt is netted out. The concept of size is thus gross of long-term debt and exceeds 'net worth' by the amount of any actual long-term debt. The symbol is K.

The next most logical thing to define is profit. Before doing so, however, it is necessary to consider the costs of growth. In loose terms these come in two parts, the investment costs of new capacity on the one hand, and the costs of organizational expansion and market development, as discussed in Chapters 2 and 3, on the other. Some subsequent writers combined both together, but because the results of the former are reflected in the firm's accounts as an increase in assets, while the latter are in practice reported as current expense, they are importantly distinct. The first are called 'investment costs'; the second, 'sustainable-growth costs'. The symbols are respectively I (being the increase in K during one year) and Π.

We then define a concept of 'basic' profit, symbolised by P_0, being the gross profits, less depreciation of tangible non-human assets, that the firm would earn from its existing markets if it was not attempting to grow. If the firm is not growing, the profit reported in the accounts, symbolized by P, is the same as basic profit, but if the firm is growing it is operating profit less sustainable-growth costs. So,

$$P \equiv P_0 - \Pi \qquad (6.1)$$

The growth-rate of the firm, which is I/K, is signified by g. In fact, g is always to be interpreted as an uncertain future growth rate, more precisely the expected (that is, the most likely) long-run value.

Then P, P_0 and Π, when divided by K, become lower case. Thus p is P/K, the reported rate of profit on assets, p_0 the 'basic' rate of profit and π, the level of sustainable-growth expenditure relative to the size of the firm. Hence,

$$p = p_0 - \pi \qquad (6.2)$$

At the end of Chapter 2 it was suggested that the motives of management might be summarized as desiring the fastest growth rate consistent with reasonable security against take-over. The danger of take-over depended on the value of the shares. The latter needs to be normalized so that the take-over risk of one firm can be compared validly with that of another. The obvious normalizer is, again, assets. So I defined V as the total stock-market value of the firm, and termed the normalized version 'the valuation ratio'[1] and gave it the lower case symbol v. The immediate task of the modelling is to find a frontier between v and g, the subsequently-named 'V–g frontier'.[2]

$$v \equiv V/K. \qquad (6.3)$$

The fundamental financial rights of ordinary shareholders are the right to an equitable share of any dividend distribution and the right to an equitable share of any capital distribution (that is, on liquidation). People buy shares in the hope of future dividends and capital gains. Unless a capital distribution is expected, however, the essential reason for long-term increases in the prices of shares is increase in expected long-term dividend flow. Thus there is an equivalence of expected dividends and expected capital gain. Of course, the expectation is highly uncertain. Therefore, in this model, we value the firm as the discounted sum of expected future dividends per share. We assume that the market does not expect new shares to be issued and that the ratio of long-term debt to assets will be constant;[3] therefore the expected growth rate of total dividends is the same as the expected growth rate of the firm. (Why? Because we assume a sustainable path of growth, with a constant rate of reported profit – maintained by appropriate sustainable-growth expenditure – so profits and assets rise together: also, with a constant growth rate, the proportion of basic profits required for investment costs – the so-called corporate retention ratio – is also constant. Hence the proportion available for distribution is constant, and dividends grow with assets.)

The rate at which dividends will be discounted will be the basic long-term interest rate plus a premium for unertainty.

So we need symbols D for the dividends and r for the discount rate.

For the time being, lacking a better assumption, we assume that the firm is expected to last for ever (!), so we use the formula for an initial stream, D, discounted to infinity at the rate r, which is:

$$V = \frac{D}{r - g} \tag{6.4}$$

But D is profit minus investment, and investment is g times K. Hence

$$V = \frac{Kp - Kg}{r - g} \tag{6.5}$$

$$v = \frac{V}{K} = \frac{p - g}{r - g} \tag{6.6}$$

This formula, which was first discovered in the above form by R. F. Kahn,[4] clearly implies that the firm has only to create an expectation of a growth rate equal to the interest rate for its value to become infinite! Obviously the trouble is the assumption of infinite discounting, an assumption made not because of its realism but for lack of a reason for choosing any particular time horizon. In what follows we use Equation (6.5) only as a framework, building on assumptions that will give a more sensible result.

ECONOMIC ASSUMPTIONS

We now make three assumptions, which were effectively embedded in the lengthy discussion of the original Chapters 5 and 6. Some subsequent writers in the field have preferred different assumptions or different mathematical modelling. Coming back to the material now, however, I have found that they also seem necessary for a reasonable account of the V–g frontier.

1. The initial absolute size of the firm is given, exogenous, and the firm can change size only by growing steadily from this position at the rate g. There cannot be 'jumps' in the size of the firm.
2. The relationship between growth costs and growth rate is non-linear. For a variety of reasons, a firm with a low growth rate is likely to be less efficient all round than a firm with a moderate growth rate. The growing firm has the advantages of faster internal promotion of staff, a younger staff and a younger capital stock. This factor, however, fights the various costs discussed in original Chapters 3 and 4, which increase with increasing effect at higher expected growth rates.
3. Faster growth rates are more uncertain than slower growth rates and this force is also non-linear. Hence the discount rate applied to an individual firm increases non-linearly with the growth rate. As expected long run growth rates become very high, their uncertainty explodes.

Using the symbol i to represent the basic (exogenous) interest rate and recollecting that π represents sustainable-growth costs per unit of assets, assumptions (2) and (3) become respectively:

$$\pi = -\alpha g + \beta g^2 \tag{6.7}$$

$$r = i + \gamma g + \delta g^2 \tag{6.8}$$

Combine Equations (6.7) and (6.2):

$$p = p_0 + \alpha g - \beta g^2 \tag{6.9}$$

Combine Equations (6.9) and (6.6) to obtain the V–g frontier:

$$v = \frac{p_0 + \alpha g - \beta g^2 - g}{i + \gamma g + \delta g^2 - g} \tag{6.10}$$

Where g, p_0 and i are positive numbers in a practical range from 0 to 0.20; α is a number of the order of 1 or 2; β is in the range from 10 to 50; γ and δ from 0 to 1.

THE DESIRED GROWTH RATE

Figures 6.1a and 6.1b respectively show the profit–growth relationship (Equation (6.9)) and the corresponding V–g for the type of managerial enterprise that was always implicitly, and to a degree explictly assumed in the original book. Rightly or wrongly, I believed it to be the dominant type of firm in twentieth-century capitalism. Now (not then) I call it the 'dynamic managerial firm'.

The firm, irrespective of its ownership structure, was strategically directed by the decisions of a group of managers who did not have ownership stakes large enough to affect their self-interest directly. They were neverthless highly motivated and devoted to the interests of the organiza-

Profit Rate %

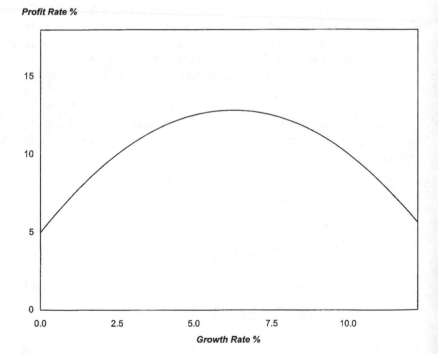

Growth Rate %

Figure 6.1a A Growth-Profit Curve for a Dynamic Managerial Firm Profit Rate %

Valuation Ratio

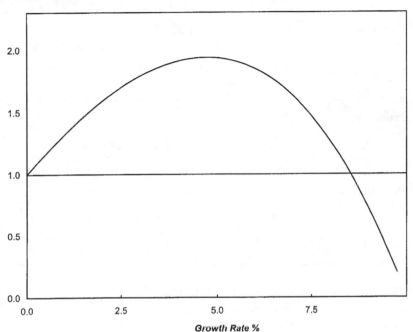

Figure 6.1b The V-G Frontier for the Dynamic Managerial Firm

tion. Because they were strongly interested in growth they were equally interested in the profits needed to finance growth. Therefore, they strove to be as efficient, in the conventional sense, as possible. Finally, they had reached their positions because they had the talent for planning and achieving sustainable growth.

Thus the firm has a generous range over which the relationship between growth and reported profitability is positive. As Figure 6.1a shows, the relationship does not become significantly negative until the growth rate reaches around 7 per cent.

Figure 6.1b shows that the valuation ratio reaches a peak at a growth rate of around 5.5 per cent. But it can be kept comfortably above 1.0 with much higher growth rates.

The original book adopted two approaches to closing the model. In the first, it was assumed that the management believed in a safe minimum level of the valuation ratio, but not necessarily 1.0; it could be higher or lower. Below the minimum they would not go, because they would regard

Table 6.1   Coefficients for the V–g frontiers of different types of firms

Coefficient	Type of Firm		
	Dynamic managerial	*Less dynamic managerial*	*Dynamic neoclassical*
Profit rate (Equation (6.9))			
p_0	0.05	Same for all firms	
α	2.50	2.0	1.70
β	20	20	5.50
Discount rate (Equation (6.8))			
i	0.05	Same for all firms	
γ	0.75	Same for all firms	
δ	0.50	Same for all firms	

the situation as being unacceptably dangerous. But once the minimum was achieved, security was of no further concern. So they would choose the maximum growth rate consistent with meeting the minimum.

For the sake of argument, assume that the safe minimum valuation ratio is, in fact, 1.0 – that is, the situation where the market value of the firm is just equal to the underlying assets. The reader can verify that maximum growth rate, subject to this minimum, is 8.5 per cent.

The alternative approach was to assume a continuous trade-off between growth and valuation. To that end I hypothesized a set of indifference curves between the two elements, spreading down from the top right-hand corner of the diagram, one of which would be tangential to the *V–g* curve and thus indicate the 'optimum' (that is, managerial utility-maximizing) growth rate with associated *v*-value (Diagram 6.6. on page 255 in the original book). Since, both theoretically and empirically, the truth must be that given levels of the valuation ratio do not create certainties of either take-over or security, but rather create *probabilities* of take-over, this approach is obviously superior: there is a smooth relationship between lower levels of the valuation ratio and corresponding increases in disutility for management. However, the smooth trade-off hypothesis is rather inconvenient for qualitative analysis, and the present discussion therefore proceeds on the more primitive minimum-*v*-level approach.

That approach was criticized by a number of subsequent theorists on an interesting, but I now perceive as mistaken, line of thought. The critics' argument implicitly perceives the typical potential take-over raider as an entity such as an investment trust. After acquiring the firm at a price above the current level but below the maximum level on the V–g curve, they will appoint new directors with simple instructions to reduce the growth rate by the necessary amount to maximize the valuation ratio and then, perhaps sell the shares at a profit. My response is that although that type of raider exists, it is only one among a number of types, and not the dominant one. As was already seen in discussing the work of Dennis Mueller in the commentary to the original Chapter 2 and in the new Chapter 5 above,[5] the most common type of raider is another managerial organization desiring to enhance its own growth. After take-over, the two organizations will be integrated and the value of the purchase will be difficult to define. The fact that the post take over performance of the shares of acquiring firms is, on average, negative confirms that value maximization is not the dominant motive. The most fundamental fact about successful acquisitions is that the acquirer has a high valuation ratio relative to that of the target. This does not mean that the acquirer is necessarily growing at a slower rate that the target. It most probably means that for one reason or another the market has more confidence in the acquirer's growth path, and therefore discounts it at a lower rate. The acquirer has more favourable (that is, lower), values of γ or δ or both, in Equation (6.8). In any event, the least likely plan that this type of acquirer will have for its victim is to slow it down!

There are numerous other institutional and motivational patterns among raiders. But the one thing they all share is love of a good deal – a bundle of material and human assets bought at a low price. For this reason it was my original prediction that at the end of the day the absolute level of the valuation ratio would remain both the most robust index of managerial satisfaction of the security motive and the most robust predictor of actual take-overs. The latter, testable, proposition has in fact been repeatedly confirmed empirically in research studies over twenty years.[6]

MICRO PREDICTIONS

The foregoing model produces the following conclusions or predictions relating strictly to a single firm in isolation, with the policies and actions of all other firms being given, as well as the general macroeconomic environment. It is assumed that management desires to maximize the growth rate subject to an absolute minimum on the valuation ratio.

1.   Any variation that creates a favourable shift of the growth–profits curve – for example, a positive variation of the basic profit rate, p_0,

or of the coefficient, α, or a negative variation of the coefficient β, will not only increase the value of the firm, but also the *growth rate* that can be sustained with a given valuation ratio. (This can be seen from inspection or analysis of Equation (6.10) or by numerical experiment with Figures 6.1a and 6.1b. The latter type of excercise will show, for example, that if the minimum valuation ratio is, in fact, 1.0, a one-percentage point increase in p_0 will increase the desired growth rate – the rate that intersects with $v = 1.0$ – by half a percentage point.) Thus, to a much greater extent than explained in the original book, this model is profit-driven. If management really does desire maximum growth subject to a given valuation constraint, then management should always be as efficient as possible. For example, in setting prices of existing, established products, managers should, wherever possible, aim for conventional profit maximization. High profit-earning capacity creates value for shareholders and discretion for managers. The conclusion is a perfect analogy for Oliver Williamson's obverse conclusion, discussed in the new Chapter 5,[7] that, when profits fall, the exercise of managerial discretion must be reduced. The difference between Williamson and myself is the difference between a static and a dynamic context. It is my opinion that the dynamic conclusion that it pays managers who have growth preference to earn profits and be generally efficient is the fundamental reason why, in the twentieth-century, the system of managerial capitalism, for all its faults, has been so outstandingly successful economically – not only growth-promoting but efficient.

2.   A negative variation in the minimum valuation ratio, reflecting forces – for example, legal or other institutional barriers – that reduce management fear of take-over, *increases* both the desired and the sustainable growth rate.

A positive variation in one or both of the coefficients, γ and δ, reflecting the effect of the growth-rate on the degree of uncertainty built into the discount rate by the stock market, will not only reduce the value of the firm but also the desired and sustainable growth rate. When management gives signals to the market indicating an expected growth rate, it also, in various ways that it cannot control, gives signals that affect the market's confidence in the plans, and so affects these coefficients. Therefore, a management which, willy nilly, gives an impression of great uncertainty, is punished by being unable to grow as fast as would otherwise be the case.

ALTERNATIVE PICTURES

Two other types of firm (among the general population of twentieth-century public listed companies) have been identified in economic theory and empirical studies. They can be called, 'less dynamic (or 'undynamic' or 'sleepy') managerial firms' and 'dynamic neoclassical firms', respectively.

The less dynamic managerial firm is illustrated in Figures 6.2a and 6.2b. As Table 6.1 (p. 128) shows, the only change, as compared with the dynamic managerial firm, is a reduction from 2.5 to 2.0 in the coefficient : the range of positive effect of growth on efficiency is shorter and weaker. The growth–profit curve is pulled down and to the left. On the new V–g frontier it would still be possible to grow at six per cent while maintaining the same minimum valuation ratio, shareholders would be better off if the rate were half this.

The essence of this story lies in the belief, supported by much convincing evidence, that managerial firms – more precisely, firms where no small ownership group holds a commanding percentage of the shares (so-called

Profit Rate %

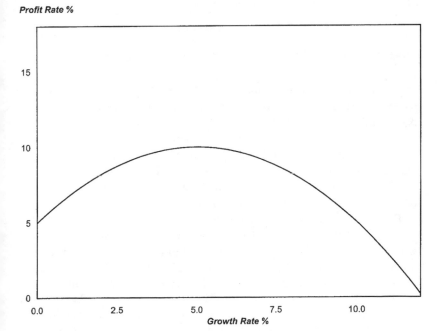

Growth Rate %

Figure 6.2a A Growth-Profit Curve for a Less Dynamic Managerial Firm

Valuation Ratio

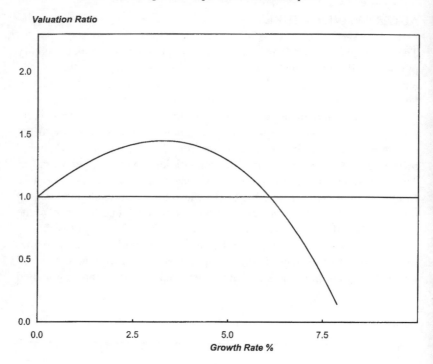

Figure 6.2b The V-G Frontier for the Less Dynamic Managerial Firm

'management controlled) are inherently inefficient. As was seen in Chapter 5,[8] this was argued strongly by Monsen and Downs and is supported indirectly in the theory and findings of Dennis Mueller.[9] It stands in stark contrast to the general picture of 'dynamic' managerial capitalism set out above and is based on the proposition that large bureaucratic organizations cannot have coherent objectives. Their behaviour is the inevitably product of their necessarily pyramidal internal organization. They are inherently risk averse, inefficient and 'undynamic'.

The dynamic neoclassical firm is illustrated in Figures 6.3a and 6.3b. It was first discovered empirically by Hugo Radice[10] and is also consistent with the idea of the 'young' firm envisaged in Dennis Mueller's life-cycle model.[11] It will tend to be 'owner-controlled' in the sense that, although it is a listed public corporation, a controlling block of shares is still held by a small group, probably the family of the original founder. These firms, whose strong existence and performance has also been confirmed by other empirical studies,[12] display high profitability and high growth. On both fronts they out-perform the average non-owner-controlled firm.

They are characterized in Figures 6.3a and 6.3b mainly by a low value of the coefficient β, permitting them to grow at high rates (see Figure 6.3a) without adverse effects on profitability: they are still riding the wave of the demand for the products' commercial and technical innovations originally created by their entrepreneur founders. In consequence, their V–g frontiers results are as in Figure 6.3b. The curve slopes upwards over a wide range where there is therefore no conflict between profits and growth. It is quite obvious that firms of this type have been the source of a great deal of the dynamism of the twentieth-century system. They are a transitional form which, in good circumstances, can take the best from the traditional and managerial forms of organization.

A SUMMING UP

Probably the majority of economists, across the political spectrum, tend to disagree with the proposition that the dynamic managerial firm has been a dominant feature of the twentieth century. They tend to see a general

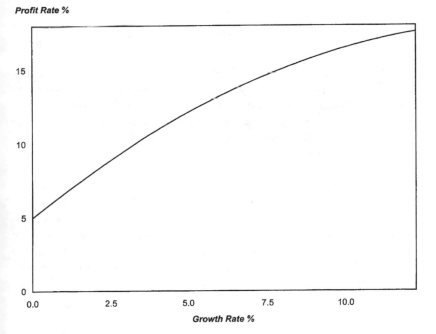

Figure 6.3a A Growth-Profit Curve for a Dynamic Neoclassical Firm

Valuation Ratio

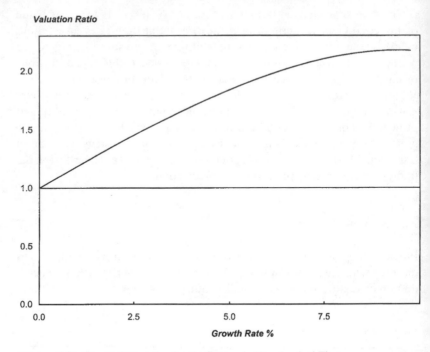

Figure 6.3b The V-G Frontier for the Dynamic Neoclassical Firm

population consisting largely of dynamic neoclassical firms and undynamic managerial firms. They suggest that the late-twentieth-century
movement to management buy-outs represents a healthy corrective tendency.[13] For obvious logical reasons the debate is difficult to test. I would
point to names such as General Motors, IBM and ICI. I would also question why, if the management-controlled firm is on average so inefficient, it
has been so persistent in both survival and growth.

But I would also concede that under the influence of the IT revolution,
the period leading up to the turn of the century is seeing great changes:
witness, for example, the story of Microsoft, a patently dynamic neoclassical firm with a total stock market value at the time of writing comparable
with that of IBM. Notice, however, that IBM, after receiving a severe
shock at the hands of Microsoft, appears for the time being to have recov-
ered and remains very much still with us.

7 Behaviour and Evidence

Here follow, only lightly edited, the first ten pages of the old Chapter 7: 'Behaviour and Evidence'. The remaining pages, concerned with empirical evidence, have been deleted in favour of the discussion of that topic now found in the new Chapter 5 – 'Managerial Theories of the Firm', above. By 'behaviourism' in economics I refer explicitly to the body of ideas founded by Herbert Simon, which are now perhaps more widely termed 'bounded rationality'. By 'satisficing' I referred to a particular class of models that Herbert Simon suggested in the second half of the 1950s,[1] where, rather than attempting to find an optimum or maximizing solution to a complex problem, the subject undertakes an heuristic search effort only until she or he has found a solution that is 'good enough'. The original text, written around 1961, follows. Although I stand by the critique I wrote then, and although I think I was one of the earliest economists to recognize publicly the richness of Simon's ideas, I believe now that I also still failed to appreciate the full power of bounded rationality over the whole of economics. The 1978 Nobel electors were more perceptive.

There is one proposition which, so far as the author is aware, not even the most ardent behaviourist would deny: namely, that no person or organization can satisfice at a utility level higher than would be obtainable theoretically from the maximizing position: a maximum is, after all, a maximum. (We admit this begs the question of the psychological reality of a preference system.) On the contrary, the drive of satisficing theory derives from the possibility that in many cases the maximizing solution may be so remote as to be of academic interest only. The author, however, believes that these cases are in practice rare. He also believes that if the behaviouristic approach were carried too far, attention could well be diverted excessively from fundamental problems towards the no doubt influential but essentially petty dynamics of the multiplicity of processes leading to sub-optimal stability in particular cases. Thus, in several extant satisficing models, there is no way of telling whether the dynamic relationships postulated are consistent with the requirements of the underlying structure of the problem under investigation. If, for example, one wishes to postulate a relationship between the time rate of change of reward and the corresponding rate of change of effort, one must also specify the static structure from which these frictional relationships are derived (for example, the static transformation curve between effort and result). To put the point another way, Professor Simon once drew an analogy[2] with a person searching for a needle in a haystack that contained not just one needle but many, all varying in sharpness. Rather than continuing until he believed he had found the sharpest needle in the whole stack, he would stop when he found one 'sharp enough' for his immediate purpose. But the economic interpretation of this is ambiguous. How do we know there is not a continuous relationship between the sharpness of the needle and the efficiency of the subsequent activity? Suppose one was in a competition to see who could find a needle and carry out a specified sewing task in the shortest total time: how would 'sharp enough' then be defined? The behaviourist would no doubt answer that even if the competitors knew the relationship between time spent in the search and the most probable sharpness of the best needle found (which, characteristically, they would not), and that even supposing they knew the relationship between sharpness and sewing speed, they would still be faced with an extremely complex game-theoretic problem. The optimum strategy in extended form might have to specify how much longer the player should continue to search after any given discovery at any given stage of the search for all given previous sequences of discoveries. What more likely than that most players would instead decide to stop searching when they had found a needle of some arbitrary minimum sharpness? Satisficing theory would then begin to bite were it able to show that, if such a game were played repeatedly, the arbitrary cut-off level would be likely to be subject to a stable adjustment process based on experience. In a maximizing theory, the adjustments would eventually result in the discovery of the strategy that maximized the expectation of a win. In a satisficing theory, by contrast, the result is not necessarily optimal, and the subject is supposed never to discover that, by behaving otherwise, he might improve his expectations. But the point we wish to emphasize is that, whether one believes the subject will satisfice or maximize, the basic structure of the problem must be specified first in order to begin any analysis: we must know the rules of the game, and, if unable to catch our haystack, at least must find our competitor. Whether the players believe it or not, the result of the game will depend on this structure, as much when they satisfice as when they maximize.

And in many cases a realistic formulation of the satisficing model implies an unstable solution, in which case it is more than likely that the system will 'explode' to the maximum. To us, therefore, the main significance of satisficing theory, in relation to long-run problems of the type with which this book has been concerned, is essentially empirical. Having ascertained the nature of optimal (that is, managerial utility-maximizing) behaviour, we shall expect empirically to observe a great deal of scatter caused by not only inter-firm differences in the positions of functions, but also to sub-optimal satisficing. The nature and direction of displacement, however, can only be suggested by specific assumptions. At present, there exists no general theory of satisficing. There are only examples.

Another difficulty is that, since its invention, the word itself has come to be used in a wide variety of senses, and one suspects, indeed, that its inventor cunningly intended just this to happen. There is one particular use that seems to us particularly confusing, if not plain wrong. This is the sense in which any form of behaviour we would describe as 'managerial' is called satisficing behaviour. The usage seems implicitly to assume that once the objective of maximizing stockholder welfare is relaxed and managerial utility permitted to count, only a satisficing theory is appropriate: management, it is assumed, cannot of its nature possess any kind of clearly defined utility function on which it might be possible to maximize. It is then usually stated that management is likely to set up satisficing levels on a wide variety of dimensions – leverage, retentions, valuation ratio, rate of return, size, growth and many others. It is rarely indicated, however, whether this behaviour is supposed to result from the existence of discontinuities in a utility function, or from what the present author would define as true satisficing behaviour (that is, behaviour arising from various forms of ignorance as to how maximum utility might be achieved). Nor is the rationality of including so many variables adequately explained. Dare we suggest that, because of contemporary prevalence of neoclassical ideology, 'satisficing' is deliberately being degraded to mean almost any form of behaviour that is, in the economic sense, non-normative? If so, we do not think this is very helpful.

None of these remarks should be taken as implying a belief that the behaviouristic approach has no application to a well-specified problem such as I have attempted to develop in this book. Far from it. We have already made considerable use of implicit satisficing concepts in the constrained levels of leverage, valuation ratio and security in general, which were deployed at various stages of the earlier analysis. Until we adopted the continuous utility function, we assumed, in effect, that security was satisficed while growth was attemptedly maximized. We could as well, perhaps, have assumed these roles to have been reversed. It is also possible for satisficing to occur on both dimensions simultaneously: satisficing levels of both growth rate and valuation ratio might be established, outside which, if either was violated, the firm would behave as if utility had become zero; inside the constraints, on the other hand, any combination meeting both would be as good as any other. Then satisfactory utility would arise anywhere along some rather arbitrarily determined segment of the valuation curve. Here, rather than some internal adjustment process, the most likely determinants of the limits would, in fact, be external: the firm would be increasingly likely to decide that a given valuation-ratio and growth-rate combination was unsatisfactory the further it deviated from the observed centre of gravity of an external population of comparable competitors. In other words, as long as we considered only firms who were at least on (rather than somewhere below) their own demand-growth curves,[3] we should expect to find them scattered along their corresponding valuation curves in a distribution that had a well-defined mode but might well be skewed: for example, it is not unlikely that the stimulus to attempt to pull back towards the centre would increase with the magnitude of the deviation more rapidly in the case of valuation ratio than in the case of growth rate; hence, we should expect more spreading of the deviations on the growth rate side than on the 'security' side. Empirical observation would then probably be unable to discriminate between this situation and the predictions of the more orthodox hypothesis, where all firms were assumed to be maximizing, but the optimum positions were disturbed by differences in data. And since we have already admitted that the utility function is necessarily conditioned by the environment, the theoretical contribution of the introduction of satisficing assumptions is here relatively slight.

As soon, however, as we let firms wander off their demand-growth curves, the picture becomes rather different. Such firms are experiencing organizational slack. They will grow more slowly for given security, experience less security for given growth rates, or, more likely, experience low security and slow growth together. In a 'bad' case, the firm would be growing slowly, be earning a poor rate of return, be compelled to adopt a relatively high retention ratio in order to finance even this modest growth rate, and hence be displaying a low valuation ratio and be in considerable danger of take-over. (*This is the 'less dynamic' managerial firm now described in Figures 6.2a and 6.2b on pp. 131–2 of the new Chapter 6, above.*) But if things became bad enough, according to the satisficing theory, the unpleasantness of the situation would eventually stimulate the taking-in of slack and some actual improvement. Oscillations would thus occur around a centre that was significantly sub-optimal, and if all firms were subject to the same type of cycle, there is no reason why the collective mean should not be sub-optimal also. No one who has worked in an administrative organisation can fail to recognize the realism of the picture.

There are, however, good reasons for believing that the chances of finding the behaviouristic norm in any given position diminish with the distance of this position from the optimum position. Because, over a wide range of quantitative assumptions concerning the values of adjustment coefficients, satisficing models tend to be rather undamped, and it is likely, therefore, that in the course of oscillation the 'ceiling' represented by the demand–growth curve will frequently be hit. But the firm must be presumed not fully to understand this cause of the apparent failure of its efforts to do better, and the reaction is therefore likely to be softened: that is, the reverse swing of the pendulum (reappearance of slack) will be less marked than if no ceiling had been present. We shall therefore expect to observe firms empirically in various stages of the process. We may also expect additional bias from the fact that the stimulus to take in slack may be more effective in relation to one variable than the other. For example, because the consequences of being taken over are much more unpleasant than the consequences of growing slowly, a given downward deviation in the valuation ratio may be more effective than a corresponding deviation in the growth rate.

So far, however, we have done no more than attempt to apply satisficing assumptions of the type characteristic in the literature, assumptions which were mainly developed for application to situations in which, however 'behaviouristic' the behaviour of the managers, the 'higher' objectives of the organization remained essentially orthodox. We now attempt to develop a satisficing model more specifically designed for the problems discussed in this book.

In my view, the essence of satisficing is human reaction to having to take decisions in ignorance of their probable outcomes. My theory not only presents subjects with a difficult maximizing problem, but also with the considerable problem of merely maintaining decision consistency. Apart from the question of how the growth rate should be maximized, there is the more elemental, but by no means easy, question of how growth is to be made sustainable – of how, that is, the firm is to ensure that decisions will be consistent with balance between growth rate of demand and growth rate of capacity. Although we have denied the possibility of a persistent trend in the degree of capacity utilization in the long run, no one can deny that short-run utilization fluctuations are not only possible, but in fact belong to the everyday experience of all business firms. Furthermore, the level of utilization is particularly likely to play the role of stimulus in satisficing behaviour, and, indeed, a wide variety of behaviouristic models have been based on this.[4]

Such models frequently make use of the idea of adjustable aspirations. The subject, faced with a problem involving effort in order to obtain reward, is supposed to set up some initial, rather arbitrarily chosen, target or 'aspiration level'. The initial aspiration level is the actual reward with which at that time he believes he would be satisfied. He then makes an effort and achieves a reward. If the result is less than the aspiration ('negative goal discrepancy'), at the next round, effort is stepped up and aspiration reduced; and the reverse occurs if the first-round discrepancy is positive. If the process continues it may in some circumstances lead ultimately to a stable solution in which effort, reward and goal-discrepancy remain constant at a level that has no particular relation to the optimum; in other cases, stability is impossible until a maximum is reached. Although the psychological literature on which such ideas as the above are based now seems rather dated,[5] their possible applications to the balanced-growth problem are evident. For example, imagine a management attempting to maximize growth subject to a minimum security constraint. But suppose they have only a most incomplete picture of the nature of the problem: not only are they ignorant of the values of the parameters, they do not really understand the structure either. They set an aspiration level of balanced growth, not necessarily the maximum. There exists a vector of policy decisions that would at least provide the aspired result, but even this they do not know how to find. Instead, they choose any set of apparently reasonable policies in the vague hope that these will prove satisfactory. In the event, the decisions prove inconsistent, growth is unbalanced and at least one of the relevant rates, the growth rate of demand, say, fails to satisfy – the firm has permitted too high a profit margin for the diversification rate.[6] As likely as not, however, the cause of the failure will continue to be misunderstood, 'demand' will appear to have been constraining growth and the supply of finance to have become excessive. If, then, rather than adjusting the profit-margin variables and diversification rate, this management, following the behaviour pattern described above, instead reduces the *aspiration level* (believing, perhaps, that they had been aspiring to the impossible), they would probably decide to reduce the growth rate of capacity in order to bring it into line with the arbitrarily-arrived-at growth rate of demand. This could be done by means of financial decisions having the effect of raising the valuation ratio to a level higher than that originally felt to represent the safe minimum. They would then satisfice at a growth rate that was in every sense sub-optimal. A similar application could be made in the case where the utility function was continuous.

A firm that had reached this kind of position would inform investigators that it was not troubled by shortage of finance, meaning it could increase the growth rate of capacity without taking risks considered likely to be excessive (or without visiting 'unreasonable' consequences on shareholders). However, had it so happened that the initial decisions had led the growth rate of demand to exceed that of capacity, although the adjustment process would have still produced a sub-optimal growth rate, it would not have produced the sensation of financial plenty. On the contrary, the firm would have pulled down the demand growth rate to match the finance supply, and would tend to report that it would be possible to grow faster if only capital were more plentiful. This may explain why, even among large corporations, much of the evidence on the subject of capital supply is conflicting, and also why there are such notable oscillations in the financial atmosphere within individual firms. It may also explain why senior executives seem to feel that, at any given time, they are usually faced with a single dominant problem: sometimes it is 'finance'; sometimes 'demand'; and sometimes 'production'.

The result is a solution entirely consistent with the dynamic outlook of the leading satisficing theorists. The problem we have posed is that of ensuring that the profits earned in Period 1 are sufficient to attract or provide the necessary capital for capacity expansion in Period 2; in terms of classical dynamics, the rate of change of profits must be in balance with the rate of change of demand. By postulating a certain pattern of reactions to dynamic discrepancies, we have shown how a solution may be found which is as much the result of the methods and accidents of the decision process as of a rational evaluation of optima. The statistical implications would be a tendency for companies to spread along demand-growth and valuation curves in a manner that had no particular relation to the utility maximum, and was not necessarily concentrated round that position. But the behaviour could also incorporate organizational slack, in which case a similar equilibrium would occur on a plane somewhere within the demand-growth curve. In reality, of course, we shall expect to observe simultaneously many examples of these various causes of scatter.

The presence of the behaviour would also be consistent with another familiar observation, namely that a substantial proportion of large corporations control investment decisions by means of a 'target rate of return'. One of the problems in sustaining balanced growth in a programme of diversification is that not only are the results of decisions uncertain, but, particularly in the case of new products, many must be taken both consistently and *sequentially*. If the firm does not know the shape of the demand-growth function (and, since the curve relates to events many of which are unique, there is a sense in which such knowledge is impossible), even if it well understands the finance–supply relationship, it will find particular difficulty in ensuring that the profits earned by new products launched today will be sufficient to support the capacity expansion required if and when today's new products succeed. In the face of this problem, an excellent method of ensuring that growth will at least be balanced is to lay down a rule that no new product should be launched unless an unbiased estimate of its prospects suggests a minimum probability of success and a minimum contribution to the firm's overall profitability position. The diversification rate arrived at then appears as an indirect consequence of the rules; provided the latter are well chosen and forecasts unbiased, at least growth in the long run will be balanced whatever the outcome. The 'target rate of return' thus appears as essentially a device for maintaining consistency. Many observers have confirmed this.

Our model provides that for every long-run growth rate there is a consistent rate of return. Therefore, every target rate of return, if maintained, is consistent with some balanced long-run growth rate. The latter may or may not be the maximum. There is no reason why, by a learning process, the firm should not find the target return associated with a maximum growth rate, provided (and the proviso is, admittedly, serious) that the optimum conditions are in the long run reasonably constant. If, as is more likely, the optimum conditions are always changing, the target rate of return and associated growth rate may well come to be settled by a satisficing procedure.

Thus 'target return' behaviour is consistent with both maximizing and satisficing in a basically managerial model. It is also apparently consistent with neoclassical behaviour – the target rate would be the exogenous 'normal rate of profit', or 'cost of capital'. The acid distinction between our own and the neoclassical explanation is this. The neoclassical philosopher simply asserts that investment is not to be undertaken for expected returns below the target rate, because to do so would be both 'non-economic', and (probably) non-optimal for shareholders. We, on the contrary, assert that investment below the target rate is not undertaken because to do so would lead to inconsistencies and probably be non-optimal for managers.

In contrast to the inability to rationalize the target in classical terms, managers are often able to give reasonable accounts of why it is necessary to set targets at all. Most of these relate in one sense or another to the problem of consistency, and not a few specifically mention the need for sustainable growth. Only a very few mention stockholders. Support for a satisficing type of interpretation is given by the fact that many respondents merely argue that something vaguely unpleasant would happen to both the firm and to themselves if profits were unduly low: profits, it is so often said, are necessary for both survival and growth, and growth is often necessary for survival. Inter-firm variation in target rates of return is therefore quite consistent with either maximizing or satisficing in our model, following the many variations in the conditions controlling individual situations. We believe these arguments to be conclusive, and with them conclude this discussion.

8 Possible Macro Implications

The purpose of the final chapter of the original book was to attempt to make useful suggestions for the reconstruction of then-contemporary post-Keynesian growth economics, based on what would now be called the microfoundations of the theory set out in the preceding chapters. The result, though seemingly clearly written, was complex and is not reproduced here with the suggestion that now-contemporary readers should attempt to trace the detail of its logic. Similarly, modern readers may find the 1950s/1960s theoretical context now has the flavour of the history of thought. No, the purpose of reproducing the chapter in full is to give a broader picture of the environment in which I saw managerial capitalism and also because, as already discussed in the new Introduction, buried in the argument are seeds of the idea of 'endogenous' growth.[1]

Unfortunately, also embedded in the argument are some concepts that were originally defined in now-deleted preceding passages of the original book. The growth–profit curve as now defined in Equation (6.9) and described in Figures 6.1a, 6.2a and 6.3a in the new Chapter 6[2] above, was partially derived from a sub-model based on a decision variable called the diversification rate. *This was defined as the annual proportionate growth in the number of distinct items in the firm's catalogue. Because a proportion of new products fail, the diversification rate was not the same as the sustainable demand-growth rate (that is, the annual proportionate growth in the firm's volume of saleable output sustainable with a constant reported rate of profit –* p*). In turn, the success rate of new products could be influenced by price policy: with lower average profit margins the firm could hope for, on average, greater success in attracting pioneers and hence a higher general possibility of demand explosion ever successive new product launches. In effect, therefore, the firm's sustainable growth rate from the demand side was an increasing function of the diversification rate and a decreasing function of the level of the average profit margin, and hence of the level of the constant profit rate. This function was called the demand-growth function. It incorporated part of the costs of growth.*

A higher profit margin means more cash flow but also an increase in growth costs attributable to failed new products. Hence it was possible to postulate the choice from possible pairs of price policies (as represented by profit margin) and growth effort (as represented by diversification) had been optimized for any given point on the growth–profit curve: for each given growth rate, the reported profit rate was maximized. The implications are in principle incorporated in the numbers presented in the upper part of Table 6.1 in the new Chapter 6 above.[3]

The term demand–growth curve *or for short 'demand curve' was then applied to a slice through the demand–growth function for a given profit margin: on a graph with the diversification rate on the x-axis and the sustainable growth-rate of demand on the y-axis there is a family of curves for given profit margins (higher for lower margins) rising but at a flattening rate from left to right. Each one of these is called a demand–growth curve.*

It is hoped that these definitions will help the reader in the original text which follows.

It was explained in the Introduction that the aims of this book lay mainly in the field of micro-theory. We wished to investigate the nature of the managerial enterprise, non-normatively, in a spirit of unrestricted intellectual curiosity; we did not want to be committed to producing a model that would necessarily be helpful in conventional ways, such as informing bases for theories of price or income determination. But we naturally hoped that the results might also be of wider interest, and we have already indicated some possible implications of departing from partial-equilibrium analysis while retaining the basic theory. We also originally believed that the theory might have significant macro implications, yet were not relying on this: we were genuinely uncertain as to what would be found when the stone had been lifted, and would have been by no means distressed had the discoveries tended merely to confirm existing orthodoxy in the area (if any such can be said to exist). However, now that the main work is complete, it does seem tempting to add, as it were by way of a postscript, some speculations as to the possible macro implications of a 'managerial' micro theory. Of course, the economic macrocosm is much less managerial than the manufacturing sector: in agriculture, services and many branches of finance, traditional capitalism remains prevalent. In the government sector there is much managerialism but no managerial capitalism. Nevertheless, in most Western countries a very considerable proportion of national output, measured from the production side, comes from organizations to which our theory applies. Almost by definition, managerial firms are above-average in size, and therefore contribute disproportionately to total production. Certainly, it is far less inaccurate to treat the economy as if it were entirely managerial than is the common practice of treating it as if it were entirely traditional. In this final chapter we therefore briefly consider the macro implications of a system that is, in effect, overwhelmingly managerial, but in which there remain a sufficient number of traditional capitalists to be capable of significantly influencing the managers' behaviour. We believe that this is, as a matter of fact, a fair description of typical mid-twentieth-century capitalism.

WORKING ASSUMPTIONS

It seems best to continue with a system in which the demand, supply and valuation curves of all firms are at all times, and throughout the economy, identical, not only as to shape but also as to position. The object of the assumption is to clear away analytical difficulties associated with differential growth rates. We well understand, of course, that we may thus be suppressing the signal with the noise. It is possible that ever-present differences between individual firms represent an essential feature of the process by which the macro-economy attempts to find dynamic equilibrium. But, if so, we shall be no worse placed than many other macro theorists, and, specifically, we assume that:

1. Every firm in the economy is at all times growing at the same rate, earning the same rate of return and displaying the same valuation ratio; the common micro growth rate is also the macro or 'national' rate.
2. The common growth rate is equivalent to the growth rate of output of real total demand and of the capital stock measured in book value at constant prices – technical progress, if any, is always neutral.
3. All firms are identically motivated – whether the utility functions are 'traditional', managerial or mixed, they are the same in all firms as to character, form and quantitative specification.
4. There exists some mechanism (for example, otherwise neutral government fiscal policy) for guaranteeing the maintenance at all times of 'Keynesian' full employment: the average utilization of capacity is always high and stable, that is, never afflicted by demand deficiency.

We then define the following analytical tools:

1. The *partial demand curve* – the common demand–growth curve of the individual firm, based on the assumption that if the firm's policy were changed, the policies of all other firms would remain constant. Associated with the partial demand curve we define a corresponding *partial valuation curve*.

2. The *partial utility function* – the firm's utility function as between val-
    uation ratio and growth rate, based on the assumption that the policies
    and behaviour of all other firms would remain constant.
3. The *general demand curve* – a demand–growth curve for an individ-
    ual firm, drawn up on the assumption that policy changes designed to
    move the firm along the partial demand curve would, in fact, be pre-
    cisely copied by all other firms; with this is associated a correspond-
    ing *general valuation curve*.
4. The *general utility function* – a utility function based on the assump-
    tion that any change in growth rate or valuation ratio occurring in the
    individual firm would lead to identical changes by other firms.

The assumptions then imply that all the above curves are at all times the
same for all firms. The 'general' curves are purely analytical conceptions,
and will not generally be known or appreciated by individual firms; they
are, however, from the analyst's point of view, both objective and, in principle, ascertainable. The experiment required to ascertain the total valuation curve would be that of inducing all firms to vary diversification rate,
profit-margin variables and financial-policy variables simultaneously and
equally, in such a way as would have been expected to produce the same
balanced movements along the corresponding partial demand curves.
Then, after allowing due time for the disturbance to subside, the observed
change in the common valuation ratio would indicate the total valuation
curve.

The shape and position of the curves is clearly affected by familiar
macro factors. A rise in the general level of prices relatively to that of
wages will raise both general and partial demand curves, even though the
micro relationships which generated these curves remained unaffected. (If
all prices rose relatively to wages, a higher profit margin could be maintained for a given diversification rate and success ratio.) And provided the
change did not in some way affect financial conditions (which, of course,
it well might), the valuation curve would be affected correspondingly. But
the valuation curve could also be shifted independently of the demand
curve by some general change in financial conditions, or, for that matter,
by a change in the supply price of take-over raiders.

It should also be noted that some movements along the general demand
curve may also imply changes in distributive shares, more particularly
changes in the ratio of profits to national income. As we move along the
demand curve we vary both the rate of return and the capital–output ratio,
and these changes in turn imply a definite variation of the average profit
margin, which is, of course, the share of profits after netting out transac-

tions in intermediate goods. For example, the position of zero growth on the demand curve is virtually the position in post-classical, long-run equilibrium – that is, the position where 'normal' profits are being earned by every firm in every industry, 'super' profits having been universally eliminated. Positions further to the right, such as, for example, the position at the peak of the demand curve, are comparable to post-classical, short-run equilibrium, generalized from the single industry to the economy at large; the short-run conditions, however, have become permanent. Profits are always abnormal, because, under conditions of growth, there are always some products that are sufficiently new that 'normal' conditions have not yet been reached in their case. In other words, at the peak of the demand curve, the 'degree of monopoly' is higher than at all positions to the left, and prices generally higher relatively to wages. We seem, therefore, to be required to distinguish between this kind of change and the kind implied in a bodily movement of the curve. But as the problem only arises to the left of the peak (to the right, the profit rate declines because capital and other costs rise while the margin remains largely unchanged), we shall more or less ignore it. We shall generally assume that a given 'position' of the general demand curve implies the same macro-distributive situation (share of profits in the national income) wherever the firms are located on the curve; provided, of course, that they are not located to the left of the peak (see above).

THE AGGREGATE RETENTION RATIO

We have already hinted that the general assumptions surrounding the micro-model seem to imply that the corporate leaders, acting collectively (but not collusively), may have considerable freedom to vary the aggregate retention ratio without running into serious restraints. In other words, it is possible that if all corporate retention ratios were to rise together, the effect on market rates of discount would be very considerably less than in the case where one ratio rises in isolation. Similarly, if all valuation ratios happened to decline together, the *ex post* decline in utility would be considerably less than where such a change occurred in isolation, because, of course, the associated increase in average individual probability of take-over would then be considerably damped. In other words, it is likely that the negative slope of the general valuation curve is considerably smaller, arithmetically, than that of the corresponding partial curve, and that the shape of the general utility function is considerably more biased towards growth than that of the partial function. But although both will thus probably be positioned more favourably to growth than the partial curves, only if the firms had some means of colluding could they necessarily take advantage of the fact.

I would also argue that, if a change in the aggregate retention ratio does for some reason occur, there will be a definite and permanent effect on the national propensity to save. This is more controversial. It means that, in the event of a rise, for example, in the ratio, any offsetting variation in the propensity to save out of *personal* income (distributed profits plus non-profit incomes) will be insufficient to offset the national effect. Looked at in this light, the propensity to save out of profits takes on some rather new colours. It is now considerably influenced by decisions of individuals who are not thereby choosing between present and future consumption in the ordinary sense. The point is of such importance as to deserve further argument.

What we are saying, in effect, is that *given* the overall distribution of income between wages and profits, the particular legal and institutional arrangements of the corporate constitution do have a definite effect on overall savings. For example, suppose a law were passed requiring corporations to distribute all profits annually, but at the same time permitting them to make automatic 'rights' issues, designed to bring in any sum up to the full amount of the dividend, on terms such that any shares not taken up were cancelled rather than reissued to the public at large. To subscribe, however, shareholders would be required to undertake annually all the transactions involved in subscribing to any new issue: they would not be permitted to make any arrangement whereby their dividend was automatically reinvested.

Evidently, investors' reactions to such a change would be varied. Some would subscribe to all their rights, some to part. Of those who did not subscribe in full, some would reinvest the difference between their receipts under the new system and the old in other securities; some would increase their consumption. (It is important to note that reactions must be different from those to typical new issues under present conditions: under present conditions, 'rights' issues raise only a small proportion of total corporate finance, and tend to be confined to situations where valuation ratios are unusually favourable.) Few would deny that a considerable redirection of funds might occur, but many would argue that the national propensity to save would remain unaffected: consumption, it would be argued, would not increase, because the savings withdrawn from the one outlet would merely be sent elsewhere, and if some individuals did increase their personal consumption, others would reduce it. The debate is important, because unless the national propensity to save is flexible, the corporations cannot, in fact, influence the growth rate through their influence on the retention ratio, except indirectly via changes in the share of profit in the national income.

If, on the other hand, the power to influence retention ratios does give direct influence over the propensity to save (we use the word direct in the sense of implying that the propensity could be affected even if distributive shares were fixed), then, when the retention ratio is collectively varied (a movement along the total valuation curve), the macro-warranted-growth conditions must be affected. The importance of this conclusion lies in the fact that, in previous growth models employing a 'capitalist propensity to save', such as Kaldor's,[4] the concept was thought of as representing (cap-italists') consumption decisions which were quite independent of invest-ment decisions. When these decisions are made by managers who are themselves major investment-decision-takers, their significance is changed drastically. The position becomes more similar to that implied in the neo-Marxist type of model, such as Robinson's,[5] where no consumption from profits is admitted at all. I believe my own view to be the most realistic, because I believe that, in the imaginary institutional situation formulated above, some families would definitely increase their consumption, and while others would not, it is difficult to see a good reason for expecting any of these in fact to save more. By generalization, we therefore presume that under the circumstances of both today and yesterday, long-run varia-tions in the retention ratio must cause long-run variations in the national propensity to save (in the same direction, of course, but smaller in magni-tude), even when distributive shares are held constant. But, as the pre-sumption is controversial, we shall also analyse the anti-hypothesis, implying, in effect, that although the general demand curve is 'normal', the general valuation curve is cut off sharply at a point that depends on the macro-distributive situation. At this point, the corporations are taking savings from the economy at a rate such that any attempt to accelerate expansion by further raising the retention ratio would inevitably be frus-trated in one way or another: to pass the limit it would be necessary to raise retentions to 100 per cent, whereupon, of course, all valuation ratios would become zero.

The alternative case, (in which I believe), I shall call only 'partly restricted', because, of course, we are not proposing to assume that, if technical conditions permitted, the managers could have any growth rate they wanted. We shall assume that the power to influence collectively the national propensity to save is a limited one, and that the total valuation curve is not, therefore, without a downward curvature. But in absolute contrast to the 'fully restricted' case, for reasons given above its down-ward curvature is less steep than that of the corresponding partial curve. In both cases, of course, the total valuation curves are based on 'given' total and partial demand curves, which means, *inter alia*, that they are based on a given share of profits in the national income. In the fully restricted case, the firm cannot move past the cut-off point in any circumstances; hence, growth cannot be increased without a change of distributive shares. In the 'partly restricted' case, the corporate sector has some freedom to vary the growth rate (subject to technical conditions), provided it is prepared to accept associated variations in the general level of the valuation ratio.

NATURAL AND QUASI-NATURAL RATES OF GROWTH

Since the original work of Harrod and Domar,[6] most contemporary growth models have been based on some development of the idea of a 'natural' growth rate. This is the maximum growth rate permitted the economy by technical and social conditions, or, more precisely, by the sum of the growth rates of population and of output per head. In the original conception, these factors were essentially exogenous: the growth rate of productivity, for example, was not affected by variables within the model, such as the distribution of income, nor was population growth governed by any kind of Malthusian relationship with the growth rate of consumption. As Harrod and Domar saw the problem, an economy need not grow at its natural rate, but cannot grow faster, and problems of considerable analytical interest arose from possible instabilities associated with conflicts between the natural growth rate and the rate consistent with a moving Keynesian equilibrium (that is, in Harrod's language, the 'warranted' rate). Subsequent writers have shown how such conflicts might be resolved by variations in the share of profits in the national income, which would lead in turn to variations in the national propensity to save, and thus to adjustments of the warranted rate itself.

Most contemporary writers, however, accept some form of exogenous growth rate, albeit with considerable modifications. In the Harrod–Domar models, as usually set out, technical progress is associated with capital accumulation in such a way that the growth rate of capital required to support the 'natural' growth rate of output per head happens to be equal to that of output, so that the capital–output ratio remains constant over time and the progress is said to be 'neutral'. Consequently, the conditions of Keynesian equilibrium also remain conveniently constant. One way of rationalizing this type of model is to imagine that at any instant of time only a single technique of production is known for each and every commodity, but that all are being improved continuously in a manner implying neutral changes in the factor ratios. Joan Robinson, and James Meade, Robert Solow and Trevor Swan,[7] provided more comprehensive arrangements in which there were always production functions – that is, ranges of alternative techniques; these, however, could shift bodily over time as a result of the development of knowledge. At any given moment in time the economy was to choose a position on the function in such a way that the rate of return was maximized at the micro level. It was then possible to show that, provided the function and its movement took restricted forms, the system could be got into moving equilibrium in which growth rates of output and capital stock were equal and constant, and so also the rate of return. Thus the apparent conditions of 'neutral' growth would be observed, but only as the coincidental result of a special condition on the trend. Disliking this feature, Kaldor,[8] introduced a 'technical progress' function, to be contrasted with a production function, in which the neutrality or otherwise of progress became endogenous to the model. If the 'attempted' growth rate of the capital stock was rapid, relatively to that of the population, labour would tend to become scarce, and the inventions adopted would tend to be capital-using (that is, to involve a rising capital–output ratio), and vice versa. There was, however, one growth rate at which neutrality was possible, and since this was the only one consistent with a stable moving equilibrium, Kaldor set out to investigate how the economy might find and maintain it. For the purpose he made use of more complex thriftiness assumptions, but the 'neutral' rate remained exogenous, and the system was thus basically similar to its predecessors.

If the dynamic technical conditions are in one way or another exogenous, the analyst already knows that one growth rate only is consistent with dynamic equilibrium. He is then left with two types of question to consider: what are the other conditions, such as distribution of income, necessary to sustain the equilibrium; and what are its stability characteristics? Most writers have to some extent attempted to answer both types of question simultaneously, but L. Pasinetti[9] has recently shown that it is often fruitful to keep them separate: he has thus been able to show that if 'workers' make savings and receive interest thereon, the conditions of dynamic equilibrium involve not only the distribution of income but also that of property, a conclusion whose further theoretical implications appear to be considerable. We shall adopt the same approach here, and shall concentrate, in fact, entirely on the first type of question, making no attempt to contribute to the discussion of stability.

Few of the previous writers were entirely satisfied with the various forms of exogenous progress with which they had been compelled to endow their models, for none really believed it.[10] As the reader is aware, we have in this book almost ignored the topic, because, at the micro level, if progress is occurring, the dynamic conditions for the individual firm do not change unless the wage–profit relationship changes: provided real wages are rising with productivity at the macro level, the micro conditions are constant. We also deliberately evaded the very considerable problem of defining progress in face of a constantly changing product list. Most readers must have realized by now that these evasions are permissible only if the rate of progress (assuming it to be capable of a definition of some kind) experienced by the individual firm is independent of all the other micro variables, and, in particular, independent of the diversification rate. In reality, this is most unlikely. When new products are created, the firm must partly invent a new production function, and if no diversification occurs, no new functions will be invented. (In the case of imitative products, the technology may also be imitated, but improvements might nevertheless occur.) It follows that in moving along a total demand curve, the associated changes in the average rate of diversification and of new product creation (these are not identical, because much diversification is imitative, and therefore self-cancelling) are likely to be *causally* connected with variations in technical progress at the macro-level. It is, in fact, widely accepted that there is a close connection between innovation on the production side of the economic system and innovation on the consumption side: the desire to satisfy newly-discovered latent needs not infrequently stimulates technical inventions, and technical inventions themselves not infrequently suggest new products and hence, ultimately, foster new wants. Let us therefore consider the possibility that the overall rate of diversification, which, it will be remembered, is the aggregated form of a genuine micro decision variable, causes changes in the rate of technical progress. For convenience, let us do without a production or technical progress function, and assume that, whatever progress does occur, it is always neutral. But this neutral, natural rate is now endogenous to the diversification rate.

The diversification rate, however, has yet other implications of macro importance. When we move along the partial demand curve, the overall diversification rate is increasing, but, as we have seen, the corresponding movement along the total demand curve is the result of successful differentiated diversification only, because much diversification is imitative. In other words, as soon as we move any distance along the total demand curve away from the origin, the implied process of macro growth is essentially the result of new product creation, of the first satisfaction of new wants, rather than of increased satisfaction of old wants. We are therefore postulating a definite macro-pattern of consumer behaviour. We are saying that, whatever the growth rate of their purchasing power, families will not accelerate the growth of their consumption expenditure beyond a certain point unless tempted by suitable new products. In the absence of temptation, the consumption function would drift downwards, and in an extreme case we might imagine that the marginal propensity to save would become unity. The economic and social reasons for this were described classically by James Duesenberry,[11] and are also implicit, of course, in the modified theory of demand developed above in Chapter 4. The implication is not so much that the diversification rate causally determines the propensity to save, but rather that, for any given growth rate of total demand, a particular diversification rate is required for any long-run stability in the consumption function. The level of the function (as given by the propensities to save out of the various forms of personal income and the distribution of income between them) may be otherwise determined, but if the level is to be free of drift it must be associated with a given diversification rate. If the diversification rate were to be too low, the function would drift in favour of savings; and if too high, in favour of consumption. The extreme case, where demand can grow only if new products are created (that is, the demand for old products is always so saturated that no increase in real income can affect it at all), is by no means fantastic. We call the overall diversification rate necessary to maintain stability of personal consumption functions (that is, stability in the national propensity to save for any given distribution of income), the 'required' diversification rate: it is a function of the desired growth rate, and can be conceived in macro terms only.

The required diversification rate is thus a function of the desired growth rate, with slope increasing in the general fashion of inverted micro demand–growth curves: as growth is accelerated, the public's palate becomes increasingly unresponsive, and an increasing proportion of new products fails. Eventually, we should assume, as the micro demand–growth curves flattened, so a point would come at the macro level where the indicated growth rate had become so rapid that no amount of innovatory effort would be capable of preventing the growth of demand from lagging behind. The effects of this non-linearity are displayed in the declining profit rate on the total demand curve, as increasing proportions of real resources are devoted to the maintenance of the optimum success rate; but this variation, we have seen, is independent of the share of profit in the national income, because on that segment of the curve distributive shares are not affected by movements along it.

The diversification rate is ultimately the result of managerial micro choices. In a sense, it measures the strength of the managerial effort to grow, and must be microeconomically consistent with the managerial utility function. We might even go as far as to say that it reflects the managers' 'animal spirits'. Is it, however, in fact free at the macro level? When managers choose their diversification rates to maximize their utility functions, are they or are they not merely choosing a position that had to be found anyway, because macro equilibrium required the various general curves (and here, associated partial curves) to find certain positions? Clearly, where a natural growth rate is exogenous this must, in equilibrium, be the case. There is only one equilibrium growth rate, so there is only one sustainable position on the general demand curve, and therefore, if macro equilibrium is to be maintained, either this curve or the utility function or both must somehow be adjusted to ensure that the partial equilibria of the individual firms in fact occur at this growth rate. What, then, is the position when technical progress is endogenous?

The answer is that we now know that steady growth requires the diversification rate and associated growth rate to satisfy two conditions: the growth rate of real output, and hence purchasing power, must be equal to the natural rate, which is in turn *determined* by the diversification rate, but every growth rate also 'requires' a certain diversification rate in order to maintain stability in the consumption function. Therefore the growth rate and diversification rate must be such that the diversification rate is equal to the rate 'required' by the growth rate, and the growth rate is, in turn, the result of technical progress at the rate consistent with the diversification rate. We call such a growth rate a *quasi-natural rate*, and the associated diversification rate a *quasi-natural diversification rate*. We do not ask how an economy may find such a rate, but do insist that it is a valid requirement of equilibrium growth. Its reality may be seen in recent economic history in the USA, where there is considerable evidence that, because the condition either has not been or cannot be met, consumers are increasingly reluctant to maintain consumption demand at the level required by the productive rate of progress.

It is thus perfectly possible that an economy may reach a situation where, until some major industrial or socioeconomic revolution occurs, no quasi-natural rate exists. Disequilibrium states will then become chronic. This is one way, in fact, of explaining the post-Keynesian condition of 'secular stagnation'. But it also seems possible that, under other circumstances, there may exist within limits a continuous range of growth rates, all of which are quasi-natural. Within the range, small changes in the diversification rate would always generate changes in the rate of technical progress that were precisely consistent with the change in growth rate of demand for which the new diversification rate was the required rate. Productive innovations would have the qualitative characteristics necessary for consumers always to want to exploit them in full. The condition might be no accident, but caused rather by a natural balance or lack of dichotomy in the two processes, productive innovations occurring because goods were wanted, and goods becoming wanted as a result of becoming available. We think it unlikely, however, that this could be true over an indefinite range of growth rates. For example, at very low rates of diversification, it would seem that the rate of technical progress should become insensitive to variations, while the demand-consistent growth rate should not. At the other extreme, at high rates of diversification it seems unlikely that the demand-consistent and technical growth rates would begin to become insensitive together, although it is not easy to think of reasons for expecting one or the other relationship to flatten first. Provided, however, that either one or the other became insensitive eventually, we should again face a definite upper limit on the growth rate, but this, we shall see, would be only partly analogous to the orthodox natural rate.

Three conditions may therefore be distinguished. There may be no quasi-natural rate; there may be one quasi-natural rate; and there may be, within limits, a continuous range of such rates. In the first case, which is pathological, the economy is unable to find any kind of dynamic equilibrium until the position is rectified in some way. In the second, provided the one rate can be found and the surrounding conditions are not unduly unstable, the equilibrium requirements are similar to those required in the case of an exogenous natural rate; either case may loosely be described as one in which the macro growth rate is inflexible. Although the partial demand curves may generally be formed in accordance with the micro theory, on the total demand curve only one position is possible.

In the third case, which we may describe as one where the growth rate is flexible, there remains an upper limit which might at first sight appear to have similar properties to those of the single rate in the inflexible case. This would represent a half truth only. The natural rate in post-Keynesian dynamics is more than a maximum. It is also the minimum rate at which the economy must grow if it is to remain healthy. In Robinson's evocative phrase,[12] an economy failing to grow at this rate is failing to meet the conditions for a 'Golden Age': only if total output is growing at a rate equal to the sum of the growth rates of productivity and population is the demand for labour growing as fast as the population; hence, if the condition is not met, employment is being offered to a continuously declining proportion of the people. Not so in an economy growing less rapidly than at its maximum quasi-natural rate. Consider, for example, a downward variation from this position. The diversification rate is reduced, so also is the consistent growth rate of demand, and also, in precise balance, the growth rate of output per worker. Therefore, the growth rate of employment remains unchanged. We are saying, in other words, that there may exist a range of growth rates, all of which, provided other equilibrium conditions are satisfied, can well be 'golden'. Furthermore, since movement among these rates is associated with variations in the overall diversification rate, which is in turn derived from a micro decision-variable, it is possible that managers, in maximizing utility, may influence the magnitude of the actual growth rate associated with macro equilibrium.

In mildly taxonomic fashion, we therefore consider four possibilities: the case of the inflexible growth rate combined with that of 'fully restricted' thriftiness assumptions; the inflexible growth rate combined with only partly restricted savings assumptions; and the two alternative thriftiness cases combined with the flexible growth rate assumption. We take them in order.

INFLEXIBLE GROWTH RATE AND FULLY RESTRICTED THRIFT

We must first be a little more specific, both about the institutional conditions and the effects on the various curves. We assume that equity shares are widely held, but the distribution of total portfolios among the population at large is nevertheless very unequal and closely associated with a corresponding inequality of personal incomes. Personal savings functions are associated with personal position in the income-and-wealth hierarchy, but shareholders, however, behave as if their functions related to a total 'income' consisting of their dividends, their equity in undistributed profits and their personally-earned non-profit incomes: any variation in the average corporate retention ratio is always precisely offset by a corresponding variation in savings from personal income. Consequently, the total savings of this class cannot be varied by the retention ratio. Then if, as we shall assume, the ratio of their personally-earned incomes to the national income is exogenous, the ratio of their savings to the national income can be endogenous only through endogenous variations in the ratio of total profits to national income; that is, only through variations in the wage–price relationship.

We have already indicated the general way in which this type of situation affects the general demand and valuation curves: the valuation curve must be so shaped as to make growth at faster than a certain rate impossible with any positive valuation ratio. With a given wage–price relationship this rate is equivalent to the Harrodian warranted rate. The general demand curve is shaped similarly to the corresponding partial curve, but the associated general valuation curve is at some point cut off sharply. When the macro wage–price relationship varies in favour of prices, profit margin associated with all given micro demand–growth curves increases, the general demand curve rises bodily and there is a corresponding effect on the general valuation curve. But, because the share of profits in the national income has also varied, so has the national savings ratio, and this leads to a secondary effect on the relationship between general valuation curve; and total demand curve, consequently, as already indicated, the vertical segment of the general valuation curve moves leftwards. But, and it is an important but, we know that no valuation curve can ever cut the horizontal axis to the right of the corresponding demand curve, because it is impossible to have a positive valuation ratio without a positive rate of return. Therefore, this sideways movement of the valuation curve is restricted by the position of the demand curve. The latter, however, cannot move sideways unless we drop our original micro assumption that the internal administrative restraint on growth at some rate becomes absolute. If we accept the absolute administrative restraint as a valid macrophenomenon (in effect, it is the maximum rate at which qualified people can be absorbed effectively into the system of organizations), then there is an absolute limit to the extent to which the valuation curve can be pushed leftwards: as such a movement develops, increasingly large distributive changes are required to produce a given displacement, because, although the profit margin is rising, increasing managerial inefficiency is also causing the capital–output ratio to rise (and with increasing severity). We call this limit the maximum administrative growth rate.

The problem of dynamic equilibrium, then, is to get the vertical segment of the valuation curve to correspond to the inflexible growth rate. If this can be achieved by distributive changes, all well and good. If not, chronic disequilibrium, or at least the failure of 'Golden Age' conditions, is inevitable. Following Kaldor,[13] we do not investigate the possible mechanism of distributive adjustment in detail, but merely assert that the existence of some such mechanism is required. It is also worth noting that 'Golden Age' conditions are impossible if the quasi-natural rate exceeds the maximum administrative rate, and while our theory is not, of course, intended for application to the problems of underdeveloped countries, there is here a clear analogy to the case of a country where unemployment is rising because 'entrepreneurial' expansion cannot keep pace with the rising population of workers. Otherwise, we merely reach the familiar equilibrium conditions: there is an equilibrium 'position' of the valuation curve, implying an equilibrium share of profits in the national income; and the latter will be higher, the higher the inflexible growth rate and/or the lower the propensities to save of the several classes.

When a transformation curve is cut off sharply in the manner assumed, it is generally likely that maximum utility will be found at this point, or at some point rather close to the corner. If so, the managerial utility function provides few additional complications. But if managers were very strongly security-conscious, this conclusion might not hold: rather flat indifference curves would find tangency on a partial valuation curve at a point corresponding to a position more to the right on the total curve. The case then merges into the one where savings are only partly restricted, which we now discuss.

INFLEXIBLE GROWTH RATE, THRIFTINESS PARTLY RESTRICTED

Consider a situation where the general demand and valuation curves are shaped more or less like the corresponding partial curves, subject only to the usual modifications of slopes caused by all firms moving together. The managerial utility function is 'normal', and, whether or not there is any effective horizontal segment in the partial indifference curves, there is no such limit on the corresponding total curves: provided all go together, there is no minimum valuation ratio which the managerial class would not be prepared to pass at a price. This does not mean that the 'traditional' raiders whom we have presumed to remain lurking in the economy are not feared at all, but merely that at no point on the general valuation curve would fear of them become infinitely intense.

Then suppose that the general and associated partial curves happen to be anywhere. Each firm, in maximizing utility, will find a tangency solution in the micro diagram, and as all the positions are, on our assumptions, the same, this implies a unique situation on the general curves. There is a unique growth rate, profit rate, profit margin and capital–output ratio. But this 'desired' rate of growth may not, of course, be equal to the quasi-natural rate. In order to find equilibrium, we must again invoke some macro distributive adjustment leading the general demand and valuation curves to set up partial curves in such a situation that the tangency solution does, in fact, produce growth at the quasi-natural rate and no other.

Assuming that such an equilibrium can, in fact, be found, the conditions do then imply several rather suggestive theorems. For example:

1. It remains true that the faster the quasi-natural rate, the greater (other things being equal) is the equilibrium share of profits in the national income.

2. But one of the 'other things' is now clearly the character of the managerial utility function, as represented in the relative strength of the desires for growth and 'security', respectively – the greater the managerial preference for growth (steep indifference curves), the lower the share of profits required to sustain any given, inflexible, quasi-natural rate and vice versa.
3. As a corollary, 'classical' behaviour (that is, a utility function containing only the valuation ratio (indifference curves all horizontal)) must always require an equilibrium share of profits greater than that required by any form of 'managerial' behaviour.

These results may be further explained as follows. When managers move leftwards through the diagram, they partly create the savings necessary for acceleration by appropriate variations of retention ratio and other similar adjustments to financial policy. But in aggregating the stock-market equations in order to generate the general valuation curve, we have not assumed that these additional savings can be obtained costlessly: they are achieved, in effect, at the cost of a rise in the 'macro' rate of interest. In effect, the 'national' propensity to save is 'determined' by attitudes of basic thriftiness, by the distribution of income, and by the interest rate, and these set up a contingent relationship between warranted growth rate and general valuation ratio. But as the result of the existence of a managerial utility function, there are restrictions on the combinations of growth rate and valuation ratio which can be consistent with individual partial equilibrium. If these are not respected, macro equilibrium will be violated by the attempts of the individual firms to adjust their partial positions, thus moving the system along the general curve. To meet the restrictions consistently with any one (quasi-natural) growth rate, the system's degrees of freedom are exhausted, and the share of profits in the national income is therefore determined.

This explains (1) above. If, however, managers have relatively strong preferences for growth, they mind less the consequences of a high interest rate and low general valuation ratios, hence more of the adjustment to equilibrium can be carried by increased retentions, and less needs to be carried by macro-distribution variation. The less the managers fear or respect stockholders, the more the equilibrium distribution of income is likely to favour those sections of society whose equity holdings are below average. This explains (2).

We then see that, in shifting towards the classical case, the implied gain in shareholder welfare is intimately associated with an increase in the distributive share of the *rentier* class. Any given natural or quasi-natural growth path generates various time paths of absolute consumption for the various classes in society, according to their distributive shares. If the shareholding class can persuade managers to pay more attention to its interests, it can induce them to take actions that imply an equilibrium macro distribution more favourable to itself: it then expresses the improvement in stock-market terms by placing a higher market value on any given collection of physical assets. In this sense, then, it is true that the managerial revolution favours the 'workers'. More precisely, the workers are favoured provided the share of executive compensation in the national income is not increased to an offsetting extent. Managerial utility associated with growth is derived from prospective gains in financial compensation, from power, from prestige, and from the satisfactions of professional competence. Provided, therefore, that the relative weight of the non-financial elements is significant, and provided the initial share of executive salaries in the national income is modest, it seems likely that institutional changes favouring the expression of more 'managerial' utility functions would be likely to yield at least some net gain for the majority of the population – that is, for the class who are neither substantial property owners nor managers. There is here, perhaps, an element of harmony of interest between workers and managers which may at least partly qualify their more apparent social and political conflicts. *Rentiers* depend on workers for their *rentes*; and managers for their livelihood. In a capitalist system, managers also depend partly on *rentiers* for capital supplies, but, as we have seen, ways have been found of greatly reducing the effectiveness of this dependence. Perhaps the managers' success in this respect reflects the knowledge that their services would be required even in a collectivist system, while those of shareholders would not.

A FLEXIBLE GROWTH MODEL

The main effect of a flexible growth rate, within the limits over which it applies, is the addition of a degree of freedom. The implications are not greatly different as between the two alternative thriftiness assumptions, so we concentrate the discussion on the second. What, then, is implied by partially restricted thriftiness and flexible growth?

The answer is extremely simple. If one degree of freedom is gained, the macro income distribution need no longer be endogenous. If the macro distribution is exogenous, as was generally assumed by Keynesians until around 1955, the system is over-determined unless the growth rate is flexible: indeed, this is one way of characterizing Harrodian instability. But the escape from over-determination via the assumption of the existence of a macrodistributive adjustment mechanism has never been entirely easy because there is so much evidence, at least in the post-1918 world,[14] that the wage–price relation is not easily changed. Monopolistic and oligopolistic behaviour on the part of both employers and workers may well lead to a carve-up of the national cake which has no particular rationality and is yet remarkably rigid. Thus, while determining the share of profits in the national income as an equilibrium condition associated with growth remains an idea of considerable charm, we can by no means be sure that it represents the solution of the mystery. (It is significant that Kaldor, for example, in some 50 000 words in all he has published on the subject, has devoted less than 5000 to his account of the *modus operandi* of the distributive mechanism: in effect, he relies on the argument that, in a system that is inherently unstable, the historical observation of long periods of Keynesian near-full employment proves the existence of a stabilizing factor, and that this can only be the wage–price mechanism – an argument, it should be noted, which is not without force.)[15]

But we are not interested here in Keynesian under-employment (that is, under-utilization of a given capital stock). We are interested in the possibility that the system might have a dynamic equilibrium at some quasi-natural rate less than the maximum. Suppose that the wage–price relation is, in fact, rigid, and that the share of profits in the national income is thus, from our point of view, exogenous. Then the micro utility function will determine a unique or 'desired' position on the total valuation curve (which is now itself exogenous), and, provided this is within the range of quasi-natural rates, such an equilibrium is perfectly sustainable. We are then back to earlier days in the history of economic thought, when distribution was thought to determine growth rather than the reverse. Alternatively, we do not have to assume that the macro distribution is totally incapable of endogenous adjustment; we may merely assume that it is somewhat 'sticky', and then let it settle down at an arbitrary level and see what happens. Provided the level is consistent with a possible quasi-natural rate, nothing happens. All the conditions for a Robinsonian 'Golden Age' are present, and no forces exist to cause disequilibrium. There is therefore no reason to suppose that the wage–price relationship will be affected by macro pressures, nor is there any special reason to expect the system to be driven to the quasi-natural maximum.

The significance of the result is that the rate of growth is then in a genuine causal sense determined not only by the distribution of income, but also by the growth propensities of the people who manage industry. This is a conclusion which would be acceptable to informed laymen, but has proved surprisingly difficult to rationalize in terms of economic theory. In both Keynesian and neoclassical models, capitalist micro behaviour has an important implicit role, but, in almost all the extant examples, the underlying properties of the system are such that equilibrium can only be found at a growth rate that is ultimately exogenous. The role of behaviour is largely confined to influencing the stability characteristics of the system, and any influence over actual growth rates then derives from the fact that, unless behaviour is stabilizing, growth rates below the exogenous maximum may well become chronic. We do not claim very much for the development suggested above. It amounts to saying little more than if the growth rate is flexible, it is flexible. But perhaps we have managed to add a little something.

SOLOW AND ODAGIRI

Two distinguished economic theorists subsequently built important models based on elements of the foundations offered in the original book. In 1971, Robert Solow published 'Some Implications of Alternative Criteria for the Firm',[16] *and in 1980 Hiro Odagiri published* The Theory of Growth in a Corporate Economy.[17]

Solow's paper represented a typically elegant contribution, which has been much admired in the economics profession. With the benefit of hindsight it can be seen as a significant contribution to the theory of general equilibrium under imperfect competition in the goods market, although, for reasons that will be seen, I personally have reservations concerning its relevance to managerial capitalism. (To be frank, the author almost certainly did not intend it to be.)

In modern terms, the model can be described as follows. The economy consists of a large number of firms, each producing, under constant returns to scale with constant capital–output ratio, a different, single, product. Every firm is engaged in imperfect competition with every other. Before introducing the theory of growth, the static general equilibrium of this type of economy can be modelled as a conjectural or Nash-competitive equilibrium in which each firm sets a price on the conjecture that all other firms' prices are constant. Equilibrium exists when, on the conjecture, no firm desires to change a price. Assume conjectural prices are set to maximize gross profits: that is, set marginal cost equal to conjectural marginal revenue. In the result, the gross profit margin (share of gross profit in price) is the reciprocal of the conjectural elasticity of demand. There is a constant amount of real capital in the economy, but it is mobile. In the process of adjusting their size for the purpose of conjec-

tural profit maximization, firms can acquire or dispose of capital. Consequently, the sizes of firms and the distribution of capital are optimized to maximize the total profit in the economy, for the given total capital stock, and thus the welfare of the shareholding class. (If the firms had identical, isoelestic demand curves, they would all be the same size.) If shares were equally distributed among households, their property income would be maximized relative to their employment income and, interestingly, so would the degree of 'excess' consumption of leisure caused by the excess of price over the value of the marginal product of labour.

Now Solow introduced a minimalist interpretation of the idea that firms, by spending money out of their profits, can influence the location of their demand curves. More precisely, he assumed that, by spending a constant proportion of their gross revenue on marketing, the demand curve could be made to grow (that is, quantity demanded at any given price) at a constant exponential rate, with the higher the marketing-expenditure share, the higher the rate. Solow then applied the famous formula set out in Equation (6.6) in Chapter 6 above,[18] subject to a restriction that the growth rate may not approach the interest rate, to choose a growth rate which, for any given initial size of the firm, will maximize its market value. He then solved the equations for a simultaneous solution optimizing both initial size and growth rate. He thus optimized the size of the firm through all points in time and thus, similarly, the total value of shares.

Apart from the obvious fact that this is a normative neoclassical model (which does not, however, produce Pareto optimality) my fundamental difficulties with it are that the firms are single-product, and that because the launching of new products is a dynamically constrained 'growth' activity, the model cannot be adapted simply to a world of diversification. The marketing-expenditure decision is also conjectural, the conjecture being that other firms' prices and marketing expenditures are constant. This results in a path of point-in-time equilibria. But surely, while firms will not anticipate this in their conjecture, their marketing expenditures will tend to cancel out and the whole effect to decay. The demand-led growth of the system will, it seems to me, then converge to some exogenously given value. In the absence of new products, it seems unlikely that the marketing expenditure will have a significant role in sustaining the growth of demand. Furthermore, because there is no 'supply-side' effect from the growth efforts of firms, there is no technological spill over. The natural rate of growth is therefore inflexible and is, in fact, the rate to which the system will converge. Given that the distribution of income between profits and wages is already determined, the way is open for an imperfect-competition version of an exogenous-growth model, perhaps a version of the celebrated model of Robert Solow which was referred to in his citation for the Nobel Prize![19]

Odagiri's major book was a tour de force *of comprehensive micro–macro modelling. It has already been partly discussed in the new Introduction.*[20] *Basing himself on a neoclassical macro production function which determined the general discount rate, he formalized the managerial utility function as maximizing the discounted value of future management earnings from the firm subject to the hazard of take-over, which latter depended on the valuation ratio and an exogenous barrier to take-over in the form of the premium that raiders must pay over the current market price of shares. Applying these concepts to the V–g frontier, he determined the managerial-utility-maximizing growth rate of the representative firm, and then boldly assumed that this would be the natural rate of the economy – the natural rate is perfectly flexible and fully endogenous. Also endogenous are a wide range of micro- and macroeconomic variables, including the distribution of income and, of course, the total value of shares.*

It is a fundamental theorem of such a model that the higher the barriers to take-over, the faster the chosen growth rate of the representative firm and the faster the growth rate of the economy! In a subsequent book[21] *Odagiri argued provocatively and interestingly, with the aid of a diagram similar to Figure 6.1B in Chapter 6 above,*[22] *that institutional barriers to take-over in Japan will have been a significant contributor to the country's original economic miracle. It is also worth noting that, since the mid-1950s, 'involuntary' take-over has been very difficult or impossible not only in the old West Germany but also in Western continental Europe generally. 'Easy' take-over has, in fact, been very much an Anglo-Saxon affair, and the 'conditional' or 'tender' offer was invented not in Wall Street but the in City of London. For the first quarter-century after the Second World War, the real performance of the West German economy was notoriously impressive. Real product per head of population grew fast, and, most significantly, so did per capita industrial output. By 1990 industrial output per head of population in the old West Germany was 20 per cent above that of the USA. And yet, the first, the very first attempted involuntary take-over in the whole history of the country did not occur until 1997,*[23] *significantly, after a period following 1990 in which, even allowing for the costs of reunification, all the economic indicators, including industrial output, went into reverse. It is now said that the German economy needs 'restructuring'. Maybe. But throughout all the time of the country's success, Germany had not one take-over. Similarly, of course, in*

Japan. The economic miracles of those two countries, and some others, were, it seems, miracles of managerial capitalism. High take-over activity is associated with slow growth. Cause or effect?

My review article of Odagiri's book was published in the Economic Journal *in November 1983. Naturally, I was, and remain, extremely favourably inclined towards it. It represents, in effect, a making of sense of my original final chapter, as reproduced above. It also made numerous improvements to the rigour of the micro theory. I suppose my main criticism would be that in the 'bold' assumption that the growth rate of the economy is simply equal to the desired growth rate of the representative firm, a fundamental question (namely, how much spill-over from firms to the economy?) is resolved by simple assumption. But it is certainly a better assumption than the one that supposes that, however hard firms try to grow, they can so so only at each others' expense, because the growth rate of the economy is fixed.*[24]

Notes and References

New Introduction

1. See Oliver Williamson (1964) *The Economics of Discretionary Behavior: Managerial Objectives in a Theory of the Firm* (Englewood Cliffs, NJ).
2. This remark was partly provoked by Frederick Scherer's flattering discussion of the topic in his 1988 article 'Corporate Takeovers: The Efficiency Arguments', in the *Journal of Economic Perspectives*, vol. 2, no. 1, Winter, pp. 69–82, but it is not entirely fair. Scherer suggested that I had found a 'third' market, after the goods market and the labour market, to close the economic system: that is, the market for corporate control. There is a suggestion that I imagined that market to be very effective, but not that I implied that it was perfect. Scherer was working from my 1963 article 'A Model of the Managerial Enterprise' in the *Quarterly Journal of Economics*, May, which preceded the publication of the book, and had not read, and did not cite, the book itself. When I re-read what I wrote in 1963, I found to my surprise that the language I used was in fact open to the interpretation in question. How our memories deceive us!
3. Edith Penrose (1958) *The Theory of the Growth of the Firm* (New York and Oxford).
4. See John Williamson (1996) 'Profit, Growth and Sales Maximization', *Economica*, vol. 33, February, pp. 1–16; Robert Solow (1971) 'Some Implications of Alternative Criteria for the Firm', in R. Marris and A. Wood (eds), *The Corporate Economy* (Cambridge, Mass. and London). Geoffrey Heal and Aubrey Silberston (1972) 'Alternative Managerial Objectives: An Exploratory Note', *Oxford Economic Papers*, vol. 24, no. 2, July, pp. 137–50; George Yarrow (1973) 'Managerial Utility Maximization under Uncertainty', *Economica*, vol. 40, May, pp. 155–73; G. Yarrow (1975) 'Growth Maximization and the Firm's Investment Function', *Southern Economic Journal*, vol. 41, April, pp. 689–94; G. Yarrow (1976) 'On the Predictions of Managerial Theories of the Firm', *Journal of Industrial Economics*, vol. 24, no. 4, June, pp. 267–79.
5. See R. Marris and Dennis Mueller (1980) 'The Corporation and Competition', *Journal of Economic Literature*, vol. 18, no. 1, March, pp. 32–63.
6. London 1997.
7. The following paragraphs represent a severe summary of my considered views on this subject. With Dr Heling Shi, I am currently under contract with Macmillan to attempt a work on the transition from twentieth to twenty-first-century capitalism, the first part of which will attempt to reinterpret the twentieth-century by means of a reconciliation of the managerial and transactions–cost paradigms.
8. A select reading list: R. Coase (1937), 'The Nature of the Firm', *Economica*, November; Oliver Williamson (1975) *Markets and Hierarchies*

166

(New York); O. Williamson (1981) 'The Modern Corporation', *Journal of Economic Literature*, December; *The Economic Institutions of Capitalism* (New York); Oliver Hart and Sanford Grossman (1986) 'The Costs and Benefits of Ownership: A Theory of Vertical and Lateral Integration', *Journal of Political Economy*, vol. 94, no. 4; Oliver Hart (1989), 'An Economist's Perspective on the Theory of the Firm', *Columbia Law Review*, November.

9. Coase (1937), p. 404.

10. The traditional method of restraining costs is the organizational structure of the pyramidal bureaucratic hierarchy. A number of writers (R. Monsen and A. Downs (1965) 'A Theory of Large Managerial Firms', *Journal of Political Economy*, June, pp. 221–36; R. Monsen, J. Chiu and D. Cooley (1968), 'The Effect of Separation of Ownership and Control on the Performance of the Large Firm', *Quarterly Journal of Economics*, vol. 82, pp. 435–51; Oliver Williamson (1970) *Corporate Control and Business Behavior* (Englewood Cliffs, NJ); James Mirrlees (1976) 'The Optimal Structure of Incentives and Authority Within an Organization', *Bell Journal of Economics*, Spring, vol. 7, no. 1, pp. 105–31.) have made much of the fact that the height of a pyramid necessarily increases with the length of the base. If the latter is considered to be a measure of the size of the firm, and the former of the length of the chain of command, it can be argued that total information error necessarily increases relative to the size of the firm as the latter increases absolutely. The problem with this law (Robin Marris and Dennis Mueller (1980) 'The Corporation and Competition', *Journal of Economic Literature*, Spring) is that it is semi-logarithmic, so the marginal effect is a diminishing one. Such a weak law might be counteracted by quite moderate opposing factors such as administrative economies of scale. Monsen and Downs argued that information errors were always opportunistically biased. Oliver Williamson, pursuing the same line of thought, provided a model in which information errors in the chain of command increased cumulatively. If the model's coefficients took on values in certain ranges, strong diseconomies of scale were predicted. But this was a particular, rather than a general model. Mirrlees discovered weak diseconomies of scale. It is my strong belief that many economists find any theory that suggests a general law of constant or increasing returns to scale psychologically distasteful. (But see *Increasing Returns*, report of a conference held at Monash University, Australia, 1985, for signs of a change of climate.)

11. Despite its title, all the examples given in Hart and Grossman (1986) relate to vertical integration. For a classic study of the role of diversification, see Adrian Wood (1971) 'Diversification, Merger and Research Expenditures: A Review of Empirical Evidence', Appendix C in R. Marris and A. Wood (eds), *The Corporate Economy*.

12. For a further discussion of the subsequent theoretical and empirical history of the theory of growth by diversification, please see the recent quotation from Dennis Mueller on page 20, I think it is fair to say that my theory has been 'rediscovered' in the comparatively new field of financial economics.

13. For an exposition of this persuasive concept, see David Teece (1980) 'Economies of Scope and the Scope of the Enterprise', *Journal of Economic Behavior and Organization*, September, pp. 223–47.

14. See F. Gibrat (1931) *Les Inégalités Economiques* (Paris); H. Simon and J. Bonini (1958) 'The Size Distribution of Business Firms', *American Economic Review*, vol. 48, September, pp. 607–17; P. Hart and S. Prais (1957) 'The Analysis of Business Concentration', *Journal of the Royal Statistical Society*, Series A, vol. 119, pp. 150–91; J. Steindl (1965) *Random Processes and the Growth of Firms* (New York).

15. Robin Marris (1979) *Theory and Future of the Corporate Economy and Society* (Amsterdam).

16. Exposition of this idea, which is not further pursued in the present volume, can be found in *Theory and Future of the Corporate Economy and Society*, ch. 2; and in Marris and Mueller, *Journal of Economic Literature*, 1980.

17. Alfred Chandler (1962) *Strategy and Structure*; and A. Chandler (1977) *The Visible Hand*, both Cambridge, Mass., Harvard University Press; plus A. Chandler and R. Tedlow (1985) *The Coming of Managerial Capitalism* (New York).

18. See my 'Increasing Returns, Constant Returns and Micro–Macro Economic', ch. 10 in Kenneth J. Arrow, Yew-Kwong Ng and Xiaofiai Ychy (eds) (1998) *Increasing Returns and Economic Analysis* (London).

19. During the period 1895 to 1915 on both sides of the Atlantic there was a rapid increase in the share of industrial output produced by public companies and a similar acceleration in the total private output share of the hundred largest companies.

20. For a good illustration of the following passage, see Bill Gates (1996) *The Road Ahead* (New York and London), p. 46.

21. See ibid, pp. 45–9.

22. Kim Cameron (1997) 'Downsizing', in *The Concise International Encyclopedia of Business and Management* (London) p. 161.

23. For further discussion see page 134 below.

24. See page 154 below.

25. Since the early 1980s papers relating to 'endogenous' growth have been appearing in learned journals world-wide at the rate of about twenty a year. The following is a very short selection of titles judged especially appropriate to the current discussion:
P. Romer (1994) 'The Origins of Endogenous Growth', *Journal of Economic Perspectives*, vol. 8, no. 1, pp. 3–22; R. Arena and A. Raybaut (1995) 'On Growth and Cycles: A Neo Kaldorian View', *Revue Economique*, vol. 46, no. 6, pp. 1433 ff; N. Gemmell (1995) 'Endogenous Growth, the Solow Model and Human Capital', *Economics of Planning*, vol. 28, no. 2–3, pp. 169–83; C. Jones (1995) 'Time-Series Tests of Endogenous-growth Models', *Quarterly Journal of Economics*, vol. 110, no. 2, pp. 495–525; N. Crafts (1996) 'Post-Neoclassical Endogenous Growth Theory: What Are Its Policy Implications?', *Oxford Review of Economic Policy*, vol. 12, no. 2, pp. 30–47; T. Palley (1996) 'Growth Theory in a Keynesian Mode: Some Keynesian Foundations for New Endogenous Growth Theory', *Journal of Post Keynesian Economics*, vol. 19, no. 1, pp. 113–35; N. Kocherlakota and K. Yi (1997) 'Is There Endogenous Long-Run Growth? Evidence from the United States and the United Kingdom', *Journal of Money Credit and Banking*, vol. 29, no. 2, pp. 235–62.

26. See pages 162–4 below.

27. See the completely revised Chapter 6 in this volume.
28. This is exactly the case made by Joseph Schumpeter (1942) in *Capitalism, Socialism and Democracy* (London). For the case of imperfect polipoly, the formal model I have in mind here is the one I computer-simulated in R. Marris (1990), *Reconstructing Keynesian Economics under Imperfect Competition* (Aldershot).
29. Chapter 3, R. Marris (1979) *The Theory and Future of the Corporate Economy*, ch. 3, Amsterdam, R. Marris and Dennis Mueller (1980) 'The Corporation, Competition and the Invisible Hand', *Journal of Economic Literature*, March, pp. 32–63.
30. See again a particularly illuminating discussion of the problem in Gates (1994), op. cit., pp. 45–9.

Original Introduction and Preface

1. That is, in the original 1964 structure; for the present structure see the new Introduction, above.
2. This did not happen exactly as described: for a general survey of empirical testing of managerial theories of the firm, see new Chapter 5 below in this volume.

Chapter 1   The Institutional Framework

1. A. A. Berle and G. Means (1932) *The Modern Corporation and Private Property* (New York), p. 285.
2. We refer to the writings of Thorstein Veblen, A. A. Berle, Gardner Means, Chester Barnard, R. A. Gordon, George Hurt, Sargent Florence, Carl Kaysen, J. K. Galbraith, Mrs Edith Penrose (listed in approximate historical order of publication). For a good general survey the reader is referred to E. Mason (ed.) (1960) *The Corporation in Modern Society* (Cambridge, Mass.) the notes to which may be used as a bibliography.
3. This was an over-simplification. One could as well argue that the invention occurred in the State of Connecticut in the year 1837. See, for example, the article by Robert Hessen (1987) 'Corporations', in *The New Palgrave Dictionary of Economics* (London). My original text was based on B. C. Hunt (1960) *The Development of the Business Corporation in England, 1800–1867* (Cambridge, Mass.) Surprisingly (to me), Hessen does not cite Hunt. I also (in 1964) insulted Hunt in my references by confusing him with Holman Hunt, the Pre-Raphaelite artist! In the third of a century since then, no one has written to me to point out the error. Food for thought.
4. This was a reference to the theory (created by Herbert Simon, who later, in 1976, received a Nobel Prize for it) now known as 'bounded rationality'.
5. See J. Downie (1958) *The Competitive Process* (London); and William Baumol (1959) *Business Behaviour, Value and Growth* (New York).
6. I have deleted the next paragraph because it was obscure. It should have said that the problems of finance, leverage and control placed a limit on the rate of growth of the firm (the maximum proportional annual growth rate, in terms of net assets, is obviously equal to the annual rate of return net of

interest and the owner's minimum take-home pay) but not on its absolute
size. The essential limit on the latter derives from the organizational capacity of the owner and his family.

7. R. H. Tawney (1926) *Religion and the Rise of Capitalism* (London).
8. Max Weber (1930) *The Protestant Ethic and the Spirit of Capitalism* (trans.
   Talcott Parsons) (London and New York).
9. James Burnham (1941) *The Managerial Revolution* (New York).
10. Thorstein Veblen (1923) *Absentee Ownership* (London).
11. For an analysis of differences in market prices as between voting and non-
   voting (but otherwise equal) shares in the same company, see *The
   Economist* (1957) London, 27 July, p. 328.
12. When I toured the USA giving seminars in 1960, because American economists at that time said they were innocent of knowledge of this type of transaction, no terminology was available. Eventually, as the facts of life became
   better known, the term 'tender offer' was coined in place of what the British
   had for some time been calling a conditional offer or simply a 'bid'.
13. The reader is especially reminded that these words were written about the
   world of the 1920s to 1960s. It is common knowledge that, in the last
   quarter of the century, management mobility steadily increased. But the
   general argument of the paragraph remains, I think, valid.
14. See also the important essay of Frederick Scherer, already mentioned in the
   new Introduction (page 166 above), in the *Journal of Economic
   Perspectives* in 1988. I have, however, a small bone to pick with my friend
   and colleague Dennis Mueller. In his paper he wrote:

> By far the most widely held view regarding the efficiency gains from
> mergers and take-overs is the hypothesis that they are motivated to
> replace managements that fail to maximize shareholder wealth by those
> that will. As first put forward by Marris, it was intended to explain hostile
> take-overs, not mergers in general, but most observers holding this
> hypothesis apply it to evidence on both mergers and take-overs (e.g.
> [Michael Jensen and Richard Ruback (1983) 'The Market for Corporate
> Control', *Journal of Financial Economics*, April, pp. 232–9.]. Following
> Henry Manne's (1965) ['Mergers and the Market for Corporate Control',
> *Journal of Political Economy*, April, pp. 110–29] appellation, it has come
> to be called the 'market for corporate control'. Those who espouse this
> hypothesis presume this market to be efficient, and thus the premia paid
> reflect the expected gains from replacing the acquired firm's management
> with that of the buyer.

Although the term 'efficient market' is being used in the technical sense,
implying that any information available to one player is also available
to all others, I feel that, as applied to myself, and in contrast to others,
the passage does not reflect the deep imperfection I saw in this market,
and without which, of course, my whole 'managerial' hypothesis would
die.

15. For example, in reporting these kinds of results, Agral, Jaffe and Gershon
   (1992) wrote, in 'The Post-Merger Performance of Acquiring Firms: A Re-
   examination of an Analogy', *Journal of Finance*, September:

A finding of underperformance [of acquiring firms] has three important implications. First, the concept of efficient capital markets is a major paradigm in finance. Systematically poor performance after mergers is, of course, inconsistent with this paradigm. Second, much research on mergers examines returns surrounding announcement dates in order to infer the wealth effect of mergers. This approach implicitly assumes that markets are efficient, since returns following the announcement are ignored. Thus, a finding of market inefficiency for returns following mergers calls into question a large body of research.

I would argue that if the hypothesis of strong managerial motivation in acquiring firms is adopted, the results are, rather than anomalous, theoretically predicted. It seems to me that, in that case, the financial markets are not necessarily 'inefficient' in the technical sense, because it is surely clear that even if research economists do not recognise managerial motivation, the markets must do so. If one asks the proverbial person-in-the-street what she or he expects after a merger, she or he (and most especially she) will say that the shares are likely to fall. The best general advice for shareholders receiving merger offers is 'take your money and run'.

16. I think that appropriate references in this context would be D. K. Datta et al. (1991) 'Diversification and Performance: A Critical Review', *Journal of Management Studies*, vol. 28, no. 5, September, pp. 531–58; L. H. P. Lang and R. M. Stulz (1994) 'Tobin's Q, Corporate Diversification, and Firm Performance', *Journal of Political Economy*, vol. 102, no. 6, pp. 1248–80; and Denis and Sarin (1997) *Journal of Finance*. The reader will recollect that in this context Tobin's Q (J. Tobin (1969) 'A General-equilibrium Approach to Monetary Theory', *Journal of Money, Credit and Banking*, 1969, vol. 1) is the concept I introduced under the name of 'Valuation Ratio' in 1964. M. Jensen (1986) 'Agency Costs of Free Cash Flow, Corporate Finance and Takeovers', *American Economic Review*, vol. 76, no. 6 (American Economic Association Papers and Proceedings), pp. 323–9.

Chapter 2   Motives and Morals

1. The footnote placed here in the original text reads: 'See Herbert Simon (1959) 'Decision Making in Economics', *American Economic Review*, June. This article gives a good general bibliography, including Professor Simon's earlier works, of which the most immediately relevant are *Models of Man* (1957) (New York) (esp ch. 14) and *Organisations* (with J. G. March), (1958) (New York).' Subsequently, in 1976, Herbert Simon received the Nobel Prize in Economics for this and other great work. The behavioural concept he created became known as 'bounded rationality' and influenced almost every area of the discipline. An introduction to his most recent thoughts can be found in Herbert Simon (1992) *Economics, Bounded Rationality and the Cognitive Revolution* (Aldershot). The references I gave above in 1964, however, still stand as the most appropriate in respect of Simon's work in organization theory.

2. William E. Henry (1949) 'The Big Business Executive', *American Journal of Sociology*, January.

3. George Katona (1951) *Psychological Analysis of Economic Behaviour* (New York), ch. 9.

4. William Baumol (1959) *Business Behavior, Value and Growth* (New York).

5. I have consolidated the original references to this section as follows: David Riesman (1950) *The Lonely Crowd* (New Haven, Conn.); Kenn Rogers (1963) *Managers – Personality and Performance* (London); W. H. Whyte (1957) *The Organisation Man* (New York); C. Wright Mills (1957) *The Power Elite* (New York).

6. The following quotation from the London *Times* of 5 August 1997 (p. 23) shows how times have changed in more than one way:

> Pearson plans to double market value in five years: Pearson, the troubled publishing group, vowed to improve its earnings by at least 10 per cent a year and to double its stock market value within five years. Marjorie Scardino, the American who took over as chief executive at the start of the year, said that last Friday's closing share price was the benchmark.

The emphasis on share value was greeted by some commentators as refreshing. There is also a poignant contrast with the sexist flavour of my original text, where, as already conceded, all managers are 'he'. A major factor in the end-of-century situation, whose significance will expand as the original text unfolds, is much increased mobility at the highest levels of management, especially for executives who seem to have a talent for rationalizing mismanaged businesses.

7. Remember that this was written before knowledge of the Japanese management culture (and its effectiveness) had spread to the West. The conventional picture now is that Japanese managers have (or used to have) *de facto* lifelong security of tenure, the adverse motivational effects of which are offset by strong moral pressure to perform, and by the practice of shifting sideways people whose chronic under-performance is likely to damage the collective.

8. See James Duesenberry (1949) *Income, Saving and the Theory of Consumer Demand* (Cambridge, Mass.).

9. At the time of writing I used 'classical', where today one would probably say 'neoclassical'. Notice also how I used the past tense, as if 'classical' (that is, neoclassical) economics was dead and buried. It never occurred to me to think otherwise. How wrong, how wrong indeed, one can be!

10. Chester Barnard (1938) *The Functions of the Executive* (Cambridge, Mass.); Norman Buchanan (1938) 'The Theory and Practice of Dividend Distribution', *Quarterly Journal of Economics*, November.

11. R. A. Gordon (1945) *Business Leadership in the Large Corporation* (Washington, DC). The references are to the 1945 edition but the passages quoted were repeated unchanged in the 1961 edition. The latter, however, had a new Preface in which the author indicated that he had found little evidence that his earlier conclusions needed modifying in the light of developments during the intervening period.

12. Gordon (1945), p. 305.

13. Gordon (1945), pp. 305–6.

14. Gordon (1945), p. 311.
15. For a contemporary comment on bonuses and other incentives, see the end of the next section.
16. Dennis Mueller (1995) 'Mergers: Theory and Evidence', in Giuliani Mussatti (ed.), *Mergers, Markets and Public Policy* (Dordrecht).
17. Michael Jensen and Richard Ruback (1983) 'The Market for Corporate Control', *Journal of Financial Economics*, April, pp. 232–9.
18. The use of this word was showing off. Unknown to most economists, it is the word used by V. Pareto for the concept that the profession now almost always calls 'utility'.
19. Pages 81–7.
20. David R. Roberts (1959) *Executive Compensation* (Glencoe, Ill.).
21. A significant econometric literature subsequently emerged. Some results favoured a neoclassical interpretation, others did not. The following is a selective list: W. Lewellen and B. Huntsman (1970) 'Managerial Pay and Corporate Performance', *American Economic Review*, vol. 4, pp. 710–19; G. Yarrow (1972) 'Executive Compensation and the Theory of the Firm', in K. Cowling (ed.), *Market Structure and Corporate Behaviour: Theory and Empirical Analysis of the Firm* (London); D. Smyth et al., (1975) *Size, Growth, Profits and Executive Compensation in the Large Corporation* (New York: Holmes and Meier); D. Ciscel (1974) 'The Determinants of Executive Compensation', *Southern Economic Journal*, vol. 4, April, pp. 613–17; J. Cubbin and G. Hall (1983) 'Directors' Remuneration in the Theory of the Firm – Specification and Testing of the Null Hypothesis', *European Economic Review*, vols 1–3, pp. 333–48.
22. H. A. Simon (1957) 'The Compensation of Executives', *Sociometry*, March.
23. See H. H. Gerth and C. Wright Mills (eds) (1946) *From Max Weber: Essays in Sociology* (New York), p. 196.
24. D. Grubb (1980) *Power and Ability in the Distribution of Earnings* (London: Centre for Labour Economics, London School of Economics) April; S. Rosen (1982) 'Authority, Control and the Distribution of Earnings', *Bell Journal of Economics*, Autumn, pp. 311–23; D. Grubb (1985) 'Ability and Power Over Production in the Distribution of Earnings', *Review of Economics and Statistics*, May, pp. 188–94; R. Marris (1996) *How to Save the Underclass* (London), pp. 150–3. In my opinion, David Grubb's statistically tested model gives the most robust explanation of the actual pattern of upper-level earnings.
    There has also been an important literature on the question of what is the optimum span of control and organizational structure generally. See, for example, M. Iviesarovic et al. (1970) *Theory of Hierarchical Multilevel Systems* (New York); James Mirrlees (1976) 'The Optimal Structure of Incentives and Authority within an Organization', *Bell Journal of Economics*, vol. 1, Spring, pp. 105–31; M. Keren and D. Levhari (1979) 'The Optimum Span of Control in a Pure Hierarchy', *Management Science*, vol. 1; Dennis Mueller (1980) 'Power and Profit in Hierarchical Organisations', *Swedish Journal of Political Science*, vol. 5, pp. 293–302.
25. J. K. Galbraith (1952) *American Capitalism* (Boston, Mass.), p. 29.
26. In an elegant paper, Robert Solow subsequently showed that this proposition contains a hidden and arguably arbitrary assumption that the possibil-

ity of selling some assets and distributing the proceeds to shareholders (that is, 'making the firm smaller') is not considered. This is discussed further below. See pages 162–3. below and R. M. Solow (1971) 'Some Implications of Alternative Criteria for the Firm', in R. Marris and A. Wood (eds), *The Corporate Economy* (Cambridge, Mass. and London). In another elegant and classic paper, James Tobin rediscovered the valuation ratio, renamed it 'q' and brilliantly deployed the concept to create a model of general equilibrium based on the existence of equity shares. ['A General-Equilibrium Approach to Monetary Theory, *Journal of Money, Credit and Banking*, 1969, vol. 1]. Both scholars, of course, are Nobel Laureates.

27. See R. M. Cyert and J. G. March (1956) 'Organisational Factors in the Theory of Oligopoly', section III, *Quarterly Journal of Economics*, February.

28. Herbert Simon went on to receive a Nobel Prize in Economics in 1976. The term 'bounded rationality' replaced 'satisficing' as a general description of his concept, which has had a profound influence on economics. In the early 1960s, however, this influence was in its infancy. I claim to be one of the first economists, on either side of the Atlantic, to appreciate its significance and to attempt to reconcile its implications with those of traditional economic theory. For a rich collection of his most recent ideas, see H. Simon, M. Egidi, R. Marris and R. Viale (eds) (1972) *Economics, Bounded Rationality and the Cognitive Revolution* (Aldershot and Brookfield, Vt). For my own latest views on the subject, see my essay, 'Implications for Economics', in the same volume.

Chapter 3   Concepts and Methods

1. William Baumol (1959) *Business Behavior, Value and Growth* (New York); Jack Downie (1958) *The Competitive Process* (London).

2. See, for example, the classic discussion of the problems of an imaginary organization set up for the simple task of cutting wood, in Chester Barnard (1938) *The Function of the Executive* (Harvard) pp. 246 *et seq.*

3. See, for example, Jacob Marshak (1955) 'Elements of a Theory of Teams', *Management Science*, January.

4. Penrose (1959) (Oxford). Leibenstein (1960) (New York).

5. But see discussion of agency and transactions costs in the new Introduction, pp. xiii et seq. above.

6. Again one concedes that late-century developments qualify this. There are no doubt some viable, very-fast-growing organizations today where most members do not know each others' names.

7. Mason Haire (1959) *Modern Organization Theory* (New York), p. 283.

8. A study of indexes shows that the frequency with which the word 'diversification' appears in titles to articles in business periodicals has displayed a consistent upward trend since the mid-1930s.

9. Penrose (1959) *Theory of the Growth of the Firm* (Oxford), pp. 212–14.

10. For updated comments on the general topic of mergers from the point of view of the acquiring firm, please see pages 19–20 of the present volume, above.

Chapter 4 'Demand'

1. Harvard.
2. Apart from Duesenberry, background reading for the following arguments includes S. Katz and P. Lazarsfeld (1960) *Personal Influence* (New York), esp. pt I, sec. 2; David Riesman (1950) *The Lonely Crowd* (New Haven, Conn.), ch. 4; and William Whyte (1957) *The Organization Man* (New York), ch. 26.
3. See Katz and Lazarsfeld (1960), pt II, sec. 2, ch. 5.
4. Since then, of course, space heating, retail refrigeration, and marketing techniques have all advanced in the UK, and so, therefore, has cola consumption.
5. See A. Kaplan, J. Dirlam and R. Lanzillotti (1958) *Pricing in Big Business* (Menasha, Ill.), pp. 59–60.
6. Kaplan, Dirlam and Lanzillotti (1958), p. 60.
7. S. Katz and P. Lazarsfeld (1960) *Personal Influence* (New York), pp. 219 *et seq.*
8. Katz and Lazarsfeld (1960), p. 236.
9. See William Whyte (1957) *The Power Elite* (New York), p. 313.
10. Whyte (1957), p. 314.
11. John Von Neumann and Oscar Morgenstern (1944) *The Theory of Games and Economic Behavior* (Princeton).
12. (New York), 1960.
13. Joe S. Bain (1956) *Barriers to New Competition* (Cambridge, Mass.).
14. S. Katz and P. Lazarsfeld (1960) *Personal Influence* (New York), pt I, sec. 2.
15. Martin Shubik (1960), pp. 214 *et seq.*
16. See R. Luce and H. Raiffa (1958) *Games and Decisions* (New York), p. 483.
17. Page 73, this edition.
18. The references were A. Kaplan, J. Dirlam and R. Lanzillotti (1958), pp. 59–60; 'Introducing and Pricing New Products', in James C. Early (1962) *Pricing for Profit and Growth* (New York); 'The Failure Rate U.S. New Products' (1957) *Printer's Ink*, 2 August, p. 20.

Chapter 5 Managerial Theories of the Firm

1. See *The Concise International Encyclopedia of Business and Management* (1997) (London), pp. 419–27.
2. By kind permission of the publishers.

Chapter 6 The Completed Micro Model

1. I conceived this ratio for the specific purposes of my micro model. Subsequently, Nicholas Kaldor, without acknowledgement, cleverly developed it into a macro concept and Nobel Laureate, James Tobin, who had not encountered it, reinvented it as his 'q' for the purpose of building a beautiful

model of the general equilibrium of the monetary system (N. Kaldor (1966) *Review of Economic Studies*, October; J. Tobin (1969) 'A General-equilibrium Approach to Monetary Theory', *Journal of Money, Credit and Banking*, vol. 1).

2. By Hiro Odagiri (1980) in *The Theory of Growth in a Corporate Economy* (Cambridge).

3. I assumed that, because of the default risk to managers, long-term debt burdens would be held to moderate levels, an assumption that was highly realistic at the time. In later times, firms have become more adventurous with debt. Oliver Hart and John Moore have argued that debt is a good thing because it restrains managerial discretion and reduces the growth rate of firms. But what is the effect on the economy? I would be willing to bet that if a law was passed compelling firms to have more debt, general economic welfare would be reduced at all future points in time! See O. Hart and J. Moore, 'Debt and Seniority: An Analysis of the Role of Hard Claims in the Constraint of Management', *American Economic Review*, vol. 85, no. 3, June, pp. 567–85.

4. See R. F. Kahn (1972) 'The Rate of Interest and the Growth of Firms', *Essays on Employment and Growth*, ch. 10 (Cambridge).

5. Pages 113 et seq. above. For convenience, the reader is reminded that the references are 'A Theory of Conglomerate Mergers', *Quarterly Journal of Economics*, November 1969, vol. 83, pp. 643–60; and 'Mergers: Theory and Evidence', in Giuliani Mussatti (ed.), *Mergers, Markets and Public Policy* (Dordrecht) (1995).

6. The earliest, and classic, studies were done in the later 1960s by Douglas Kuehn (1969) 'Stock Market Valuation and Acquisitions: An Empirical Test of One Component of Managerial Utility', *Journal of Industrial Economics*, April, vol. 17, pp. 132–44; and D. Kuehn (1975) *Takeovers and the Theory of the Firm: An Empirical Analysis of the United Kingdom, 1957–1969* (London). The most recent, also classic, study was by J. W. Bartley and C. M. Boardman (1986) 'Replacement-Cost-Adjusted Valuation Ratio as a Discriminator among Take-over Target and Nontarget Firms', *Journal of Economics and Business*, vol. 38, pp. 41–55. Kuehn postulated that the critical level of the valuation ratio at which a take-over occurred would vary between firms according to underlying factors that could not be observed statistically. If, however, it could be assumed that the critical value was statistically normally distributed, the statistical relationship between the valuation ratio and the observed probability of take-over would form an S-shaped, or Logit, curve. Mathematical techniques for testing Logit-curve hypotheses were applied to the British data, with very positive and significant results. Among the several contributions of Bartley and Boardman was the deployment of replacement cost instead of historical cost to represent the denominator the valuation-ratio fraction. This contributed a major improvement in the robustness of results. Using multiple discriminant analysis they studied a carefully matched sample of US target and non-target firms to discriminate between the valuation ratio and other possible predictors of targetability, and found that the absolute level of the valuation ratio was in effect the only clear discriminator between target and non-target firms.

7. Page 112 above.
8. Page 118 above.
9. Page 116 above.
10. H. Radice (1971) 'Control type, profitability and growth in large firms', *Economic Journal*, vol. 81, September, pp. 547–62.
11. See Chapter 5, pages 113, 115 and 117 above.
12. For example, those of Hunt, and Hill and Snell, cited in Chapter 5 on p. 118 above.
13. See, for example, Michael Jensen (1984) 'The Eclipse of the Public Corporation', *Harvard Business Review*, 61, Sep–Oct.

Chapter 7 Behaviour and Evidence

1. See, for example, H. Simon (1959) 'Decision Making in Economics', *American Economics Review*, June.
2. See James March and Herbert Simon (1958) *Organisations* (New York), pp. 1, 41.
3. For definition, see Chapter 8, page 144, below.
4. See, for example, Richard Cyert and James March (1956) 'Organizational Factors in the Theory of Oligopoly', sec. III, *Quarterly Journal of Economics*, February.
5. See, for example, K. Lewin (1944) 'Levels of Aspiration', in McV. Hunt, *Personality and the Behaviour Disorders* (New York).
6. For an explanation of the terminology, see Chapter 8, page 143 below.

Chapter 8 Possible Macro Implications

1. For the original discussion, see pages 153 et seq. below.
2. Pages 126, 131 and 133 above.
3. Page 132.
4. For a bibliography of the successive developments of the 'Kaldor model', see Note 12 below.
5. Joan Robinson (1956) *The Accumulation of Capital* (London).
6. R. F. Harrod (1948) *Towards a Dynamic Economics* (London); Evesey Domar (1957) *Essays in the Theory of Economic Growth* (Oxford).
7. Robinson (1956); James Meade (1956) *A Neo-Classical Model of Growth* (London); Robert Solow (1956) *Quarterly Journal of Economics*; Trevor Swan (1956) *Economic Record*.
8. See Note 12 below.
9. L. Pasinetti (1962) *Review of Economic Studies*, no. 2.
10. See Robinson (1956), p. 100.
11. J. Duesenberry (1949) *Income, Saving and the Theory of Consumer Demand* (Harvard).
12. Joan Robinson (1956), p. 99.
13. See Note 12 above.
14. See R. G. Lipsey (1960) *Economica*, p. 1.

15. This statement is based on an analysis of the following: N. Kaldor (n.d.) *Essays on Value and Distribution*, pp. 228–36; *Essays on Economic Stability and Growth*, pp. 256–300; and in *** *The Theory of Capital* (1961) (London), pp. 177–220; also N. Kaldor and James Mirrlees (1962) *Review of Economic Studies*, June.

16. An essay in a conference volume: R. Solow (1971) *The Corporate Economy*, R. Marris and A. Wood (eds) (London and Cambridge, Mass.).

17. (Cambridge).

18. Page 124.

19. Robert Solow (1956) 'A Contribution to the Theory of Economic Growth', *Quarterly Journal of Economics*.

20. Page xix above.

21. H. Odagiri (1992) *Growth through Competition and Competition through Growth: Strategic Management and the Economy in Japan* (Oxford).

22. Page 127.

23. See 'The Dam Busters', article in the London *Sunday Times*, Business Section, p. 3, describing an attempt (immediately denounced by Germany's head of government) by Krupp to take over Thyssen.

24. For an important and fruitful attempt to quantify the relationship see Laura Rondi and Alessandro Sembinelli (1991) 'Testing the Relationship between the Growth of Firms and the Growth of the Economy', *International Journal of Industrial Organization*, vol. 9, pp. 251–9.

Author Index

Subject Index